P9-AQA-446

Soviet Society and the Communist Party

Contributors

Karl W. Ryavec
University of Massachusetts, Amherst

George W. Breslauer
University of California at Berkeley

Robert W. Campbell
Indiana University

Paul M. Cocks
Stanford University

Erik P. Hoffmann
State University of New York at Albany

Donald R. Kelley
Mississippi State University

Sanford R. Lieberman
University of Massachusetts, Boston, and Russian Research Center, Harvard University

David E. Powell
Russian Research Center, Harvard University

Peter H. Solomon, Jr.
University of Toronto

Soviet Society and the Communist Party

Edited by Karl W. Ryavec

The University of Massachusetts Press Amherst, 1978

48631

Copyright © 1978 by The University of Massachusetts Press
All rights reserved
Library of Congress Catalog Card Number 78–53179
ISBN 0–87023–258–4
Printed in the United States of America
Designed by Mary Mendell
Library of Congress Cataloging in Publication Data
appear on the last printed page of the book.

The essay, "Specialists in Policymaking: Criminal Policy, 1938–1970," by Peter H. Solomon, Jr., is excerpted from *Social Scientists and Policy Making in the USSR,* edited by Richard B. Remnek. Copyright © 1977 by Praeger Publishers. Reprinted by permission of Praeger Publishers, a division of Holt, Rinehart and Winston. This essay is also based on material in Peter H. Solomon, Jr., *Soviet Criminologists and Criminal Policy: Specialists in Policy-Making* (New York: Columbia University Press; London: The Macmillan Press, Ltd., 1978).

Contents

48631

Acknowledgments

A number of persons and groupings provided aid and encouragement to the project out of which this volume developed. I appreciate the assistance given by John N. Hazard, Andrzej A. Korbonski, M. George Zaninovich, Jerry F. Hough, John A. Armstrong, George W. Hoffman, S. Frederick Starr, William Zimmerman, Donna L. Bahry, Robert E. Blackwell, Abraham Brumberg, Paul K. Cook, Jerome M. Gilison, Alexander J. Groth, Darrell P. Hammer, Nancy W. Heer, Roger E. Kanet, James A. Kuhlman, Ellen P. Mickiewicz, Joel C. Moses, John W. Parker, Jane P. Shapiro, Philip D. Stewart, Curt Tausky, the Research and Development Committee of the American Association for the Advancement of Slavic Studies, the American Enterprise Institute for Public Policy Research and Robert J. Pranger, the Office of External Research of the United States Department of State, and the Cremona Foundation and Norton T. Dodge. In transliterating Russian terms, an attempt has been made to use the system followed by the *Current Digest of the Soviet Press.*

Karl W. Ryavec

Introduction

¶ The CPSU, Institutions, and the Political System

This joint effort is part of a renewed interest in the political importance of institutions and change, an interest very different from the former legalistically oriented approach. Whereas the study of institutions or large-scale stable sets of interlocking human relationships once emphasized formal or concrete structure, legal processes and stability, the present approach recognizes that institutions are far more fluid and political in operation than can be shown by the descriptive presentation and examination of only formal structure and process. This new perspective cannot be labeled easily, although studies of the dynamics of large organizations and groupings provide a useful major intellectual orientation, one that is used below. Institutions of government are themselves minor political and social systems, not merely obedient and perfectly programmed cogs. They are given to internal conflicts involving values and power and to a sort of interinstitutional politics as well. Although specialists among the proponents of the behavioral approach to the study of Soviet politics say correctly that "it is necessary to concentrate on the functions performed by the [political-KR] system rather than on governmental institutions," [1] these institutions ought not thereby to be neglected and all attention diverted to the study of the performance of political functions without reference to the formal and lasting "concrete" structures of government. At the least, institutions and their leaders will tend to channel and control the political process. Institutions are a permanent feature of all modern political systems.

This is only an obvious and natural corrective to the view that politics can exist without government.[2] Logically, it can so exist and certainly has done so in preindustrial societies, but thus far it has not in industrial societies, except perhaps for periods between governments. Although it is recognized that the formulation of the concept of political system is an advance over some previous efforts in political theory, it must still be recognized that the institutions of the state, however "state" is defined, are generally becoming larger and more active in most political systems, notwithstanding the dominating ideology. To bring the point home, has there ever existed a Russian political system without a powerful and heavily bureaucratized state apparatus? The only times in the past four or five hundred years when such an apparatus has been lacking have been periods such as the Time of Troubles or the Civil War, certainly not historical moments people hope might recur. Possibly a defining characteristic of Russian politics is the institution of the state. We must recognize, then, that thus far at least Russian politics seems to presuppose the existence of a large state that tries to be omnicompetent through concrete institutions. The latest Russian variant of this type of political institution is the Leninist party, no doubt a major and original contribution to politics. Students of Soviet politics cannot ignore it. (Russian political patterns have survived in the USSR for a variety of reasons, one of which is the high political status accorded Russians and Russian values since at least the mid-1930s.) Macridis's statement regarding the imperatives for political research is most appropriate for the study of politics in the USSR: "We must study the structures and organizations and mechanisms through which the elites gain political power and exercise it, that is, the parties and other political associations. . . . we must be concerned with the governmental institutions through which demands are channeled, or, just as often, by which they are generated." [3]

Both suggestions fit the CPSU, the channel for recruitment of the future Soviet political elite and the institution with which the present political elite exercises its "supercoordinating" powers. The realistic study of Soviet politics requires well-substantiated and incisive analyses of the political roles of, and the processes at work within, the major political institution—the Communist Party. The ways in which it maintains its position are necessarily objects of any study of Soviet politics that aims at making a significant statement of its processes, moving forces, and probable course.

¶ Definition of the Problem

These articles analyze the changing nature of the Communist Party in the Soviet Union as an institution of cultural and social control. It is assumed that the variety of problems existing in the sociocultural milieu of the Soviet Union at a given time will affect the mechanisms that the CPSU employs for control purposes. The basic research goal of these articles has been to consider how any given set of environmental forces that operates within Soviet society has been or is related to changes in

Party structure as well as Party strategy. It is assumed that an optimally adaptive structure will increase the likelihood of CPSU survival (retaining its essentially unitarist nature) as the control mechanisms are modified to meet new problems and new demands emanating from the environment. Consequently, this approach tends to reverse that facet of the traditional literature on Party systems in Communist societies which sees adaptations by the Party as negligible despite the appearance of major changes in the society at large. Rather than assuming that the social and cultural milieus will bend easily and fully to the will of the CPSU, this analysis proceeds by anticipating that the Party may change some of its parameters as a result of the pressure of its own survival needs. We analyze the various mechanisms and instruments of cultural and social control developed by the Party as they respond and change in relation to changes in the nature of Soviet society.

¶ Supporting Rationale

In considering the CPSU, several perspectives might be used in examining its relationship to key elements and processes in Soviet society. The term "Party control" will not be employed here, in order to avoid prejudging the issue at the start. Some analysts, for example Jerry Hough, consider the power of the CPSU to control persons and processes to be generally overstated. As a result, to focus upon the Party's "relationships" to other societal forces is both more neutral and more realistic than to speak of the unqualifiedly determining role of the CPSU. After all, "power" is fundamentally a relationship, not a material substance. The view held here is that the Party apparatus must be seen as subject to change through processes fostered by societal problems and issues. The focus on the interaction of the CPSU and groupings in society also speaks to the dynamic nature of the adaptation process, since *neither the Party nor these other elements* in Soviet society have ever been dormant or unchanging. The overriding task is to determine the pattern of interaction between the CPSU and these sociocultural forces and the way in which these forces have affected changes in the Party's structures and strategies.

The timeliness of this general topic is enhanced by the practice within Soviet leadership circles of emphasizing the maintenance of existing political principles and practices while at the same time attempting to modernize Soviet society and the economy, particularly stressing efficiency and high-quality products. The leaders seem to be trying to return to the *political* situation that existed during the mid-1950s, the period just before the appearance of political opposition, widespread samizdat, political neutralism among professionals (such as scientists), and implicitly antiregime theses in literature and the theater. The CPSU would in this respect seem to be culturally and ideologically conservative or static, while at the same time trying to be economically and scientifically progressive. Stated otherwise, there is an attempt to create a more developed economy and a more educated population, while still holding to a type of politics that existed during an earlier period of considerably less economic and cultural development. This approach has been tried in Russia before. The present attempt is a contemporary version of Tsarism's similar effort to match the West in technique and weaponry while preserving the autocracy. The critical question here is what CPSU adaptations become necessary to deal with pressures arising from newly created and energetic social and cultural elites and new social and economic processes.

Several approaches have made unique contributions to our understanding of Soviet political processes. The present study seeks to add a new dimension by viewing the CPSU as dependent upon (or, more exactly, structurally responsive to) societal forces. In this respect, we hope to begin to fill the need for a thorough analysis of the CPSU as it relates to Soviet society.

¶ Organizational Maintenance

Each of these essays deals with the CPSU as it continually faces one of the most severe challenges to any governing group attempting to rule, in an active sense, not only a large number of its own native citizens but an almost equal number of people of other nationalities in the largest politically defined land mass on earth. These papers are concerned with the related issues (and problems) of organizational maintenance and change. To be more exact, they deal with change, permitted and fostered by the Party leadership, that allows or is supposed to allow maintenance of the Party as an organization with a high degree of wide-ranging social control, while certain goals of the Party, both ideological-utopian and more specific goals deriving from the ideology, are implemented. The pattern desired by the leadership is one of corrective changes allowing the Party's political or power position to remain essentially unaltered while changes are introduced in society.

The fundamental question is whether this process of maintaining political stability in the midst of social and economic change can continue or, easier to answer, whether it has continued until now or continues at present.[4] I reject the romantic view sometimes put forth that the Soviet political system is in the midst of a transformation in the direction of liberal or even social democracy. I also reject the possibility of political development in the transformational sense and assert what to me seems self-evident: once a political system is formed as a complete (however simple) structure, its essential character continues unimpaired unless it either collapses as a result of intolerable internal stresses or is physically restructured after conquest from the outside by a different kind of political system. Even in these latter cases, change is not total, as the examples of both Germanies, Japan, and, say, Poland since 1945 show. And collapses such as that of Russia in 1917 often do not allow a thoroughly new start; cultural values underlying political processes seem to be able to survive almost any social shock.

The literature on organizational maintenance and change applies readily to the CPSU. It is, after all, an organization—"a system of coordinated activity, and thus a more or less uniform pattern of behavior." "Maintenance" is, "in short, producing and sustaining co-operative effort." [5]

We are often unduly influenced by what at first glance seems to be the rigid, authoritarian, growth-oriented, and seemingly unchallenged and ostensibly successful rule of the Soviet Communist Party. We tend to forget or not give proper weight to the severe tests that the activist core of the Party and of the system as well has faced and has perhaps only barely overcome. Here we come to a question of philosophy and reasoned outlook. What might be a balanced and honest view of the ability of the CPSU not only to stay in power but to mold Soviet society to its image to some degree? It would be as incorrect to say that the Party made it through crisis after crisis—the Civil War, collectivization, World War II, and the succession to Stalin—only through dumb luck, and just by the skin of its teeth, as it would be to claim that some variant of the totalitarian model applies to Soviet politics so strongly that the Party can do, and sometimes does, anything it desires, gets away with whatever it does completely, and is always clearly successful.

If we combine the main points of what we know about the Soviet Union, about other authoritarian systems—such as Hitler's Germany and Mao's China—about the great empires of history, and about politics today in industrialized societies, we must inevitably, if we are fair with our knowledge, come to recognize that despite the Party's institutionalized forceful will, grandiose goals, and powerful instruments, it does not achieve its aim completely. A long-term observer of the CPSU notes that it grapples with the same problems again and again. The problems or limitations on the Party's goals recur continually. Since Amitai Etzioni has found that no organization is able to attain its goals fully—to provide services or products with the least possible expenditure of resources, while maintaining the support of all members and clients—it is by extension logical to note that an organization like the CPSU, with such varied and ambitious goals, is inherently bound to fail to do all that it sets for itself.[6] Of course, by stifling both formal opposition and its vocalization and operating "by campaigns" (*po kampanski*), the Party is able to "rotate" its political maintenance about the whole range of social groupings in a nearly continuous fashion, without losing ground irrevocably in any one area. The major problems include the peasantry's attitude toward working for the state, the competition among the Party elite, the exact place to be on the centralization-decentralization continuum in administrative organization, and the tension between "red" and "expert." The full list is much longer; some of its elements date from the 1920s and others from the Tsarist period. The authors of the papers in this volume discuss questions of continual political significance and controversy.

The Party is unavoidably threatened by organizational "strain" in various forms, and its leadership, like those of all organizations, strives to minimize this strain. In doing so it engages in a struggle with its environment, Soviet society itself, and it courts, although perhaps only in the distant future, the abandonment of its special goals and powers. "In the long term . . . all organizations seek some form of accommodation with their environment. . . ." [7] Certainly, in the CPSU's case, the environment has both domestic and foreign dimensions.

One mode of accommodation would be for the Party to give up trying to order the environment and allow itself to be ordered by it to some definite degree. (Of course, the social environment has already powerfully affected the Party, but not to the point of making it abandon its unique Leninist goals.) But by the time this "long-term" possibility is visible we may all be dead. Although Trotsky said forty years ago that the reversal had already happened,[8] perhaps all he saw occur was, in James Q. Wilson's terms, a change of the Party from a "redemptive" organization, which tries to transform its own members, to an "ideological" one, which tries to implement the rest of the goals deriving from its ideology within society at large. Certainly the CPSU has not become an organization aiming to implement only a few specific and circumscribed goals. It remains a "purposive" organization in a major, ideological sense—notwithstanding an abundance of evidence to the contrary—since its goals still posit the transformation of human society in a qualitative way. Despite the Party's apparent concessions to aspects of the present state of Soviet life, it has not conceded its transformational role publicly and refuses to allow the groupings within Soviet society either to put forward their views on their own or to combine freely for social and economic, much less political, purposes.[9] The Party is also, in Etzioni's terms, still a "coercive" organization.[10] Incidentally, where the totalitarian model of Friedrich was open to criticism (much of it overdone) was in its assertion that totalitarianism actually existed to some great degree; it would have been more realistic to base the model on totalitarian intent, the serious attempt to realize this intent, and the consequences of the combination of intent and the political pressure accompanying it.

This quest to transform Russia, or at least this goal of not allowing Russia to find its own way, however diluted it has become, is itself a primary cause of the organizational strain buffeting the Party. As Wilson suggests, "The . . . function of sustaining the organization is especially difficult in purposive associations. Only rarely do ideological organizations attain their ends. . . ." [11] This is a fundamental problem of the CPSU; it cannot give up its transformational or totalistic stance without in effect consigning itself to the dustheap of history. Any fallback to a status as a mere regulatory agency would be an admission of defeat and would constitute a signal to other groupings and indeed to its own factions to find their respective levels. Of course, any such step back might well be only temporary. For example, the League of Communists of Yugoslavia returned emphatically to an activist level in 1971, after having tried to be an ideological guide and limited regulator for some years. Why would a Russian Communist Party, with its and its culture's traditions, do less? As Leslie Lipson says, Russia and Spain, of all the European countries that have exercised a significant historical role, "are the two whose political systems have stayed, continuously and decidedly, authoritarian and retain this character today. . . . Neither Spain nor Russia has contributed anything of significance to democracy. On the contrary, in their different ways both can be said to typify democracy's antithesis." [12] History suggests that democracy in its usual forms is a most unlikely prospect for Soviet Russia and can be ruled out unless an improbable and unusual cataclysm forces its introduction.

Although the Party retains its transformational role—partly as a pretense and partly as a protection against the beginning of unstructured political activity that could not be in its interests—it nevertheless runs into a severe and continuing tension between its stance and its accomplishments, one that affects its power. This is a basic contradiction: its aims are too great to be accomplished within human society without the aid of such means of changing human behavior as envisioned, for example, in *Brave New World* and *1984*. However, the attempt to realize the aims must be allowed to continue if only in the form of elaborate pretense praised in the state-controlled communications media. If the change-oriented activity were allowed to cease, the Party could no longer operate even as imperfectly as it does now. Undoubtedly, the CPSU commands vast coercive and manipulative resources. If its failure to do all it is supposed to do were revealed and freely discussed, the absurdity of the present political arrangements would be so apparent as to be caustically erosive. It is for reasons such as these that the great power of the CPSU fosters both a lack of realism and a fear among its leaders. The power deceives even the Party leadership into thinking success may be at hand if only the old methods are used again and again and the old slogans continually shouted. The fear, which alternates with the dizziness of power, derives from the consciousness of what might happen to the Party and its leaders' perquisites if its powerful instruments were not forcefully used. The Party apparatus, then, might be seen as energetically playing an elaborate game of shadowboxing, while its own spokesmen stridently announce one victory after another. The proto-opposition, both within the Party and within society at large, is continually kept off balance, being forced to witness one nonvictory after another while so deafened by the cheers of the controlled media that there is no place in which to think of alternative patterns of action. This combination of power and fear is a strong and painful spur to political activity. As a result we see continual, massive, and occasionally frantic CPSU activity that never fully achieves its purposes.

In trying to implement the vision of ultimate transformation, or perhaps of perfect social control (maybe the same thing to a bureaucratic Communist leadership), the leadership always faces the undesired but unavoidable risk of changing itself into a new kind of organization, one less totalistic or ideological in aim. All the Party's activity holds the threat of forcing it to live with the relative intractability of its environment or of being transformed through its close relationship with that difficult environment. In fact, the Party already has been so changed to some degree—Trotsky's overstatement in that regard has already been mentioned—and more change is constantly and unavoidably threatened. No organization can do so much daily with so many social groupings and diverse technical processes without being influenced by the very elements it is trying to control and change. Since power is not an artifact but requires an ongoing relationship between human beings, even those supposedly without power in a relationship do have some ability to affect those with power. The Party's wide-ranging attempts to affect society also affect the Party. This does not mean it is not vastly powerful, just that even vast power has its limits in actual human situations. There exists, in Schelling's terms, a very real "coercive power of the weak."

At the extreme, people can refuse to recognize power's weight—of course, usually to their peril. More commonly, people learn how to avoid being totally constrained by power's directives and so make their lives more bearable. Soviet life is replete with informal behavior that creates a seemingly proscribed but nevertheless vital grey area of significant semifree activity.

What change and adaptation of the CPSU is then possible or likely in the short term? This is a much easier question to deal with than the more challenging but esoteric one of what is in store for the entire Soviet political system. That question draws a steady stream of answers, even though we cannot tell which is in fact an answer until the future arrives. The larger question then belongs in the realm of utopian literature. Despite this gap in our intelligence, since the future of the Soviet political system is inextricably bound up with that of the CPSU and indeed depends on it, the questions of the two futures are linked and, however unsatisfactorily, the reasonings followed in pursuing both are similar.

Speculation on the Soviet political future can be subdivided into three general positions: change will not occur; change will be slow, incremental, and "within system"; and change is inevitable and will have a decisive nature. Usually this last possibility is presented as a move toward democratization, but a change in the reverse direction, toward active, total neo-Stalinism or "retotalitarianization," cannot be automatically excluded, however unlikely. All sorts of shadings and combinations occur in the literature, as do the reasons given for any point of view.[13] Unfortunately, we still lack the "general theory of political change" called for by Dankwart Rustow in dealing with change in Communist political systems.[14] I doubt that pluralism involving the masses or freely formed interest groupings will be seen in the USSR in the next few decades, unless the political system falls prey to a catastrophe, an unlikely occurrence given the innate caution of the leadership. At the most, I think, we can look forward to a widening politics of oligarchy and of the enlarging power of present social elites within the current limits of the Soviet political framework. Maverick movements and ideas of widespread effect are precluded by social as well as political considerations; Soviet society is "conservative" or conventional in its style and outlook in many ways.

¶ Change

Every political system has some unique processes.[15] The most important aspect of the Soviet Union's uniqueness is its Communist Party and its totalistic effort. The Soviet political system interlocks so closely with the form and activities of the CPSU that change in the latter would change the "interlock" and then the system as well.

One impediment to accepting the idea that change is common in formal and bureaucratic organizations is the realistic but often overemphasized knowledge that such social institutions resist change. This resistance, often very powerful and at times supposedly successful, obscures the changes organizations undergo. Even seemingly successful resistance to change often conceals what is in fact change as adaptation or a way of maintaining the organization.

Any government is linked with its environment and, since "most environments may change very considerably, . . . only self-changing and self-enhancing systems and organizations are apt to survive eventually." [16] It is well to remember that "since the perfect adaptation of organizational structure to external conditions or internal operations is rarely if ever achieved, and since these factors are also changeful, the potential for experiencing organizational change is ever present." [17] Moreover, any of the party's recurrent shifts in focus and intensity of activity raises the possibility of setting in motion "unanticipated consequences with meaningful effect on it." [18]

Again, as Michel Crozier puts it, "any organization, whatever its functions, goals, and environment, has to face change from within and from without." And, "while a bureaucratic system or organization resists change longer than a non-bureaucratic system, it must nevertheless resort to change often in our adaptive modern society." [19] The big question, raised by Crozier and others, is what prompts change. He supplies one answer, a crisis of dysfunction recognized and acted upon by the "higher level," often resulting in further centralization. In other words, adaptation can be an effective authoritarian or at least nonliberal response to challenge. The French mode of bureaucratic adaptation offers a fascinating possible parallel to the Russo-Soviet. Are "isolated" and separate castes of higher civil servants analogous to the Party apparatchiki? In capability for independent, authoritative action, they may be. What the comparable Soviet "caste" lacks is the image of middle- or upper-class origins and impartiality.[20]

Wilbert Moore lists several sources of organizational change, at least three of which are applicable to the CPSU. First and most generally, both goals and means must be specified and in the process become subject to dispute, including dispute among factions. Second, attempts at the solution of problems provoke "new strategies of competition and conflict, . . . new procedures, new distributions of power, influence, prestige." In addition, the process of deliberately changing procedures, products, and even public opinion, a function common to large, modern organizations, has additional organizational consequences. "These include new functions and opportunities for disputes about goals, means, and jurisdictions." [21] This is the very stuff of politics when the organization changing is the CPSU. An indicator of this development is provided by Erik Hoffmann's essay on new methods of information handling within the Party. Generally, then, we have to recognize that organizations can assimilate elements of change into their operational assumptions and procedures. Of course, they do so to allow their own survival. But they must do so eventually to avoid extinction. Whether "absorption without resistance" is "change" and "absorption with resistance" is "reform" is not necessarily a meaningful differentiation.[22] It is difficult to imagine meaningful organizational change not encountering some resistance.

Ironically, the CPSU has already undergone significant change. Perhaps these changes made the Party go from bad to worse for liberal democracy, but they occurred nevertheless. The times when these changes occurred vary according to the person discussing them, but it would not be wide of the mark to suggest the years 1918–19, 1921–22, 1927–28, 1934–35, 1956–59, and 1969 to the present. The changes that took place in these years may not have been total, systemic, or "qualitative," but they were meaningful nevertheless for the Party's work, its members, and its opponents at home and abroad. Changes that arrest or even reverse the course of a social movement cannot completely forestall the cumulative effects of small changes on the larger system, particularly as the passage of the years multiplies the number of small changes until they form a new ruling pattern. Sanford Lieberman's essay on the Party's response to the challenges posed by World War II may indicate an example of absorption of stress without lasting change; but if the Zhdanovshchina had not been imposed after the war, perhaps the Party would have changed at that time. Such powerful inhibitions on the course of change cannot be imposed successfully more than a few times, and probably not at all in such a complex modern society, without striking at a central element of the real Soviet ideology, economic growth and continuing rationalization of production processes. Indeed, T. H. Rigby says that in some of those areas of Soviet life where "professional decision making" is the necessary rule, "the Party has had to learn to confine itself to the tasks of overall policy making, indoctrination and reconciling technically necessary innovations with the official ideology." [23] He does not, however, provide any examples. Robert Campbell's article deals with a similar issue.

In general, there are three alternative paths for any organization to traverse over time: development, stasis, and decline. Stasis is ruled out for the CPSU in the short run, since it rules a still developing complex society with a wide variety of foreign commitments. And, although I agree with Wilbert Moore that the probable ultimate course of organizations is "decline through demise," [24] realistically this result is not even dimly in sight for the CPSU. The path of development, necessarily involving survival-oriented change—albeit change intertwined with continuity of much of its structure and role—is the only possibility in the short term, say the next few decades or perhaps beyond. The leadership and some of the rest of the apparat will most likely strive for some effectual combination of continuity and change.[25] The question is what in its structure and role will change, particularly since challenges met and incorporated within an organization through adaptation strengthen the organization. Thus, change of a limited nature is in the Party leadership's interest. The Party's continuing rounds of confrontations with problems provide it with "testing crises"; it is this process and the question of what in the Party changes that this volume examines.

Part I

Theory and Policy

George W. Breslauer

On the Adaptability of Soviet Welfare-State Authoritarianism

Specialists on the USSR have for decades searched for organizing concepts that would best characterize the nature of the Soviet system or the direction in which it has been moving. For many years the totalitarian model provided such a concept. With the field's increasing dissatisfaction with the totalitarian label, however, has come a series of efforts to find substitutes. Terms such as "mobilization system," "mono-organizational society," and "institutional pluralism" have been offered. Other terms suggested capture not the nature of the current system but the extent of deviation from the totalitarian syndrome; in this context such terms as "change" and "adaptation" have been offered to characterize the direction of metamorphoses since Stalin.[1]

Some scholars undoubtedly experience frustration with the proliferation of concepts and must wonder about the pay-off. Why don't we simply abandon the search for organizing concepts and get on with the task of empirical research? Such a reaction is understandable but somewhat shortsighted; it ignores the fact that we all employ organizing concepts in our work, implicitly or explicitly, articulated or unarticulated. The concepts we choose guide the types of questions we raise and the components of the political order to which we direct our attention. The problem with the totalitarian model, for example, was that it directed our attention almost exclusively toward the political control network and thereby blinded us to sources of political and social support for the regime. The problem with such concepts as "adaptation" and "change" is somewhat different: they are so broad as to be almost meaningless. Adaptation of what to what? Change of what, in which directions, and with what consequences?

This last question implies the need for standards by which to judge the performance of a system—lest the mere documentation of changes or "adaptations" become an end in itself. It also implies the need for a definition of "system," identifying political, social, and ideological bases, that will then allow us to specify when systemic or within-system change has taken place. Such useful labels as "institutional pluralism" deal with only one dimension of change since Stalin: the political process. The concept of a "post-revolutionary oligarchy," [2] focuses upon both the political process and changed political goals, but ignores the socioeconomic base that buttresses the regime. An alternative to the totalitarian label is needed, lest we ignore the fundamental character of change since Stalin, but it should broaden our perspectives to incorporate both the character of regime politics and the direction of its social policies. Let me characterize the Soviet regime under Brezhnev, therefore, as "welfare-state authoritarianism." [3]

Although this concept has obvious shortcomings for use in the comparative analysis of one-party systems, it can be useful for Soviet specialists in clearly differentiating the Brezhnev regime from the Stalinist, as indicated by their respective approaches to political participation, social transformation, and material standard of living. Accordingly, I view the contemporary regime as authoritarian rather than totalitarian for a number of reasons. First, it has moved far in the direction of a form of "corporate pluralism" within the political elite.[4] Second, it has expanded and regularized opportunities for specialist input into decisionmaking processes on social and economic issues. Third, it has abandoned the use of mass terror as an instrument of policy, has depoliticized many realms of social life, and allows a considerable measure of physical security and privatism for the politically conformist. Thus, whereas the regime has retained its mobilizational character, it no longer engages in totalitarian forms of mass mobilization.

I label the regime a "welfare-state" because its policy includes a basic commitment to minimal and rising levels of material and social security, public health, and education. Equally important, its commitment to welfare includes an egalitarian commitment to job security and subsidized prices for basic commodities—even at the cost of considerable economic inefficiency and failure to develop entrepreneurial initiative. The level of material welfare, or the quality of public health, might not accord with many Western definitions of a "welfare-state," but the term strikes me as useful in differentiating the social policies of the Brezhnev era from both Stalinism and alternative approaches currently under discussion within the Soviet establishment.

Hereafter, I shall refer to the approach to political participation, social transformation, and material welfare just outlined as the basic social and political "contract" of welfare-state authoritarianism. It is not a contract in the liberal-democratic sense of an authoritative agreement between equals; what it represents is the pattern of political, social, and material benefits offered by the ruling authorities since Khrushchev's dismissal, both to regulate relationships among themselves and to elicit compliance and initiative from groups in society. This package of benefits and constraints differs from that offered by Stalin and Khrushchev and may not survive the Brezhnev succession. However, it does define the boundaries within which policy changes have taken place during the Brezhnev era. Thinking of a contract helps us to avoid the inordinate ambiguities associated with defining the "nature" of the Soviet "system." Those seeking to evaluate the adaptability of the Soviet "system" would be better advised to explore the durability of this contract and the realistic alternatives to it.

Three alternatives come to mind as responses to the tensions inherent in this contract: (1) varying types or degrees of public disorder ("instability") resulting from economic shocks or centrifugal ethnic pressures; (2) pressures from within the political elite for the constitutionalization of political relationships among the corporate groups comprising that elite (but without mass democratization), coupled with a social policy that allows massive material differentiation and managerial autonomy for the sake of economic efficiency (an alternative I have labeled "elitist liberalism"); (3) pressures from within the political elite for a right-wing reaction against the compromise, secularization, and lack of "discipline" that characterize welfare-state authoritarianism in the eyes of many a neo-Stalinist. This third, fundamentalist alternative would return to a "contract" based upon autocratic rule—or highly exclusive committee rule—and economic austerity, mobilizing the masses through such nonmaterial values as Russian chauvinism and antiintellectualism.

Any of the three alternatives would constitute "systemic change," if "system" is defined as the social and political contract of welfare-state authoritarianism. We who are concerned to explore the prospects for "within-system" change in the USSR must examine the range of policy alternatives possible within the bounds of the contract. We must investigate the trade-offs possible among the conflicting goals of efficiency and equity, scientific expertise and the political docility of scientists, material incentives and Party activism, military-industrial might and consumer satisfaction, and managerial discretion and political intervention. Moreover, we must delve into the *political* feasibility of different combinations of values. Can the political elite build coalitions that will maintain a stable bargaining structure supportive of the continuation of this contract in one form or another? Evaluating the durability of the contract requires an appreciation of its adaptability; and this assessment, in turn, requires an investigation of the levels and types of polarization within the political elite, of the ways in which elite groups define their interests, and of the compatibility of the decision-premises advanced by different interests. The more compatible these premises, the greater the prospects for shifting coalitions and alliances within the context of the basic contract of welfare-state authoritarianism.

These are the big questions for students of the Soviet present and future, and although they cannot be answered definitively at this time, the cause of cumulative research requires that we gather evidence with an eye to addressing them. The purpose of this essay will therefore be twofold: (1) to explore the character of regime policies during the Brezhnev era, in order to justify the characterization I have proposed; and (2) to explore the character of policy *changes* within the Brezhnev era, in order to illuminate the linkages among issues and the trade-offs possible within the contract of welfare-state authoritarianism. What makes the exercise all the more interesting is that the Brezhnev era today may fruitfully be divided into two phases (1965–69 and 1970–78), which differ importantly in the mix of approaches and the character of policies.[5] The two phases may be distinguished by analyzing the regime's approaches to issues of political participation, social transformation, and economic achievement, as these have affected the treatment of workers and peasants, members of the intelligentsia, and Party and state officials. Phase One constituted a mix of policy premises weighted in the direction of a left-wing version of welfare-state authoritarianism. Phase Two was characterized by a backlash against that particular direction of movement, a shift in the mix of premises, and a selective retrenchment to the political right.

¶ The Brezhnev Era, Phase One: Political Participation

The dismissal of Nikita Khrushchev in October 1964 brought in its wake a cluster of policy changes. Khrushchev was no welfare-state authoritarian, though he was also not a Stalinist. On the one hand, he shared and sponsored post-Stalin emphases on consumer welfare, an expanded amount of consultation with empirically oriented scientists, the abandonment of mass terror, and collective leadership. On the other hand, his commitment to radical and rapid social transformation, his efforts to circumvent the constraints of collective leadership, his attempts to redefine the terms of political participation by combining a personality cult with populist efforts to mobilize the masses against their hierarchical superiors, his erratic economic and administrative policies—all combined to shape a regime quite different from welfare-state authoritarianism. These tendencies alienated Soviet officials by threatening their personal security and political prerogatives, alienated many members of the scientific intelligentsia by failing to regularize specialist impact on policy, and alienated many workers and peasants by threatening their hopes for privatism and material security.[6]

After Khrushchev's overthrow, his successors moved quickly to redefine the terms of political participation, social transformation, and economic achievement. In the realm of political participation, the new regime immediately took measures to reassert the political autonomy of Soviet officialdom from personalistic rule and public, unregulated, mass criticism. The bifurcation of the Party apparatus was immediately revoked; the rotation of officeholders was suspended; the Party-State Control Commission was transformed into an organization that would leave the Party apparatus to check up on the behavior of its own; the practice of expanded plenary sessions attended by non-Party specialists was dropped, and, after the March 1965 session on agriculture, stenographic transcripts of the proceedings of the sessions were no longer published. In addition, most of the "diploma specialists" recruited into the apparat during 1962–64 were purged shortly after Khrushchev's overthrow, and the importance of training in a Party school before advancement into, and within, the Party apparat was restored. Further still, the role of the non-Party population in the adult political education program was rapidly reversed. In sum, Khrushchev's tendency to "go public" and to circumvent normal channels in legitimizing and implementing policy was rejected, as were his attempts to diminish or close the gap in relative political status between the aktiv and the apparatchiki.

Political participation in the uppermost, ruling circles was also placed on a new basis. Criticisms of Khrushchev's "subjectivism," "voluntarism," and "hare-brained schemes" implied, among other things, a commitment to *proceduralism* in the conduct of collective leadership and a determination that stable norms for political interaction among the members of the Politburo would be developed and respected. Although much discussion must have occurred behind the scenes in defining these norms, the most important example of this commitment of which we have gained knowledge is the Central Committee resolution of October 1964 declaring that henceforth the posts of Party first secretary and chairman of the Council of Ministers would not be combined in the same person. Moreover, informal understandings were apparently also reached, limiting the ability of the first secretary to dominate the allocation of patronage and establishing a norm against disproportionate Politburo representation by either the Party Secretariat or the Council of Ministers.[7]

The combination of restored political status for Soviet officials and collective leadership at the top made clear that Khrushchev's successors would cater to the most basic yearnings and interests of Soviet officialdom. Indeed, the new leaders were quite explicit in signaling to the Soviet political elite that Soviet officials would be the beneficiaries of a retreat from "unremitting pressure as a principle of rule.[8] Thus, numerous statements during 1965–66 indicated formal rejection of Khrushchev's contention that policy failures were a consequence of the administrators' lack of will or competence. At the Twenty-third Party Congress, Brezhnev gave such assurance to Party cadres, when he declared that "the development of the principle of democratic centralism has found expression in . . . the manifestation of *complete trust* in cadres. . . ." [9] Similarly, Kosygin, in his presentation of the economic reforms of 1965, described the regime's changing posture toward its managerial executives by reassuring them that "the party and the people value the country's experts and executives *whom they fully trust and support in their difficult work* for the good of society." [10] The two critical words in this statement are, of course, "trust" and "difficult." The conception of trust indicated a formal rejection of the earlier notion that mistakes by officials would be taken as indications of their lack of social consciousness. Moreover, the recognition that their work is difficult accorded cadres the assurance that some mistakes are acknowledged to be in the nature of the task and that these will not be interpreted simply as gross incompetence.

Although the regime avoided ideological redefinition during 1964–66, it did diminish the salience in public literature of ideological conceptions with antiofficial, Khrushchevian overtones. By 1967, however, there began to appear in *Pravda* and *Kommunist* articles and official statements indicating a redefinition of the "State of All the People." These statements still spoke of "self-regulation" as the ideal and even as the best way of describing the current reality. But this concept was no longer viewed as in any way contradictory to the notion of "strengthening" the state, using it as the "organizational principle in solving problems of communist construction," or using it as an instrument of "discipline." [11] This change was part of a larger effort to reaffirm both the professionalized character and political status of state officials: "There functions in a socialist state a specialized apparatus, consisting of officials who are professionally concerned with questions of administering public affairs." [12] This perspective stood in marked contrast to previous doctrine, as expressed in the 1961 Party Program's contention that work in the state bureaucracy could "cease to constitute a special vocation." [13] Thus, the terms of mass political participation were being redefined, a tendency that complemented the policy changes listed above and reinforced both a reduction in opportunities for mass criticism of the terms of political participation and a crackdown on cultural dissidence.

Yet within the context of reasserting the political autonomy of Soviet officialdom, the regime also sought to upgrade the quality of specialist input into decisionmaking processes by changing both the channels of access and the ethos of the regime. Scientific commissions were attached to Party committees, and bureaus for "concrete sociological investigations" were established throughout the country. A resolution calling for expanded public opinion polling had already been passed at the October 1964 plenum. The state and Party bureaucracies also moved to rationalize information flows between the Academy of Sciences and the political authorities at the top.[14]

At the same time, both the policy premises and the ethos of the regime were altered in order to create conditions under which expanded specialist input might be processed and find its way into policy outputs. Accordingly, the new regime immediately rejected Khrushchev's overly optimistic and arbitrary approach to planning, criticizing him for "actions based on wishful thinking, boasting and empty words."[15] More to the point, speeches by Soviet leaders suddenly included a ceaseless repetition of the need for "realism" in planning. Target setting was no longer to be a process of anticipating the unprecedented so much as a process of judging possibilities on the basis of past performance. Or, as Brezhnev put it in September 1965: "In brief, everything must be done to put an end to voluntarism and subjectivism in planning. Workers in the planning agencies must be guided in their work exclusively by objective economic calculations, and they must have the possibilities for this."[16] These perspectives, in fact, found expression in the targets for the Eighth Five-Year Plan (1966–70), which, compared with the Seven-Year Plan (1959–65) and the Party Program of 1961, reduced the gap between aspirations and capacities to a very great extent.

A corollary to the need for "realism" was the persistent call for "scientific decisionmaking." It is true that Party leaders had always claimed special, scientific insight into the laws of historical development, based upon their ideological legacy in Marx's "scientific socialism." Used in that way, however, the term was basically a cover for the definitional function and political autonomy of Party officials, who would provide the direction and basic goals for the nation. What was occurring after Khrushchev was something different: a redefinition of the meaning of "scientific decisionmaking" in the direction of a more open-ended, empirical approach that did not excessively prejudge conclusions.[17] The task of communicating this redefinition to Soviet officials fell to Pyotr Demichev, CPSU Central Committee Secretary for Ideological Affairs:

> Lenin saw a truly scientific approach to lie in a precise evaluation of the facts of life, of the existing situation, of the correlation of class forces. . . . He often repeated that a concrete analysis of a concrete situation is the soul of Marxism. . . . It ill becomes a scientist to forego the truth under the influence of the political situation or other attendant circumstances. In their struggle to discover and know the

> truth, to put the fruits of scientific work at the service of the interests of the people, the interests of peace and progress, Soviet scientists will always have the complete support of the Party and the government.[18]

These words (and others like them) should not be dismissed as mere rhetoric: not only were they consistent with policy changes at the time, but they also had behavioral consequences in serving to assure specialists that their efforts to conduct empirical research, and to gain access to officials, would receive political support at the top. It would be remarkable indeed if many specialists were not emboldened by such assurances. They now had further ammunition to bring to ongoing political conflicts: they could cite the authorities' stress on realism, scientific decisionmaking, the "scientific technological revolution," and the ever-increasing "complexity" of problems to support the cause of expanded empirical input into decisionmaking processes.[19]

¶ The Brezhnev Era, Phase One: Social Transformation and Economic Achievement

The political contract of the first phase of the Brezhnev administration, then, entailed a dual commitment to institutionalizing the privileged political status of Soviet officialdom and expanding specialist input on social and economic issues. The social contract, in turn, entailed a repudiation of Khrushchevian efforts to use campaignist pressure against yearnings for privatism and security. The premises for these changes, in fact, were reflected in Soviet leaders' speeches almost from the time of Khrushchev's overthrow. In November 1964, for example, Brezhnev declared that "Now more than ever the necessity is evident for the wide application in our country of economic stimuli in the development of production."[20] One month later, Kosygin amended the Party Program's earlier emphasis on the role of collective rewards: "Despite the growing role of public consumption funds, the principal source for satisfying the people's needs in the conditions of socialism remains payment according to labor, which derives from the principles of socialism."[21] In April 1965, Demichev chimed in, pointing out that "the augmentation of the wealth of the collective farms and the growth on this basis of the personal incomes of the collective farmers do not contradict the interests of socialist society."[22] And at the Twenty-third Party Congress (April 1966), Kosygin noted that "*the main thing in our labor-payments policy* is a steady rise in the stimulating role of wages in solving the major production tasks of the five-year plan."[23] Although there must certainly have been conflict within the political elite, and the Politburo itself, over the *extent* and the *structure* of material incentives and individual rewards, it did not prevent a distinct shift in perspective and emphasis in the direction of each.

Indeed, major policy changes at the time reflected these premises. A comprehensive program for improving agricultural production, unveiled in March 1965, represented a clear break with Khrushchev's commitment to optimism and pressure.[24] Production norms were reduced and made more uniform, and promises were extended that they would remain stable from year to year. Khrushchev's restrictions on the private sector were lifted, and the peasant was given financial incentives to raise productivity in this sphere. Procurement prices were raised dramatically, and a vast program of state investments was announced. Most significantly, increases in procurement prices for most products reflected the regime's attempt, much more serious than in the past, to adjust prices to previous years' *costs*. Indeed, after outlining these measures, Brezhnev gave a principled justification to the new approach: "We proceed on the premise that (these measures) will allow us to place the grain economy on a firm basis, and to put an end to the low profitability of grain production on the collective and state farms in a number of the country's zones." [25]

The industrial reforms announced in September 1965 had a similar emphasis on economic rationalization through appeals to personal material gain and stable expectations. Accordingly, the role of profits was to increase substantially and "to constitute the principal source of managers' and workers' bonuses." [26] Moreover, these bonuses were henceforth to constitute a greater percentage of total earnings, as larger and more varied bonus funds were introduced. Decision-rules were changed so as to lead managers to pursue profitability and salability as their primary success indicators. The number of success indicators was reduced drastically, and the amount of discretion formally accorded the manager in manipulating resources within his enterprise was increased. In contrast to the traditional Stalinist emphasis on detailed directives and unremitting pressure, the reforms of 1965 were based upon a greater faith in "automatic levers," through which managers would be induced to exercise entrepreneurial initative. In contrast to the Khrushchevian penchant for frequent administrative reshuffling, these reforms promised officials a more stable and predictable task environment in which to work. The doctrine of "trust in cadres" was thus supplemented by a doctrine of administrative stability: frequent reorganizations, Brezhnev declared, "created an atmosphere of nervousness and bustle, deprived managers of a long-range perspective and undermined their faith in their abilities." [27]

The expanded emphasis on individual material rewards, instead of political pressure, as a means of spurring initiative among workers, peasants, and administrators was accompanied by other changes that further sacrificed Khrushchevian social values. The regime moved quickly to remove many restrictions on private housing construction and to make a commitment to vastly expanded production of private automobiles, at the same time abolishing, as noted, many restrictions on the private sector in agriculture.

The regime further sacrificed goals of radical social transformation to those of immediate economic achievement in its approach to educational access. The educational reforms of 1958, which had called for polytechnical education for all and work in the factories for almost all who aspired to a university education, were formally revoked, allowing a return to relative elitism in the universities.[28] Children of the intelligentsia would henceforth increase their proportions at the universities, since their generally superior preparation and motivation tended to give them a competitive advantage on entrance examinations. The achievement-based needs of the scientific-technological revolution, it seems, were at the time perceived to be more important than the egalitarian pay-offs resulting from rapid social mobility for the underprivileged.

Indeed, all these changes in the political, social, and economic realms were accompanied by interesting trends in the philosophical literature related to the concept of "social interest." According to the traditional Soviet monolithic image of society, "there is no room for particular purposes that diverge from those of society." [29] By this interpretation, the interests of one were the interests of all. Harmony between state and society reigned supreme. The individual's "interests" were defined by his class affiliation and were therefore considered to be objective characteristics, interpreted for him by the state. Unremitting pressure on factory managers was justified by the demand that they place "state interests" over "personal" or "enterprise" interests. The goal of radical social transformation legitimized a simplified view of society that did not accord recognition to the "interests" of social groups within classes. The independence of the political elite from unregulated social forces was legitimized by the Party and state's exclusive right to define the public interest, a task that was not viewed as problematic.

After Khrushchev's dismissal, however, all these assumptions became open to question. The sociological and philosophical literature introduced a significant revision of the traditional, "solidary" conception by acknowledging the existence of differentiated interests in society. Society began to be viewed as being composed not simply of *classes* but of *groups* and *strata* with interests of their own.[30] Similarly, and in line with the thrust of the economic reform, factories and other organizational units were viewed as having distinct interests, with the role of the state being to coordinate and harmonize those diverse interests.[31] The philosophical literature also moved toward a revision of traditional doctrine, and many theoreticians embraced a movement away from the notion that interests are "essentially" objective phenomena to a definition of interests as "the unity of the objective and subjective." Because the notion of "unity" was vague, it began to be equated with "correlation," which led to calls for using concrete sociological research to determine the correlation in Soviet society between the objective positions of certain groups and their subjective definitions of their group or class interests.[32] The implication was that the regime recognized the profoundly problematic nature of the task of defining and enforcing the "public interest." The regime acknowledged that it could not manipulate society effectively without taking into account the existing level of consciousness among various groups of society, a process that required learning more about how people themselves define their interests. In a sense, there was a temporary victory of "system management" over "revolution from above."[33]

These philosophical changes had many practical policy consequences. After Khrushchev's overthrow, social scientists were given greater latitude to explore the distinctive characteristics and "interests" of groups and strata in society, in part through the public opinion polling noted above. Sociologists expanded their inquiries into the character of intraclass mobility and intraclass differentiation. Jurists expanded their discussions of ways to define the rights and responsibilities of Soviet citizenship, while economists delved more deeply into the role of material incentives and administrative rationalization in spurring economic efficiency. At the same time, the authorities expanded their efforts to revise methods of mobilization in line with their more complex appreciation of societal differentiation. The role of politinformator was developed to supplement the traditional agitator in political education.[34] Politinformatory would be more educated and specialized mobilizers, whose sophistication would make them more effective in relating to the more highly skilled and educated strata of the population. In a similar vein, the regime sought to revise public lecture programs to infuse them with a more "differentiated" approach to their audiences. In short, Khrushchev's successors combined a reemphasis on statism with a diminished emphasis on radical transformation, but tried to upgrade the capacity of welfare-state authoritarianism for social engineering.

¶ The Elitist Liberal Illusion

The cluster of policies and premises that followed quickly on the heels of Khrushchev's removal pointed in the direction of a left-wing version of welfare-state authoritarianism.[35] By upgrading the importance of political institutionalization and proceduralism, specialist input, managerial autonomy, material incentives, privatism, and social differentiation, these measures raised questions in the minds of Western observers of whether the Soviet leadership had abandoned its traditional values to become pragmatic or technocratic in orientation.[36] At the same time, these changes initially raised the hopes of many members of the Soviet intelligentsia that further movement to the left might be forthcoming. Some hoped for further political institutionalization—or even constitutionalization; others looked forward to further development of the spirit of the economic reforms, allowing for substantial managerial autonomy in industry and agriculture, coupled with massive income differentiation designed to spur worker and managerial initiative. "Libermanism," the Shchekino experiment, and the link system in agriculture provided their rallying cry. In sum, to many liberalizers within the Soviet establishment, the changes immediately following Khrushchev's dismissal provided hope of further development toward elitist liberalism.[37]

Yet the hope turned out to be an illusion, and not only because a backlash later set in—as we shall see below. The mistake came from an overestimation of the strength of these new premises and a view of them, in many cases, as potential *substitutes* for earlier orientations. If we reexamine what was happening at the time, we find that what took place was a shifting of the weights within a mix of premises. The industrial reforms, for example, were severely limited by the continued commitment to political intervention and an egalitarian social policy. Administrative forces within the system continued to prescribe managerial behavior in great detail, and the size of bonuses allowed managers engaging in successful innovation was deliberately circumscribed. Unwilling to create a system in which managers would be free of political intervention and pressure, or in which managers' incomes would exceed still more greatly those of the workers in their factories, the regime created conditions under which "automatic levers" would be stifled or undermined, even as they were being extolled as the harbingers of technological innovation.

Most of the other changes noted were also constrained or supplemented by competing premises. Material incentives and the possibilities of private accumulation for workers and peasants were increased but remained far from sufficient to elicit a significant rise in labor enthusiasm or individual responsibility. Regime aspirations in the Eighth Five-Year Plan (1966–70) were considerably lower than the targets of the 1961 Party Program, but they remained, nonetheless, ambitious enough to require mobilization and pressure for their attainment. The ability of specialists to ensure or anticipate responsiveness to their input was constrained by the simultaneous reinforcement of the political status of Party officials, apparent efforts to rehabilitate Stalin, and the prosecution of an antirevisionism campaign after the trial of Sinyavsky and Daniel in February 1966. The economic reform challenged the traditional conception of Party activism in the factory, but the regime simultaneously worked to *extend* Party agitation in residential areas,[38] and primary party organizations began, already in 1966, to seek ways of recovering their traditional mobilizational role in the factory. Achievement criteria were stressed in university admissions, but some "affirmative action" programs remained, and the regime continued to expand construction of specialized secondary educational establishments as a means of encouraging mobility out of the less-skilled, blue-collar strata. The material privileges of top officials, which had been challenged by Khrushchev, were restored, but measures were taken to strengthen the overall post-Stalin trend toward income equalization among the classes.

Thus, the post-Khrushchev adjustments represented a shifting of weights among the premises that comprise the basic contract of welfare-state authoritarianism, but *within the context of* an ongoing commitment to political intervention in cultural, economic, and social affairs, resocialization of the populace, and a relatively egalitarian social policy. The more realistic question under these circumstances would have been not whether post-Khrushchev changes presaged a breakthrough into elitist liberalism but whether the changes could survive a backlash. Indeed, during 1966–68, the pressures of mobilizational, anti-revisionist, and egalitarian premises expanded. By 1969 they crystallized and a backlash set in, ushering in still another selective shifting of weights.

¶ The Brezhnev Era, Phase Two: Political Participation

After 1969, changes initiating a selective retrenchment and movement to the right could be observed in each of the dimensions of political participation under review in this essay. At the top, the delicate balance within the collective leadership appeared to shift. Brezhnev visibly expanded his role, acquiring primary supervision over foreign policy.[39] By most Kremlinological evidence, the general secretary became the most visible and central figure in the collective leadership, with levels of adulation rising steadily through the 1970s. Indeed, by 1976 one could speak of a genuine personality cult, expressed in paeans of praise in newspapers, journals, and speeches of other leaders. By 1977 the general secretary had gone still farther, acquiring the titles of marshall of the Soviet Union, supreme commander of the armed forces, and chairman of the Defense Council of the USSR. Also in 1977, Brezhnev crowned the expansion of his political base by dropping Nikolai Podgorny from the Politburo and himself stepping into Podgorny's post as chairman of the Presidium of the Supreme Soviet.

Paralleling Brezhnev's rise has been the steady expansion of both the ideological status and the administrative role of Party organs in relation to state administrators.[40] Ideologically, the concept "Party of All the People" has been effectively dropped from the doctrine, being replaced by a formulation that emphasizes the Communist Party's privileged political status. The Party is therefore now routinely declared to be "the political leader of the working class, of the working people, and of the entire Soviet people."[41] Similarly, the new Soviet Constitution, finally completed and ratified in 1977, placed exceptional emphasis on the leading role of the Party in all spheres of Soviet life, a feature that distinguished this constitution from that of 1936.[42] Augmented status has also been accompanied during the 1970s by an expanded role: since 1971, primary Party organizations within ministries, scientific research institutes, and certain other state institutions have for the first time been given the formal right to exercise supervision over state officials within their domain; in like manner, there has been expanded penetration of central ministerial decisionmaking processes by representatives of the Central Committee apparatus and an expanded role for December Plenary sessions of the Central Committee in supervising ministerial affairs.[43]

All these developments have been accompanied by the formal rejection of the major premises underlying the Kosygin reforms of 1965. Brezhnev sounded the death-knell of those premises at the December 1969 plenum, where he seized the initiative on economic and administrative reform. Referring to the Kosygin reforms, he exclaimed: "These measures have yielded good results. But naturally they still have been unable to solve the problem of increasing the efficiency of the economy as a whole."[44] From this time forward, the entire ethos of regime articulations about the responsibilities of cadres began to change, reflecting a repudiation of the earlier emphasis on "automatic levers." The literature on "scientific management of society," for example, now emphasizes systems analysis and selective application of pressure from above and below as the means of introducing new technologies, while criticizing earlier approaches as fostering "spontaneity."[45] In practice, the authorities have returned to a centralist-prescriptive form of public administration, supplemented by campaigns to overcome human and bureaucratic inertia.

Under these circumstances, the "contract" between the political authorities and the administrators has also been redefined. Since the December 1969 plenum, speeches by leaders have been filled with criticisms of "bad management," "wastefulness," and "lack of discipline." Enterprise directors and ministers alike have been criticized for behavior arising from causes that "cannot be considered objective." [46] The earlier emphasis on "trust in cadres" is now almost always supplemented by the caveat that such trust must be combined with "principled exactingness toward them," indicating that such trust is contingent on adequate performance and that none of them have the right to keep their positions indefinitely.[47] Under these conditions of expanded use of pressure to induce administrative responsibility, the regime has made a concerted effort to recruit young, technically competent individuals into the apparat, while vastly expanding the enrollment of Party and state officials in courses devoted to both practical skills and ideology. The stress on technical competence for Party officials is meant to ensure upgrade of their abilities to supervise technical administrative affairs. The stress on ideology for state officials is meant to expand their awareness of their responsibilities and thereby to increase their responsiveness to pressure. Indeed, an additional measure taken during the early 1970s was an exchange of Party cards, a step ostensibly designed to weed out Party members who had been defaulting on their social responsibilities.

The redefinition of the political contract of welfare-state authoritarianism was extended to the regime's relationship with the intelligentsia as well, and at about the same time. A Central Committee resolution of 1970 was the signal for an intensified antirevisionism campaign in scientific research institutes.[48] Since 1971, scientists have been required to take part in larger numbers of ideological seminars, as a means of countering any narrowly pragmatic tendencies. Also in 1971 the regime announced that primary Party organizations in scientific research institutes would be given a greater role and augmented authority to approve the lists of research topics and to demand displays of political conformity from scientific personnel. In 1972, Party officials purged the Institute for Concrete Sociological Research, scattering the liberal-minded sociologists who had worked there among various institutes. Since then, Soviet sociology has been developed "intensively" rather than "extensively," with a narrower range of topics and conclusions gaining access to publications of wide circulation. Moreover, through the 1970s, there has been an escalating crackdown on overt political defiance ("dissent"), which has resulted in a Constitution placing extraordinary emphasis on "the interests of the state," the "interests of society," and the obligation of the citizen to subordinate personal interests to state interests. Finally, one can detect in Soviet leaders' speeches during the 1970s a much increased use of the term "scientific decisionmaking" in its traditional normative meaning and a diminished use of the term in its newer, more empirical meaning.[49]

¶ The Brezhnev Era, Phase Two: Social Transformation and Economic Achievement

During this period, the regime has also expanded the use of pressure on workers and peasants as a means of increasing labor productivity. Soviet leaders' speeches since the December 1969 plenum have had a persistent refrain: "automatic levers" are not the only means of increasing labor productivity; a crucial factor is the attitude of the individual toward his job and his social obligations. Typical of the messages was Suslov's warning that "our party has never believed and does not now believe that the action of economic incentives is the only action that produces results. . . . Disregard for moral factors is capable of causing just as much national-economic and political damage as ignoring the principles of material interest." [50] The stress has not been simply upon moral incentives, however, for in leaders' speeches there has been an even greater concern for "discipline," "organization," and "responsibility."

Buttressing this change of ethos has been a series of policy changes pointing in the same direction: (1) continuing campaigns for mobilizing reserves, socialist competition, Stakhanovism, and a "regime of savings"; (2) administrative measures designed to reduce labor turnover and increase the penalties for lax performance; (3) a resurgent role for the agitator in pressuring workers on the job; (4) increased pressure on the Party aktiv to adopt "social assignments" and to exercise "iron discipline"; (5) the spread of an industrial tutelary movement (*nastavnichestvo*) geared toward increasing the benevolent supervision of younger workers by older ones; (6) personal productivity plans for workers, specifying their responsibilities and expanding the regime's capacity to monitor poor performance. All these changes, we should bear in mind, have taken place since 1969–70.

The resurgent emphasis on pressure has also led to the demise (however temporary) of such administrative experiments as the Shchekino innovation and the link system.[51] The legitimacy of each has been undermined by resistance to the wide material differentiation they would require and the threat to lower-class job security they would entail. In addition, in the case of the link system, such a reform would threaten the political prerogatives of the rural Party raikom. In a period during which pressure has been gaining ascendancy over "automatic levers" in the mix of policy premises, and in which the political status of Party organs has been reinforced, it should not come as a surprise that these experiments have been undercut.

Egalitarian premises also experienced a comeback in 1969 on questions of social mobility. In September of that year, the regime passed new laws facilitating entrance to universities for children of peasant background, demobilized soldiers, and the working class. "Preparatory sections" were established for people from these categories, and those who successfully completed the course of study were promised admission to the university without entrance competition. As one Western scholar observed, "The post-Khrushchev leadership evidently found that active intervention in this important social process was needed in order to counteract the marked elitism which Soviet institutions of higher education [that is, universities], like those of many other lands, seem to engender." [52]

¶ The Fundamentalist Illusion

Indeed, the cluster of changes in policy and premises represented something of a right-wing reaction against the leftist form of welfare-state authoritarianism that was taking shape in 1965. It would be a grave mistake, however, to overstate the extent and character of this backlash through the indiscriminate use of such labels as "neo-Stalinism." Just as we saw that the orientations of the mid-1960s represented a subtle mix of premises weighted at first in the leftist direction, so we now find that the backlash since 1969 constitutes a selective retrenchment through a shifting of weights within a cluster of premises. The shift did *not* violate the basic contract of welfare-state authoritarianism, for it did not entail a return to austerity, terror, or arbitrary, personalistic rule. It *did,* however, reinforce those forces opposed to further movement in the direction of elitist liberalism, which would have constitutionalized collective leadership,[53] ensured managerial autonomy, and encouraged much wider social and material differentiation and social insecurity for the sake of economic performance. It behooves us, therefore, to reexamine this backlash in order to define its character more precisely.

Let me begin with realms of policy relating to political participation. At the top of the policymaking pyramid, Brezhnev's role expansion should not be overstated. There is no evidence to indicate that he has acquired widespread purge powers, or even the ability to push through far-reaching policy changes challenging the prerogatives of major institutions. In fact, his domestic policy program for budgetary reallocation and administrative reform has been resisted by the political and administrative elite.[54] Moreover, after assuming Podgorny's post, Brezhnev felt constrained to reassure the political elite that he would not engage in arbitrary behavior or personalistic rule,[55] and his behavior as general secretary during the 1970s has conformed to the image of a leader who respects (willingly or unwillingly) stable procedural norms in the conduct of policymaking. I conclude, therefore, that Brezhnev's accumulated power has been largely self-protective and defensive in character, allowing him perhaps to weather political storms that others might not survive, but not allowing him to violate the political contract of corporate pluralism within the ruling elite.

Party intervention in administrative affairs has also been selective, in no way approaching the degree of interventionism practiced under Khrushchev. To the contrary, mobilization premises have been accompanied by an ongoing effort to define more clearly the rights, responsibilities, and jurisdictions of administrative personnel as a means of fostering administrative responsibility.[56] As Brezhnev put it at the Twenty-fourth Party Congress in 1971: "At all levels of management . . . extensive rights with little responsibility create opportunities for administrative arbitrariness, subjectivism, and ill-considered decisions. But extensive responsibilities with few rights [that is, the Khrushchevian pattern] is no better. In such a situation, even the most diligent official often finds himself powerless, and it is difficult to hold him fully responsible for the job assigned." And at the Twenty-fifth Party Congress, Brezhnev reiterated this concern and upgraded its importance still further, dubbing it "the essence of organizational questions" and the "foundation of foundations of the science and practice of administration." At the same Party Congress he continued to call for rationalization of administrative success indicators, indicating the problematic character of establishing administrative responsibility in the absence of such rationalization. Success indicators, he averred, "must harmonize the interests of the worker with the interests of the enterprise, and the interests of the enterprise with the interests of the state." [57]

This admission that augmented pressure cannot solve the problems of administrative control in an irrationally planned command economy has had an important political corollary. Unlike Stalin or Khrushchev, the current regime, in its criticisms of managerial behavior, has not gone so far as to equate "bad management" with "antistate" behavior. It is not questioning the *loyalty* of its personnel, nor does it feel the need to devolve all responsibility for economic difficulties. At the Twenty-fourth Party Congress, for instance, Brezhnev rejected a return to earlier definitions of "discipline" and called instead for "discipline that is not based on fear or on methods of ruthless administrative fiat, which deprive people of confidence and initiative and give rise to overcautiousness and dishonesty. What is involved here is discipline that is based on a high level of people's consciousness and responsibility." [58]

This subtle shift in premises should not be written off as political rhetoric, for it has been accompanied by policies consistent with its thrust. Thus, the authorities have not engaged in a purge of the administrative elite. Indeed, the exchange of Party cards during 1973–75 resulted in expulsion of only about 1 percent of the Party membership.[59] Moreover, the selective reemphasis on pressure has not prevented a rather steady effort to diminish the imbalances in the Five-Year Plans. The Tenth Five-Year Plan (1976–80), in fact, is especially noteworthy for its unprecedented degree of congruence between aspirations and capacities (though it is ambitious nonetheless).[60] The expanded emphasis on "demandingness" toward cadre, therefore, does not imply either purge or a "great leap forward" mentality.

The retrenchment has also been selective and ambiguous with respect to specialist input and the status of the intelligentsia. The normative definition of "scientific decisionmaking" has acquired increased prominence, but it has coexisted with continued deference to the empirical definition. Moreover, since the early 1970s, the regime has simultaneously upgraded the ideological status of science. Science is no longer just *becoming* a direct product force, as was declared in the Party Program of 1961; it now has become such a force, according to official Soviet doctrine.[61] Then too, officially articulated deference to the "potential" and "complexity" of the "scientific-technological revolution" continues unabated. All these items reflect an ongoing commitment to the development of a knowledge industry relatively unencumbered by dogmatic preconceptions.

But there are strict limits as well. Scientific empiricism is called upon to play a distinctively instrumental role, helping the authorities to better understand the environments they are trying to manipulate. Scientists will be accorded official status only in return for political docility. Thus, whereas scientists have had to attend more philosophical seminars, and their research projects have been subjected to closer scrutiny, the priorities of economic progress have not been sacrificed. Rather, the current message appears to be that in return for a certain latitude in research and regularized access to officials within their fields of specialization, the scientific community has a reciprocal obligation to: (1) focus its research on problems related to the priorities defined by the regime, and (2) compartmentalize its critical faculties, exercising them within scientific fields of inquiry but not extending them to critical questions of political authority. In short, the regime has committed itself to creating conditions under which scientists can be experts, but it expects them not to become public intellectuals.

The backlash on questions of social transformation and economic

48631

efficiency has also been a limited one. The renewed emphasis on regimentation, exhortation, and obligation has not constituted a return to the philosophy of deferred gratification or economic austerity, notwithstanding ideological criticism of the "cult of things and the standards of the notorious consumer society." [62] There has been no cutback in the material reward that one can earn for hard work; if anything, material incentives have been continually expanded in an effort to spur productivity. In addition, the regime has expanded its investments in agricultural development to massive dimensions (now investing more in agriculture than do the United States and Western Europe combined). In a similar vein, the authorities have committed scarce foreign currency to the importation of varying types of consumer goods and have expanded very greatly the availability of consumer goods other than food. Then too, in 1971, when the campaigns for "moral incentives" were gaining momentum, Leonid Brezhnev proposed to the Twenty-fourth Party Congress a program for inducing heavy industrial enterprises to expand their production of consumer-oriented products.[63] In the light of these trends, the conclusion is unmistakable that the backlash entails a subtle redefinition of the social contract: the regime attempts to increase the availability of consumer goods at measured rates and maintains its commitment to meeting consumer expectations; in return, however, the authorities demand that consumers keep these expectations within strict bounds and respond with labor contributions to the current levels of material incentives. Political and social pressure, in turn, are counted on to supplement material incentives and make them effective. Indeed, such pressures are directed against the attitudes vividly expressed by the Moscow workers' saying of the 1970s: "As long as the bosses pretend to be paying us a decent wage, we'll pretend we're working." [64]

Nor has the regime taken actions reminiscent of Khrushchevian campaigns of social transformation. The backlash since 1969 has hardly—if at all—affected the post-Khrushchev commitment to privatism. Pressure on the agricultural private sector has not been notably increased. Housing and automobile production have proceeded at levels sufficient to give many urban dwellers the hope of some day having a single-family apartment and a private automobile. As for social mobility, the educational reform of 1969 was significant, but although it may be further developed in the future, it has thus far not been as detrimental to the aspirations of children of the intelligentsia as were the reforms of 1958. Young scientists are not being asked to work in the factories before entering the university. Preparatory sections do not appear to have caused a major shift in the social composition of student bodies.[65] The current approach, then, is clearly a compromise between the meritocratic de-

42631

mands of the "scientific-technological revolution" and the more egalitarian, mass-oriented basis of early Soviet political culture.

Finally, the resurgent emphasis on both regimentation and the privileged political status of official organs should not be interpreted as a return to Stalinist methods of control. Contemporary calls for "discipline" lack the paranoid component of the Stalinist era. Today, "discipline" usually means that the masses are expected to be politically conformist and to remain sober, arrive at work on time, labor hard and conscientiously, upgrade their skills, and participate in such occasional rituals as subbotniki (donation of off-work time to state projects) and political lectures. Moreover, while the political prerogatives of official organs have been restored since Khrushchev and enhanced since 1969, there has been no systematic return to the commandist and heavy-handed leadership orientation of earlier years. Quite the contrary: the right of trade unions to protect workers against being fired has been reinforced and reaffirmed. Moreover, the new Constitution contains an extraordinary article to the effect that citizens who feel they have been subjected to arbitrary official behavior may appeal for redress of their grievances beyond the bureaucracy in question to the courts. It remains to be seen how this system will work in practice, but this feature of the Constitution, combined with a pervasive emphasis on "legality" in the document and contrasted with the Constitution's simultaneous emphasis on the "interests of the state," provides an important clue to the strategy of the authorities for maintaining political stability. They appear to be attempting to isolate the mass of politically conformist workers from the dissenters by providing a less austere and repressive daily life for the masses, while cracking down on the dissenters. As Brezhnev put it in his closing words to the Twenty-fourth Party Congress, his regime was creating an atmosphere in which people who do not become dissenters can "breathe freely, work well, and live quietly." [66]

¶ Policy Clusters and Political Support

Ambiguity remains, however, about the precise reason for the shifting mix of premises since 1969. If we accept conflict as a universal feature of oligarchic rule, but nonetheless view the Soviet Politburo as a *relatively* unified elite possessing multiple goals (efficiency *and* equity; expertise *and* political docility on the part of scientists; political autonomy *and* expanded input; military-industrial might *and* consumer satisfaction; material incentives *and* Party activism), then we explain the changes as resulting from a learning experience: in response to the Khrushchevian experience, the actor pays considerable attention to one set of premises during 1964–68, finds that his actions have unanticipated consequences violating his other goals, and takes corrective measures. Interpretations that point to environmental changes as mediating factors also employ this unitary image. Thus, a scarcity of resources in the late 1960s could have triggered regime attention to the need for cheaper, mobilizational approaches to productivity. Similarly, the Dubček movement in Czechoslovakia could be viewed as an impulse leading to greater distrust of Soviet intellectuals and expanded emphasis on the political status of Party organs, and worker riots in Poland might have alerted the regime to the desirability of increasing attention to consumer welfare.

On the other hand, one might argue that the changes resulted from a shift in political alignments, with those forces favoring the leftist movement of the mid-1960s suddenly finding themselves on the defensive. Environmental factors, such as events in Czechoslovakia and Poland or domestic problems, would then be viewed as triggering a shift in *political coalitions*. If the changes at the turn of the decade reflect a political change, then the current mix of premises (as well as the mix of 1965–66) might be interpreted as a *resultant* of bargaining and compromise rather than a result of rational calculation by a more or less unified Politburo.

To decide the issue would require evidence of a different sort than that collected in this article. Content analysis of leaders' speeches, or careful examination of discussions among academics and officials, might help us to evaluate the extent to which occupants of different positions view the premises under discussion here as incompatible or antithetical. This analysis would move us beyond two of the gravest weaknesses in Soviet studies to date: (1) the tendency to impute the interests of different groups and deduce their political postures, thereby largely ignoring the possibilities for coalition-building across institutions; and (2) the failure to differentiate among types and degrees of political conflict within the political elite, assuming instead that all observable conflict must necessarily be severe and potentially destabilizing.[67]

The Brezhnev era provides an especially intriguing case for investigation along these lines. The backlash of 1969, however selective and measured, was nonetheless real, and it occurred across such a broad range of issue-areas as to suggest a high degree of linkage among policy premises within the Soviet political elite. At the same time, the very selectivity of the backlash suggests that the linkages are not fixed and that trade-offs among the premises are possible.[68] Also intriguing is the remarkable stability, despite the shift, of the composition of the Politburo. From April 1966 to April 1973, no individual was removed from full membership in the Politburo. And between December 1965 and

May 1977, the inner core of that body (Brezhnev, Kosygin, Podgorny, Suslov, and Kirilenko) did not change. Those positing an unusually high level of overt conflict, or perceived *incompatibility* among policy premises in the eyes of the decisionmakers, cannot explain these trends.

And what of the future? It is undeniable that within the broader Soviet attentive public there exists support for both elitist liberalism and for a fundamentalist reaction.[69] How broad that support might be and how much of an echo it finds within the political elite, however, remain open questions. The record of the Brezhnev era suggests considerable support for the social and political contract of welfare-state authoritarianism, with conflict focusing largely upon differences along a left-right continuum within welfare-state authoritarianism. I have argued elsewhere that a rightist version of this regime-type would have little chance of mitigating social and political tensions within society-at-large and that it would probably result in increasing polarization within the elite.[70] A centrist or leftist version, however, would perhaps be viable. Whether changes during the Brezhnev succession will be marked by another within-system shift in the mix of premises, or whether they will result in disorder, elitism liberalism, or a fundamentalist reaction cannot be predicted. Much will depend on circumstances, accidents, and personalities. But much will also depend upon the extent to which different groups find the social and political contract of welfare-state authoritarianism to be tolerable and the extent to which policy premises within that contract are viewed as compatible. Then too, much will hinge on the lessons drawn by members of the political elite from fourteen years of experimenting with a constrained set of policy options.[71] Insofar as the present and past can be a guide to the future, the evidence adduced in this essay constitutes a first step toward a research strategy for evaluating the adaptability of welfare-state authoritarianism.

Robert W. Campbell

Economic Reform and Adaptation of the CPSU

¶ Introduction

The topic of adaptation by the Communist Party of the USSR to societal change is of great interest to the economist. Economic development is a pervasive and influential force for general societal change. Forty years of economic growth in the USSR have transformed the environment for economic growth, and the transformation has led to changes in the goals and the strategy of growth, which in turn has led to pressure for changes in the institutions that embody and implement that strategy—that is, for economic reform.

But experience with economic reform in the Soviet Union and in other Soviet-type economies has led to some doubts about the adaptive potential of the system, its ability to reform itself. The Party is intimately involved in this process, of course. It is so central an institution in the economic and political order that economic system change is bound to affect its role and functions; on the other hand, the Party has the final say over the kind and extent of reform that can take place. One of the explanations commonly offered for the failure to achieve significant economic reform in the sixties is a fear among Party leaders of an erosion of its power.

¶ Depoliticization of Planning and Management

One of the main themes of the analysis and discussion of the reform effort in Eastern Europe and the USSR is that a fundamental requirement for improved operation of the economy is "depoliticization" of economic planning and management. This is a familiar enough slogan but, in order to make clear how the term is used below, some elaboration is required. The Soviet political-economic order and the Soviet strategy of development have always been characterized by a fusion of political and economic functions. Moreover, the Soviet leaders have always approached their problems in a *strategic* manner. That is, we can conceptualize the world with which the Soviet leaders have been trying to deal as involving a hierarchy of means-ends relationships. The broad objectives of the leaders—growth, national security, personal power, and so on—can be conceived of as dependent on a variety of rather general policy variables that can be considered as means—growth of the steel industry, allocation of resources between defense and investment, and so on. Any one of these intermediate level variables can alternatively be thought of as a goal to be pursued in turn by a variety of more detailed means. Some proximate goal—development of the steel industry, for example—can be pursued by such means as different locational patterns, domestic or foreign technology, or alternative combinations of capital and labor. It is also useful to distinguish in this hierarchy two broad domains of variables that might be characterized as "allocational-operational" and "institutional-constitutional." The split between consumption and investment, general priorities within the fuel sector, and technological emphases are examples of the first, whereas collectivization, the principle of the foreign trade monopoly, and ministerial versus branch organization are examples of the second.

The economist would like to order this hierarchy in a way that would neatly separate means and ends. Parallel to this separation would then be a distinction between the political process of setting goals and the technical processes of choosing efficient means for achieving those goals. Economics provides much of the technical discipline for this latter process, but some of the issues are illuminated by political and administrative science, sociology, and other social sciences.

It has always been a hallmark of the Soviet system that the leadership at the top has tried to keep this distinction between means and ends muddied. The leaders like to express their decisions in policy variables associated with the middle ranks in this hierarchy, that is, variables that embody a considerable prejudgment about means. Rather than simply setting performance goals for agriculture, they also specify an organizational means—collectivization. They have always gone beyond the high-level issue of the split between consumption and investment to concern themselves also with the relative rates of growth of Industry *A* and Industry *B*. They like to specify allocations of capital between sectors of the economy, such as industry and agriculture, rather than limiting themselves to specifying the relative size of industrial and agricultural output.

There are numerous reasons for this approach. One is that the distinction between means and ends is not always clear. Some policy ranked in the hierarchy as a means to some other goal may be seen as an end in itself, as is the case with collectivization. This is particularly true of constitutional-institutional variables.

There have often been ideological prohibitions against techniques that would permit the separation of tasks into a goal-setting function and the technical function of choosing the means. For example, the kind of cost effectiveness calculations that would settle the optimal input mix to achieve a prescribed output was not acceptable ideologically, so the leaders treated input allocations as a goal within their jurisdiction as political leaders.

One very important reason for this mixing of means and ends is probably that it is one way to exercise power, in the very literal sense that the exercise of power strengthens it. One of the significant grounds claimed for the Party's legitimacy has been that the Party alone has the judgment and the vision to manage society. Therefore, it has been important to follow through on this claim by arrogating to the Party generalists questions that were really the province of technicians. Stalin showed his belief in this principle by destroying a whole generation of economists and a significant number of the managerial experts.

This technique partly reflected Stalin's megalomania, but it can probably also serve some functional purposes. When the leadership operates in an environment of uncertainty and hostility, detailed interference is seen as necessary to ensure that the leaders can guide the direction in which the economy is moving and to ensure the achievement of priority goals. Procurement targets for agricultural products, for example, were seen as more likely than output targets and prices to get the leaders the deliveries they wanted. Also, some of these middle-level variables are very direct and operational, as in the case of determining the main sectoral priorities through the investment allocation. This is also an expression of a common feature of Soviet planning, that is, considerable redundancy (in the sense of communication theory), a feature understandable in a transmission process where inertia and hostility introduce a lot of noise into communication channels.

Economic reform and rationalization have always meant a retreat from this stance of confusing political and economic decisions. The acceptance of input-output analysis has made clear to an increasingly large circle of planners that the leaders need not concern themselves with setting gross outputs for all the branches of the economy but can limit themselves to the structure of final demand. Specification of final demand can fully embody the preferences of the leaders about resource use, and the computer can then find out what this final output structure implies about gross outputs for each sector. Similarly, it is now generally accepted that, once the structure of output is set, then the allocation of capital is basically a technical issue to be settled by capital effectiveness calculations according to a theory devised by the economists. The higher levels of the power structure have reluctantly given up some arbitrary specification of the variables involved, but there are still numerous areas where they refuse to be persuaded. For example, the proposition that the output mix of consumer goods or the input mix for any producer could be settled effectively by profit calculations is a notion it has not yet been possible for the reformers to sell.

On all those issues, the decision to retreat can be posed and resolved as a trade-off between two kinds of power. The argument a reformer can make in favor of any such move up the means-ends hierarchy is that, by giving up their petty tutelage over some instrumental variable, the leaders get more real control over the big issues and, as a result of rational rather than arbitrary decisions, more economic resources with which to pursue the big objectives. Another rationale for moving attention up the hierarchy is often that it is no longer necessary to intervene in lower-level issues, because socialist development has altered the resource base and the class situation. A reformer would argue that the invention of input-output analysis and linear programming represent successes of socialist Soviet science that permit the task of planning to be approached in a new way. The creation of a truly socialist cadre of managerial personnel imbued with the spirit of socialism permits more decisionmaking to be entrusted to them. The reformer can argue that, unlike the peasant with his inherently petty-bourgeois ideology, the present-day Soviet kolkhoznik is a supporter of the Soviet regime, so that it becomes possible to organize the state's dealings with him on a price basis, as was not possible when agriculture was in the hands of the class enemy.

But the closer any reform proposal gets to a constitutional-institutional issue, and the closer one moves toward the higher reaches of the means-ends hierarchy, the more sensitive the Party people become. It is virtually impossible to touch the collective farm or such basic institutions as the foreign trade monopoly or to discuss rationally considerations that should govern the split between consumption and investment.

¶ Need for a Parametric Stance toward Management

Further reform of the system is crucially deadlocked over a constitutional issue, that is, the degree of entrepreneurial involvement by the Party and the central apparatus of state power through which it operates in the management of the economy. But a considerable digression is needed to demonstrate this difficulty.

In reviewing past experience with economic reform and interpreting its failures, many analysts have come to the conclusion that one of the greatest problems that must be overcome, but has not yet been faced, is the bargaining stance of the center toward operating management. In thinking about the weaknesses of economic performance in the Soviet-type system, we might distinguish two kinds of waste, two kinds of performance failures. One might be characterized as planning errors—misallocations of inputs among firms or industries, failures to balance supply and demand, uneconomic location choices, and so on. These failures can usually be interpreted as stemming from deficiencies in the informational inputs into decision processes or from reliance on invalid criteria in the making of choices. It is precisely these kinds of deficiencies to which most economic reform measures thus far have been directed and on which current strategies focus. Price reform, the acceptance of input-output and linear programming logic, and the current program of introducing the computer in automated systems of management and planning are all concerned with problems of this nature.

The other type of failure might be described as administrative friction —a failure of the incentive system that leads to defensive, noncompliant, and even obstructive behavior by managers at various levels. Examples include concealment of capacity, bargaining for an easy plan, hoarding materials, unwillingness to innovate or introduce organizational improvements, and so on. A case could be made that the second type of failure is the major source of disappointing performance in the Soviet economy. This sort of behavior leads to underutilization of capacity, low productivity, slow technological progress, and waste of manpower. And it is this kind of behavior that distorts information as it flows up the hierarchy in a way that leads many of us to doubt that the computer by itself will be able to solve the information problem. Soviet writers typically point to the resolution of such administrative frictions as offering the hope of great increases in output, but these reserves somehow never get mobilized.

There is indeed a great potential increment in output from these reserves, and one would think it a simple matter to get this increment produced just by offering the managers a share in it. This extra output or income is a rent or a surplus in the economists' definition. The gain to be had is far bigger than the amount that would have to be paid to managers to compensate them fully for their efforts in producing it. That it is not forthcoming suggests some defect in the contract relationship, in the bargaining process between the top level of the system and the managers in working out the terms under which the latter are going to operate. We can think of this negotiating process as a game of the mixed cooperative-competitive type, with the Party and the managerial class as the players. And it is a variable-sum game in which the total benefits available to the two sides together may be dependent on the outcome of the bargaining interaction over the distribution of the total.

An idea now widely accepted is that this relationship needs to be converted from its present strategic bargaining form to a "parametric" form. The Party leadership and its agent, the state (which, for the moment, we will describe as a single entity, the center), ostensibly have the stronger position in this negotiation and can impose whatever terms they like. The center does, indeed, insist on playing a very active bargaining role with managers, insisting on continual renegotiation of terms and on separate bargains with each participant in the discriminating monopolist tradition of dealing with each client separately and leaning on him as heavily as possible. In this behavior, the center treats the management of the system as a zero-sum game in which anything given up in the way of material rewards to managers subtracts from the resources available to be used to advance goals important to the leaders, and any rights given up represent a corresponding reduction in the power and authority of the center. But it seems to me that this is a misreading of the situation. In the setting of Soviet-style planning, managers possess what Thomas Schelling calls "the coercive power of the weak." [1] In mixed conflict-cooperation games, the bargains reached are determined by the kinds of threats and promises each side can make, and the weak partner can often use the fact of having less at stake to make threats credible. (It was this kind of situation that gave South Vietnam so much control over U.S. actions.) The main defense the Soviet managers have against arbitrary exactions by the center is insistence on their limitations and substantiation of them by mediocre performance. Those who respond to the bait of attractive incentive plans are likely to find that the terms are unilaterally renegotiated in the next round to make their positions rather worse than before.

As Schelling points out, it is often a useful strategy in this situation for the stronger player—the one with the most at stake (the center here) —voluntarily to choose a limited maneuverability as a way of making promises and threats more credible. This player announces the terms offered once and for all, indicates that they are going to be applied uniformly to all comers without fear or favor and then gives this stance credibility by adherence to it in successive rounds. This is what is meant by saying that the center needs to change its present bargaining stance for a parametric stance. I should add that there is no implication here that terms have to be so rigid as to be fixed permanently; an alternative is to supplement the announcement of terms by stating parametrically the basis on which the current terms will be renegotiated.

Now, although these ideas are advanced as aspects of economic bargaining, they have profoundly political implications in either a Marxist or a traditional framework. They are akin to the notions of the rule of law, due process, and constitutional constraints on Party and state power. They suggest the notion of treating managers as a *class* rather than as individual stewards of state property and imply a move to "propertify" or constitutionalize the relationship of management to the means of production.

It will be useful to substantiate and illustrate the importance and *aktual'nost'* (timeliness) of these issues in the experience with economic reform. But the reader may prefer, for continuity's sake, to skip the detour that follows here and go on to the next section.

¶ Concern with Parametric Instruments in the Economic Reform

There are numerous hints in the reform experience of all the Soviet-type societies that this shift to a parametric stance is crucially important but that the Party has never been willing to accept this change in its relationship to management. A Czech economist who participated in designing the first, unsuccessful installment of the Czech economic reforms concluded that much of the problem was in the failure of the reformers to make the terms concerning tax deductions and bonus formulas parametric. Enterprises were, therefore, inclined to invest more effort in negotiating advantageous values for these instruments, allowing for their "special" situation, than in working hard under stated terms. Their argument was always that they could not survive under the stated terms (the coercive power of the weak); and since the government saw itself as responsible for the survival of the enterprises, it was vulnerable to this argument. He concluded that reform would never work unless the center so dissociated itself from the fate of its wards that it could accept their bankruptcy with equanimity and could restrain itself from arbitrary exactions if enterprises should do well under the stated terms. In the USSR the acceptance of bankruptcy was argued by some as important for success of the reforms, but this idea was always rejected by the more conservative and political figures. Another perceptive writer on economic reforms in Eastern Europe, J. Zielinski, came to a similar conclusion—that as long as the institution of annual target setting (and, thus, the opportunity for frequent renegotiation of terms) remained, no fiddling with the bonus formulas could have any significant effect.[2]

In the Soviet Union it is clear that many of the participants in the reform discussion recognized that the terms of payoff formulas once set should remain unchanged for an appreciable period. It was recognized that, if these incentives were to do their work, enterprises would have to feel that they would persist and would not be renegotiated in a discriminatory way to favor firms with poor performance and to penalize those that responded to the offered incentives with great improvements in performance and, hence, won large rewards. But the Communist leaders cannot quite accept the idea of letting some enterprise managers obtain windfalls or the prospect of others failing under hard terms. In practice, the designers of the reform were careful *not* to announce some simple general terms on which the gains from improved performance would be shared (like giving enterprise directors 10 percent of all profits earned) but instead worked out for each firm or group of firms a detailed formula that would have generated in the first post-reform year about the same payoff as the previous formula did, but on the basis of the new criteria. The new formulas also made payoffs a function of certain planned variables, so that payoffs would depend on the planned targets for profit and output to be negotiated in the future. But there have been many complaints that, although the norms and coefficients in the payoff formulas were supposed to remain fixed for several years, the ministries subsequently readjusted them to extract windfalls and to ease terms for enterprises in trouble.

The discussion concerning the rent payment introduced in the oil and gas industries as part of the reform suggests that managers are not only interested in security of terms but also aware of the importance of specifying terms for renegotiation. Some directors of the regional *obedineniya* (amalgamations, combines) in the oil industry did not like the proposed fixed rent payments on the grounds that, as the fields in their regions moved from flush production to secondary recovery, fixed rent payments would narrow the profit they could hope to show and, hence, limit the bonuses they could expect. One of them made the interesting suggestion that rent payments should change over time in accordance with changes in output per well (on the grounds that this output was the main determinant of cost). This suggestion indicates the usefulness of a parametric basis for renegotiating the terms and the importance of due process as a demand of the managers.[3]

¶ Marxian Interpretation of Party-Management Relationship

In Marx's view of social change, economic development plays a crucial role. Soviet ideologists would deny that the intra-elite relationship described here (between the center and the managers) is a Marxian class relationship or that it could be the basis for an "antagonistic contradiction" and class conflict within the system. But bargaining over the terms of stewardship of socialized property is clearly a class relationship, and the antagonism between the bargainers is a fetter on production. In the usual Marxian view, a ruling class never resolves these conflicts by voluntarily giving up its power; it is deposed only by a revolution carried out by the new class it has created.

The role of the Party in the Stalinist development strategy offers a good parallel to the Marxian idea that the ruling class is doomed to create its own gravediggers. The Party's role was like that of the board of directors in an all-inclusive structure in which political power and economic strategy are fused. Legitimacy for the Party in this dual role was argued on the grounds that only a dictatorial Party could enforce the discipline needed for catching up with and surpassing the advanced countries and that crucial decisions about economic planning and management could not be left to the economists and managers.

Development has undermined both those grounds of the Party's legitimacy. First, the USSR has not yet caught up with the United States in total output, but it spends as much for military purposes and has a bigger investment program. So it is implausible to argue that the Party must enforce the suppression of consumption by iron discipline while the USSR is building the material-technical basis of Communism and seeing to its security. At the same time, growth has created a new managerial-technical elite, which undercuts the Party's pretension that it must control everything from the center. And the increased complexity of the economy has forced the Party to acquiesce in the creation of a new generation of economists, who are taking away from the central Party authorities a large range of economic questions.

The notion that the Party is somehow involved in a class conflict with the managers is one that Soviet spokesmen would certainly deny, and it is also a very dubious proposition to many Western analysts. Jeremy Azrael, for example, does a painstaking job of refuting it in his *Managerial Power and Soviet Politics.*[4] Such a cleavage has not been evident in the past, and he considers it unlikely that it will emerge in the future. It does not exist, he says, because there is a big overlap of membership in the managerial-technique elite and the Party. Also, within the managerial-technical elite there is an important division between those on the top and those on the bottom of the bargaining process. Those at the top are really speaking basically for the Party, while the operating managers at the bottom are more concerned with the prerogatives and rewards of managers proper.[5]

This overlap is a consequence of careful design, of course, and it is because the Party does not want to interfere with this design that it is so reluctant to entertain the kind of reform in the Party-management relationship that I have suggested is needed. This is what we mean when we try to locate the political obstacles to reform or when we try to think about the political consequences of adapting the management of the economy to the changing conditions that go along with economic modernization. The interesting question is whether the Party could willingly initiate such a differentiation between itself and the managers or could be led into it by accident. Reflection on this question first requires analysis of the nature of the Party's "power."

¶ Would Propertification of Management's Status Diminish the Party's Power?

Would the Party lose political "power" through constitutionalizing its relationship with management? In *economic resource* terms there is a significant increment in output to be gained by making the relationship parametric. Although this change might open the way to some income gains for management, it would simultaneously leave the Party with a significant increment in resources to achieve a superior position under its own objective function, at least insofar as its objectives can be furthered by more resources. It is possible to object that the leaders may not see this as an improved position if income distribution is an important aspect of their objective function (they would not like to see managers get rich in a way they did not control) or if the change altered their standing in relation either to workers or to party functionaries. But these are not real problems: other instruments (such as taxes) can be used to control income distribution, and other resources ensure that the party apparat can keep its relative income standing. To design those instruments is the function of the technicians. That a more complicated system would result is of course to be expected.

It is a cybernetic commonplace that control processes must have "variety" equivalent to that of the phenomenon controlled and an economic cliché that a policymaker with fewer policy instruments than variables to be controlled is in trouble. After all, that is what is wrong with the present situation in the USSR: the center is trying to control both managerial performance and income distribution by juggling the payoff coefficients—which is one goal too many to be pursued with a single instrument. This, incidentally, is a common failing of Soviet *economic* control, and one would suspect that it is a point equally applicable to much of the rest of the Party's approach to *societal* management. In general, one aspect of Party adaptation will have to be the multiplication of instruments to cope with a more varied goal structure.

It is not clear what constitutionalizing its relationship with management would do for the Party's monopoly on political power. But this *is* the way the issue is usually posed; discussions usually tie the question of what the Party will accept in the way of change to the effect of the change on the Party's power. But how are we to measure or even conceptualize power? If we were to pursue the analogy with the economic resource situation, we might ask whether the generation of power through politics is a zero-sum game or a positive-sum game. Exploring that idea might be productive—along the lines of a hypothesis that the amount of power is not a fixed sum but can increase parallel to the degree of political participation allowed to all political resource holders. Enfranchisement of the managers would increase the aggregate amount of power in the system, so that increased power for managers would not diminish the preponderant role of the Party.

Some of the literature on power in society seems to operate with this notion. Talcott Parsons says that power is exercised by making commitments, engaging in promises, rousing expectations, and enlisting energies.[6] The focus is on power as the product of a process. Breakdowns in the process lead to defensive behavior in which the interacting parties all try to cash in their claims and protect themselves against the claims of others. They retreat to fortresses buttressed by their private resources, and the total of power is reduced. The difficult ambiguity with the present problem is whether the Party aspires to power as an end in itself or as an instrumental value to be used in the furtherance of still higher objectives—perhaps national, ideological, altruistic. In the first case, Party people would be very bearish—more interested in defending their fortress than in the extension of power through enlarged commitments as in the Parsonian concept. In the second, the Party would be more willing to make adaptations that would enable power to be diffused but expanded, in the aggregate, to permit better fulfillment of the Party's ultimate goals. It would be an intriguing task to try to make those ideas operational in evaluating how the power position of the CPSU has changed over time.

¶ Corporate Base for Managerial Independence?

If the center were to take toward the class managers the kind of parametric stance described above, how might it go about doing so? What kind of dynamics might lead to this state, and how might it be institutionalized? Consider the implications of some changes in the organization of management that have taken place under the reforms or are being discussed.

In all the Soviet-type economies, one of the outcomes of the decade of reform in the sixties seems to have been the strengthening of the intermediate level organs of administration at the expense of the lower levels and, to some extent, of the center. A feature especially of the Eastern European countries, the process seems to have occurred in the USSR as well. The original expectation at the time of the 1965 reform in the USSR that there would be a decentralization of power from the center to the enterprise level and the introduction of market methods to coordinate them was not realized in practice. Perhaps such expectations were unrealistic, given the leaders' limited goals for reform; but in any case, the outcome is not surprising. Enterprises were too small and weak to handle the functions that had been handled at higher levels or to win in a competition for power with the newly reconstituted ministries. But what has happened, partly independently and partly as a way of coping with the inability of the enterprises to handle these tasks, has been amalgamation of units and functions into bigger organizations. Enterprises have been combined into *firmy* (firms), and obedineniya have been given operational management authority over what were formerly *khozraschet* (independently accountable) firms. One ministry (the Ministry of Instrument-building, Automation Equipment, and Control Systems) has been busily taking away functions and rights from the enterprises under it to remake itself into a kind of supercorporation. Throughout, there has been much interest in the American corporation as a model for these new units.[7] There was apparently a proposal in 1974 to reduce the existing number of ministries to a smaller number of larger units and give them some of the functions of the Gosplan (State Planning Commission), a move that might be interpreted as de-operationalizing the Gosplan. The enlargement of ministries would also necessarily reduce their operational role and leave more room for the obedineniya to increase their independence. This general trend is likely to be helped along by the process of computerization: the current strategy is to master the computer in the form of branch systems of automated planning and administration, which is likely to strengthen the hands of the combines not only against enterprises but against the higher levels as well.

Might such units—a Soviet version of the corporation—turn out to be a vehicle for institutionalizing managerial independence? Much depends on how the environment in which they are to operate will be designed, whether central allocation of materials will be retained, how much financial independence they will have, and so on. But these units *are* being given more functions and more responsibilities. It is conceivable that they could be given much more general charters and subjected to more general forms of guidance than enterprises have received and that they might then be regulated by much more general economic levers. If this process should occur, it would give the managerial group a secure organizational base, income security, a more easily defensible material status, and an arena within which the professional norms of behavior would control advancement.

An interesting paper by Donald Green[8] suggests that the corporation could be set up with a board of directors chosen by the Party and including Party representatives. This procedure might solve two problems at once. It would give the Party a voice and would provide a device for buying off many of the functionaries now operating in high-level executive roles. Positions on these boards would give these people income, status, and a chance to use their experience. This suggestion seems a little difficult to accept but gains interest in light of the controversy now taking place in the USSR over the principle of edinonachalie and the possible introduction of collegia in the ministries; these collegia would include Party representatives and could overrule the minister. The argument is being carried on in a rather veiled way (I am basing my statements mostly on the Kremlinological analyses of Christian Duevel at Radio Liberty), and it may be that this idea of collegia with party representation is being considered for lower-level units as well. The interpretation generally accepted is that this proposal is being advanced by Brezhnev as a way of asserting Party power over management and is but one feature of a generally retrograde policy on reform. But the collegium bears a certain resemblance to Green's board of directors, and it is conceivable that, even if these boards were the Party's way of asserting its control over management, this control could be of a policy-making rather than a management kind.

¶ The Party's Stake in Preventing Intra-Elite Differentiation

The discussion so far has treated the Party as the real power behind the center, which is in conflict with another entity, the operating managers. Even if this relationship were constitutionalized, the Party would still exist as the shadow state and would still control the processes of setting priorities, resolving disputes among sectoral and regional interests, and regulating the framework. The only change would be the Party's willingness to redefine its role and change the style of its overlordship.

The relationship of the Party to management is more complicated than this description indicates, however. The Party is not just a central body but is organized as a hierarchy. The Party-management relationship is thus a relationship between two hierarchies, and the implications of untangling economic administration from Party work are highly ramified. As suggested in the Marxian interpretation above, these two hierarchies are closely intertwined, because many of the elite who perform managerial functions are also Party members and because there is movement back and forth between the two groups. Thus, a Party person may work for a time in management and then be shifted to full-time Party work (apparently, the reverse rarely occurs). This interchange happens at all levels of the hierarchy. Depoliticizing the economy implies a symmetrical "de-economizing" of the polity and the Party. What are the prospects that the CPSU would give up this part of its activity and its involvement in the economy to permit some new, more constitutional relationship between the Party and managers?

From the literature on the functioning of the lower levels of the Party,[9] it appears that the CPSU would be very reluctant to let that adjustment happen. It is not that the Party's control over economic activity is exercised at this level. The decisive allocational and institutional policy plans are made at the top; and Party guidance flows downward through the state hierarchy, rather than downward through the Party hierarchy, and thence laterally to operating management. Nevertheless, the activities of the lower levels of the Party apparatus are very heavily oriented toward economic work, such as involvement in the day-to-day business of the enterprises in the region covered by the lower-level unit. The relationship of the Party officials at this level to enterprise management is as likely to be cooperative as to be one of imposing outside direction. Yet it becomes clear that the Party gains much of its power by this involvement, especially by its ability to control the career prospects and progress of people at all levels of the management hierarchy through the nomenklatura system. Indeed, it might be said that it is the nomenklatura system that keeps the Party alive: if one could make his way up the economic hierarchy without membership in and constant discipline and review by the Party, then there would be little motivation for the skilled elite to join the Party; and the authority of the Party at the top, as it confronted the upper levels of the administrative hierarchy, would be gravely weakened.

To return, then, to the original question of the relationship between economic reform and an evolution in the role and functioning of the CPSU, we are left with a contradiction. There is a very clear, economic need for the Party to adapt, to reorganize its relationship with the managerial-technical elite in the interests of better performance. On the other hand, as we try to see how this new relationship might be institutionalized and how the Party might retreat somewhat from its entrepreneurial role in the running of the economy, it is difficult to visualize a "de-economized" version of the Party that would be able to remain vital and that could justify and defend its claim even to make the political decisions about goals to be implemented by the managerial-technical elite.

Administrative Rationality, Political Change, and the Role of the Party

Paul Cocks

The desire to impose rationality on human affairs has long captivated systems designers and social engineers, not to mention students of political development and bureaucracy. This desire has led to a search for the optimal instrument by which to achieve and administer planned change. In the USSR the quest has resulted in one of the distinctive and unique features of the Soviet regime, namely, the existence of a dual system of administration with separate Party and state hierarchies of authority and command. Although much has been written on this subject, the historical roots and functional ramifications of the Party-state duality still remain insufficiently explored.

This essay seeks to illuminate some of these gaps in our knowledge and understanding of Party and state in the Soviet system. It focuses on the only example in Soviet history where a party institution was amalgamated with a governmental organ into a single joint Party-state agency, a primary purpose of which was to promote administrative rationality and modernization. This was the merger of the Central Control Commission (CCC) with the Workers' and Peasants' Inspection (RKI or the *Rabkrin*), which took place between 1923 and 1934. What were the significance and consequences of the fusion of Party and government functions and structures for the development not only of the CCC-RKI but also of the political system more broadly? What light does it shed on the problems and dynamics of organizational adaptation and political change during the twenties and early thirties as the Bolsheviks wrestled with the dilemmas of Russia's backwardness? Before taking up these questions, we will discuss briefly some trends and views on adaptation and change in Western organization theory in order to place in perspective the significance of the Soviet historical and organizational response to the problems of modernization.

¶ Organizational Change and Organization Theory: Recent Western Views

Since World War II modern organization theory has been beset by a persistent "paradigmatic crisis" evoked by the insufficiency of the paradigm of Weberian rationality inherent in traditional administrative doctrine.[1] Advancing technology and the changing world of complex organizations have generated anomalies that challenge a whole set of prevailing assumptions and beliefs. They have forced a fundamental rethinking about organization, administration, and leadership. In the process, old concepts have been extended, modified, or abandoned in favor of new images and metaphors. Generally speaking, the thrust of theoretical reconstruction has dealt with issues of change, conflict, and interaction: these are the real forces inside the organizational world.[2]

With the "change to change" in the study of organizations, the notion of rigid, permanent, "mechanistic" structures has given way to an emphasis on flexible, temporary, "organic" systems. Such systems are viewed as open rather than closed, with considerable capacity for innovation and adaptation to change. The organization is more and more regarded as a self-modifying, adaptive, creative organism, distinguished by a high degree of uncertainty. This conception of organization is a significant departure from classical doctrine, which stressed the predictability of organizational behavior. Indeed, uncertainty appears to the modernist as the fundamental problem for complex organizations. Growing attention is given, therefore, to problems of managing change in organizations and of developing adaptive subsystems to deal with planned and unplanned change.[3]

There has also been a sharp reversal of attitude toward conflict in organizations. Given their bias toward harmony, order, and predictability, classical administrative theorists tended to view conflict as a sign of imperfection. They saw it as undesirable and detrimental to the organization, both to its stability and to its goal maximization. More recently, however, modern organization writers have come to regard tension as not only normal but also desirable and functional. As one authority notes, "At one time the ideal amount of conflict was zero and the common decision was 'eliminate it.' Now the questions are what are the limits within which conflict is useful and how does one manage conflict." [4] The functional character of disorder relates to adaptiveness: conflict can provide checks and balances to a system and can promote innovation and change among organization members.

Still another major theme of contemporary theorists is the systems concept, which stresses notions of interdependency and complexity. In general, classical and neoclassical theory were preoccupied with the internal dynamics of organization. Modern systems analysis, however, emphasizes the organization's external relationships and interactions as well. The environment constitutes one of the basic sources of uncertainty for organizations; at the same time, organizational change is perceived to be increasingly induced by external factors.[5] How an organization depends on, transacts with, and adapts to external pressures figures prominently in its ability to learn and to change. Current theoretical concerns have refocused, therefore, on the issues of how to identify the organization's boundaries and how to describe the organization-environmental interface.[6]

As a result of these conceptual reformulations, the very notion of rationality has also been modified and broadened. Because uncertainties pose major challenges to rationality and the environment is a main source of uncertainty, classical writers tried to achieve rationality by eliminating uncertainty through conceptual closure of organization. They sought to protect the organization from exogenous influences. By assuming that goals are known and excluding external variables, they placed stress on the manipulation of system inputs. Rationality thus came to mean a narrow kind of technical rationality devoted almost exclusively to the discovery of means, or to the elaboration of techniques. As such, rationality became practically synonymous with efficiency. It tended not only to neglect ends generally but also to stress "techniques of organization which are essentially neutral and therefore available for any goals rather than methods peculiarly adapted to a distinctive type of organization or stage of development." [7]

The Weberian paradigm of rationality, as often interpreted, is based on a closed system of logic—closed by the elimination of uncertainty and exogenous variables—and is clearly insufficient for evaluating organizational adaptability. Such a theory of bounded rationality can become, as Vincent Ostrom notes, "a theory of bounded irrationality." [8] Administrative behavior is bounded by constraints other than those internal to the organization. Reference to these external constraints figures prominently in more recent conceptions of and criteria for organizational rationality. Such "open-system" theories are predicated on the expectation of uncertainty; indeed, they focus on variables not subject to complete control by the organization and not contained in a closed system of logic.[9]

Within the context of these revised norms of rationality, the concept of leadership has similarly acquired new meaning. Today the crucial problem for organizations is perceived to be not coordination but adjustment to constraints and contingencies generated by exogenous variables beyond their control.[10] For the adaptive organization, leadership and influence will fall to those who seem most able to solve problems of coping with uncertainty and change, rather than to those who fill programmed role expectations.[11] A key element of effective leadership is "creativity," the ability to go beyond both efficiency and routine in choosing methods appropriate to changing goals and situational demands.[12] Recent conceptions of leadership also recognize the importance of a political perspective and the capacity to conceive problems in terms of the realities of partisanship and the use of power.[13] In this sense, they differ markedly from those interpretations of Weberian doctrine which contend that bureaucratic rationality is best served by excluding politics from the routines of administration. The predominant opinion in classical theory stresses the use of authority as a means of influencing behavior and deemphasizes power as such a means. In fact, power assumes a very negative connotation, being linked to domination and coercion. The utility and functionality of *consensus* is the logical corollary of the classical view about the disutility and dysfunctionality of *conflict* in organization.[14]

Finally, with respect to organizational design, there has been considerable movement away from the stereotype of monocratic bureaucracy as the paradigm of rationality. Concerned about organizational innovation and adaptability, modern theorists have aimed at developing structures that can, in effect, enable the organization to "institutionalize flexibility." "The name of the game for organizational design has changed from trying to discover the ideal one best way to trying to discern what is an appropriate design given a discrete set of goals, known material and human resources, a more or less turbulent environment, and captive technologies and programs." [15] Consequently, the trend has been away from an ideal of bureaucratic structures toward an array of designs.

The most appropriate form for adaptive-organic structures, according to modern management thought, is not the monocratic organization but a so-called matrix or overlay system. The distinguishing feature of the monocratic type of organization is its accent on vertical hierarchy as the means of assuring predictability, accountability, and coordination. Duties and jurisdictions are narrowly defined so as to avoid ambiguity and duplication. The concept of a matrix organization, on the contrary, entails a more untidy and fluid structure to secure cooperation and integration of effort in solving complex and crucial problems. Designed as a "web of relationships" rather than a pyramid of strict line and staff functions, this model allows for overlapping responsibilities and duplicating efforts. Built around specific projects, the matrix organization provides for temporary project teams drawn from more permanent departments, so interdisciplinary efforts can be concentrated on key problems cutting across functions. Paramount to the way of thinking and working in this type of organization is a "management by objectives" approach to decisionmaking and problem-solving.[16]

¶ Soviet Administrative Thought in the Twenties: Evolution, Crisis, and the Emerging Stalinist Paradigm

This brief outline of the main directions in recent Western organization theory provides a useful framework for viewing the evolution of Soviet administrative thought in the twenties and early thirties. Generally speaking, Soviet thinking during the first decade of Bolshevik rule closely followed then-prevailing Western trends. Toward the end of his life, Lenin concluded that Russia's path to modernity and socialism lay in her learning and applying advanced capitalist technique and managerial know-how, especially from America and Europe. Subsequently, the administrative rationalization movement of the twenties, devoted to remodeling the cumbersome bureaucratic machinery inherited from the tsar, came under the strong influence of Western schools of public administration led by such men as Henri Fayol and Frederick Taylor. Indeed, the foreign flavor of the whole movement led ultimately to the charge leveled by the Stalinist machine that Soviet administrative doctrine included "a bouquet of anti-Marxist theories." [17]

Given the growing determination of Stalin and company to propel Russia forcefully and rapidly into the industrial age, it is not surprising that the inadequacies of monocratic bureaucracy as an instrument for planned change—let alone for totalitarian social engineering—surfaced much earlier and more starkly in the USSR than in the West,[18] because of the Soviet push for superindustrialization and forced collectivization. The overriding concern became how to enhance the capacity of the administrative superstructure to cope more effectively with rapid change, conflict, and a turbulent environment. The ultimate organizational design advanced by Stalin for the political system resembles in many ways the matrix type of structure advocated by modern Western theorists for adaptive organizations.

A full description of Soviet "management science" in the 1920s is outside the scope of this essay. Briefly, the rationalizers from the beginning concerned themselves with narrow technical details, with "administrivia," and adopted a highly apolitical and excessively mechanistic approach to administration. Despite repeated criticism from prominent politicians, many of them continued to build abstract models, to be preoccupied with techniques, and to neglect politics.[19]

The leader of this mechanistic school of thought, Elena Rozmirovich, headed the Institute of Administrative Techniques—Rabkrin's "think tank" on rationalization. She expounded the theory that administration turns increasingly into a technical problem only. The exercise of managerial functions in a government office was called its "production." According to this "production interpretation" of administration, any person—including the class enemy, opportunist, or political saboteur—could work in the state apparat, since his personal views and ideological complexion did not directly affect his performance. As Rozmirovich claimed, "The personality of the worker and manager little by little ceases to influence the results of his work." Rationalization theory similarly disparaged the need for leaders and for a strong directing hand.[20]

Needless to say, the parallels with classical administrative theory and the scientific management movement in the West are striking. At this time the West, too, was concerned largely with human engineering problems and simple physical operations performed on the factory floor or in clerical offices. Representative of the movement and the period were the time and methods studies in industry by Taylor and others, which focused mainly on the use of men as adjuncts to machines in the conduct of routine production jobs and on cost reduction and efficiency. Thus, the whole flavor of the movement was at first highly attractive to the Soviets, who in the mid-twenties sought the means to finance Soviet Russia's industrialization largely through a campaign for economy and thrift. Classical management doctrine, like early Soviet rationalization theory, neglected or passed by the psychological and behavioral aspects of humans in organizations. These Western ideas, therefore, fed and reinforced Marxist and Soviet biases and blindspots.

Ironically, politics forced the rationalizers to have nonpolitical concerns and to focus on techniques. In delivering the Organizational Report of the Central Committee to the Twelfth Party Congress, Stalin made plain that the Soviet machine was basically sound and that only some of its component parts had "distortions." Above all, its "political line" was correct. The political decisionmakers determined the general complexion of the Soviet administrative system and controlled its development. The rationalizers were to deal only with the organization of administrative methods; they were not to decide fundamental issues of policy and power. In short, rationalization did not extend to politics.

Despite this ruling to restrict rationalization to technical matters, those working in this sphere were also warned against neglecting political concerns. As the journal of the CCC-RKI stressed: "If NOT [*nauchnaia organizatsiia truda,* or scientific organization of labor] remains "apolitical" and "cool" to the burning tasks of the revolutionary movement, its contradictions with the major organizational problems of Soviet power will continue to exist and even grow. They will grow because a purely handicraft, technical NOT will not and cannot give any firm gains from scientific organization to our state and economic apparat." [21] The rationalizers were caught in contradictory crossfire, between politics and administrative rationality, between power and technique.

Another major error of rationalization theory elaborated at the Institute of Administrative Techniques was an understanding of administration as an aggregate of functions, rights, and responsibilities, rationally distributed and delineated. This "functional" view of administration came steadily under attack, and it was eventually overthrown at the Seventeenth Party Congress in 1934, in favor of the so-called production branch principle. By differentiating and giving equal emphasis to a number of administrative activities, such as planning, control, and so on, the functional system in effect diffused leadership and fragmented power precisely at a time when one-man command and concentrated authority were becoming decisive in Stalin's eyes.

After 1932 and the closing of Rozmirovich's institute, increasing attention was given to Molotov's statement, "Putting in order the verification of fulfillment [control] and ensuring effective leadership [power] are essentially two sides of one and the same question." [22] According to this formulation, which became the basis for the 1934 reorganization of the control organs and of the Soviet administrative system, there was no longer any need for an independent function of control, especially as a possible restraint and check on the misuse of power.

Basically at issue between the rationalizers and Stalin were conflicting control strategies and organizational models for the Soviet system. This "administrative debate" was, in turn, integrally tied to the "industrialization debate" that was waged between the political protagonists. Here it is important to remember that an economic development policy is not just an economic strategy but also a whole set of institutional devices, techniques, and assumptions that go along with it. Certainly the interrelation between the methods of industrializing and the essence of the political system loomed large in the Bolshevik mind during the economic debates of the twenties.[23] Stalin saw clearly that behind the administrative model of the rationalizers lay, in part, an attempt to preserve the basic framework of NEP. It was not by accident, then, that he had rationalization theory declared in 1932 "a right deviation in politics" and linked directly to Bukharin's *Economics of the Transition Period.*[24] Stalin also understood well that success in control was as essential to Soviet industrialization as were purely economic strategies.[25] Yet it was precisely in this area that he saw the main weakness of the rationalizers' model. For his purposes and plans, the theory of administrative rationality that was espoused by many at the CCC-RKI was "a theory of bounded irrationality."

The rationalizers, on the one hand, sought primarily to pattern control through structural arrangements in a harmonious and static model. It was a model premised essentially upon a peaceful, gradual, and spontaneous road to socialism, and it was geared preeminently for a post-revolutionary era and a fully institutionalized system, with regularized machinery and routinized behavior. As such, it was indeed more suitable to the Rightists who, Stalin remarked in 1930, "think that socialism can be built 'on the quiet,' spontaneously, without class struggle, without an offensive against capitalist elements." Already, two years before, he had warned against such a peaceful mentality regarding Soviet development. "We have been advancing smoothly as though on rails," said the general secretary. "And the effect of this has been to induce the belief in some of our officials that everything is going swimmingly, that we are as good as traveling on an express train . . . nonstop, straight to socialism." [26]

The strict departmentalization of tasks in the functional system, which the rationalizers propounded, tended to eliminate the problem of coordination and the possibility of conflict. Viewing administration as a production process, they tended to see individuals as inert cogs automatically fulfilling their assigned roles. People were regarded, then, as an unproblematical "given" rather than as a "variable" in the system. The whole administrative apparat resembled for the most part a giant but simple machine with a set of predictable responses. The class struggle, conflicts of power, and dysfunctional consequences simply had no place and did not arise in such a model.

Stalin, on the other hand, sought to impose control on a highly hostile and turbulent environment. Fully aware of the noncompliance of individual behavior, he knew that his policies generated massive discontent and resistance. To implement them, he required a set of extensive and effective, indeed impelling, control mechanisms. "Collectivization without coercion was impossible," notes Alec Nove, "and rapid industrialization was bound to cause stresses and strains." [27] Stalin's "revolution from above," Lewin also points out, "was an immense improvisation guided by the rule of thumb, hunch, and all too often by despotic whims." [28] It was the unplanned character of the whole process, he adds, that led ultimately to the disappearance of rational planning and to the growth of ever more administration and control. To borrow apt phrases from Alvin Toffler, the years 1928 to 1934 were indeed a time of "future shock" when "adhocracy" became the order of the day.

For these reasons, therefore, the general secretary switched to a different strategy and organizational model for achieving control. Instead of demarcating precisely functional roles, he deliberately blurred lines of responsibility. Ultimately he created and relied upon a system of duplicating and parallel hierarchies, each checking and cross-checking the other in an atmosphere of institutionalized suspicion. The whole system was built with the aim of securing not efficiency but organizational and leadership effectiveness.[29] Those who got results, no matter how ruthless the methods and terrible the costs, were the ones who climbed up the administrative ladder.

In addition to a maze of institutional controls, Stalin also relied heavily on supervisory influence, externally imposed and highly personalized.[30] The substitution by the Seventeenth Party Congress of the slogan Cadres Decide All for the formulation Technique Decides All, which had been adopted at the Sixteenth Congress, captures well the fundamental change in the nature of control and the underlying character of the Soviet system as it moved into its Stalinist and totalitarian stage. The seed for the highly personalized system of control plenipotentiaries that Stalin adopted as the basis for the reorganized control machinery in 1934 was germinated in 1928. Already at that time he predicted that this institution of the control agent would have "a big future." In many ways, the figure of the plenipotentiary, of the roving judge and prosecutor, captures well the growing interventionist role of the Party official more generally as "political trouble shooter." [31]

It is important to stress the significance of Stalin's "revolution from above" for political system-building and not just economic development. As Moshe Lewin so aptly states, "The new state system which emerged in Russia in those years became the most important product of the *pyatiletka,* more important even than economic planning itself." [32] It was during the years 1928 to 1934 that the political system finally crystallized into its matrixlike shape.

¶ The Dual System of Party and State Administration: Soviet Polity Viewed as a "Matrix Organization"

The rise and persistence in the Soviet Union of two distinct administrative hierarchies, of separate Party and state bureaucracies, has long confounded Western analysts. The assumption is commonly made that such duplication is wasteful and "irrational." Moreover, it is the inclusion of the Party in the administrative system, according to this view, that introduces the deviation from rationality. The Party—or more properly speaking, the Party apparatus—injects "ideological" and "power" factors into the administrative equation, which upset and prevent a rational calculus of decisionmaking.

In the last few years, however, a number of scholars have begun to contest this interpretation, contending that a functional basis does underlie the Party-state dyarchy. Jerry Hough, for example, sees the Party "not as an intrusive element that interferes with the effective operation of the administrative system, but as an integral part of the system—one which, in fact, has played an important role in promoting its effective operation." [33] T. H. Rigby similarly emphasizes the significance of the Party for the adaptive aspects of the system's functioning. The duality of Party and state administration resembles in important respects, he points out, Burns and Stalker's dichotomy of "organic" and "mechanistic" systems of management: "As the prime bearer of authoritative messages about approved innovations and current priorities, the Party tends to embody the organic aspects of the system, while the state bureaucracy, primarily responsible for effective routine performance, tends to embody its mechanistic aspects." [34] The role and raison d'être of the Party are seen from this perspective to be directly related to the capacity of the system to respond to conditions of change and stress generated in the course of development and social engineering. Rather than to inject irrationality, the Party's primary task, in theory at least if not always in practice, is to eradicate and rectify the dysfunctionalities and deviations of "rational" bureaucracy.

The idea of a completely rational-technical bureaucracy is itself an illusion. The perfect bureaucracy about which many an administrator dreams, notes Meyer, can only be one from which human beings have been eliminated.[35] Bureaucratic machines are necessarily subject to and exhibit certain "dysfunctionalities" and "irrationalities" that derive only in part from the human frailties, limitations, and idiosyncracies of the men who run them. They are also generically rooted in the very structure and technical functioning of the rational organization. Adhering too strictly to the principles of rational administration, for example, can itself result in chaos and a kind of tyranny, the arbitrariness of rules. Overorganization and overregulation breed their own peculiar variety of bureaucratic evils, "the ills of pathology of planned and rational management," to use Meyer's terminology.[36] These can be particularly debilitating for a bureaucracy whose primary task is social engineering, for rules and routines by their very nature go against change and can easily turn into paralyzing poisons.

To help avoid the trap of rational bureaucracy, Soviet organization theory posits the need not for a monocratic or single-centered model but for a dual system of Party and state administration. The Party's tasks are not administrative and technical but preeminently organizational and political. The job of administering the economy and societal affairs belongs formally to the governmental bureaucracy and state agencies. They are indeed expected to discharge their responsibilities according to all the rules of scientific management. But in doing their job, the Soviet managerial elite, like administrators everywhere, tend inevitably to suffer from a kind of bureaucratic myopia. They begin to develop a fixation on technique and efficiency that causes them to lose sight of the larger political universe of which their administrative world is but a part. Whether or not they carry Party cards, they tend in time to identify with and to promote the parochial interests and goals of the organizations and sectors to which they are assigned. As Reinhard Bendix notes about bureaucracies more generally, "Concern with administrative efficiency puts all policy considerations affecting the use of power outside the pale of bureaucratic competence. Bureaucracy is, therefore, all powerful and at the same time incapable of determining how its power should be used." [37]

In the Soviet system it is precisely the responsibility of the Party, especially of its bureaucracy, to compensate for and to correct this deficiency of rational bureaucracy. While the intrusion of Party authorities into the administrative process often results in their exercising petty tutelage over and issuing commands to economic executives and government officials, this is not its intended purpose. Rather party intervention is designed to reassert the primacy of politics over administrative efficiency, to ensure that broader policy considerations and priorities are brought to the fore in decisionmaking and implementation. Or, as *Pravda* put it in an article entitled "The Political Vanguard of Soviet Society," "[The Party] prevents the reduction of managerial functions to the accomplishment of mere technical and technological tasks." [38] The right of the Party to function as the leading force in society is predicated on the assumption that its higher political consciousness enables it to have better vision and knowledge of the long-term needs and general interests of society. Only the Party is capable of determining how power should be used. Accordingly, one of its primary functions is to control the misuse and misdirection of power by the regular administrative bureaucracy, to ensure that the flow of power is not diverted or its ultimate effect subverted by the technical means and administrative hands through which it must necessarily pass.

The Party is a counterweight to rational-technical bureaucracy in another important sense as well. By its very nature, the world of administrators tends to be static, though often intolerably hectic. This is especially true of administrators in the Soviet Union, because of the peculiar conditions and constraints under which they operate. Constantly wrestling with vast arrays of almost impossible problems, they are forced to live from day to day and consequently develop a short time horizon. Their work and success revolve inexorably around fulfilling the Plan—meeting production targets, output deadlines, delivery schedules, and so on. The demands of efficiency place a high premium on order, predictability, and harmony. The quest for efficiency leads them to value and to seek routine, above all. Planners, too, tend to develop an "incremental" perspective that favors building on "the achieved level." Throughout the administrative world the resistance to change grows; routine threatens to turn into a rut.[39]

Development, on the contrary, entails and requires the initiation of change and the resolution of conflict that results from the breaking of both order and routine. Particularly for organizations and political systems bent on social engineering, rational problem-solving "can be achieved only by transcending routine, by taking initiative, by experimentation, innovation, and the breaking of rules." [40] Routine brings political complacency, which Stalin contemptuously labeled "a belch of the Right Deviation. . . . Victory never comes by itself," he stressed. "It has to be dragged by the hand." [41] A fundamental feature of the Soviet regime is that it has tried to cope with the contradictory needs and conflicting pressures for both routine and change in social engineering by its dual system of organization and a differentiation of the functional roles of the Party and state hierarchies. While the latter takes charge of routine administration, the former bears primary responsibility for initiating change, coordinating policies, and resolving conflicts. If the tendency of the managerial elite is toward routinization, the task of the party bureaucracy is to shake up the apparat, to fight Oblomovism, and to combat routine.

In both conceptual design and behavioral dynamics, this dual management system bears strong resemblance to the "modern" matrix organization. The latter emerged in the 1950s as a hurried improvisation of the American aerospace industry to the need to develop and produce large projects in the shortest possible time. It provided the adaptive capacity, in an ad hoc way, to handle the complexities and uncertainties inherent in large-scale planned activities.[42] Concerned with maximizing organizational effectiveness in the allocation and use of resources, the matrix, or mixed, organization tends to bifurcate the management system into functional and project roles and structures. It has a formal functional hierarchy for normal routine decisionmaking. Superimposed on this primary authority structure is a secondary authority network and project-focused organization. The latter cuts horizontally across vertical functional and organizational lines. Its purpose is to insure the achievement of common interorganizational objectives through the functional organizations and over their specialized interests.[43] The project organization is primarily a problem-solving entity that handles nonroutine "crisis management" situations.[44] Describing this mixed structure, the president of a small aerospace firm noted, "What we came up with is an organization within an organization—one to ramrod the day-to-day problems; the other to provide support for existing projects and to anticipate the requirements for future projects." [45] Such a description fits well the respective roles of Party and state administration in the USSR.

In a sense, the overall decisionmaking responsibility of the Party is similar to the role of corporate or general management in the matrix form of organization. The Party's second main function is to supervise the implementation of decisions and general performance by the regular administrative bodies. This regulatory task is primarily the job of the Party apparatus and its secretarial hierarchy. On a somewhat different level, it is the main responsibility of local Party organs to ensure the execution of plans and priorities set by central authorities. It is this general supervisory role of Party agencies, resembling the project management function and structure in the matrix organization, to which this discussion mainly refers.

The matrix organization is, above all, a fluid structure. The mixture can lie anywhere between the two extremes of standard functional organization and pure project management. Different types of organization represent varying degrees of authority and responsibility assumed by the project manager and splintered from, or shared with, the functional manager. The exact shape of the structure is determined by the project-functional interface and by changing task requirements. Typically, the project manager acts as an assistant and adviser to the functional organization in a staff capacity, with no direct or line authority over project participants but broad functional authority. Close organizational proximity to the chief executive and general management gives the project manager significant influence. Basically, though, in this restricted staff capacity, the project manager is more a monitor than a true integrator and decisionmaker.[46] This is generally the relationship of the CPSU official to governmental bodies. At times, however, circumstances may arise that require the project organization within a matrix structure, like Party agencies in the Soviet system, to intervene increasingly and even to usurp momentarily the responsibilities of functional management. In such a situation, the legitimacy of the task dominates all other business considerations. The project organization virtually displaces the regular authority structure and becomes the focal point for decisionmaking and execution.[47]

Underlying the operation and philosophy of the matrix structure, however, is the fundamental notion that no one organization can take over the role of the other and become paramount: the functional organization must not overpower the project organization, or vice versa. The success and survival of the whole system depends on the preservation of a delicate though dynamic balance of power and focus between the two structures. "The unbridled use of power, then, is something to be resorted to only in extreme cases in the matrix form," observes Donald Kingdom. If the two parts become disjointed, the management system will lose its ability to set goals and to link them.[48] A better description of the basic dilemmas and dynamics of the Soviet system is difficult to find. This one captures well the problematical roles of the Party and state administrative hierarchies, as well as the constantly shifting and fluid relationship that has existed between them over time.

This view of the Soviet political system as a matrix organization is illuminated further if we look more closely at the role of the CPSU functionary as essentially that of a project manager extraordinary. Interestingly, the forerunner of the Western project manager was designated "project expediter." This person did not usually perform line functions but rather informally motivated those persons doing the work. Concerned mainly with schedules and obtaining the requisite supplies, the "project expediter" depended on personal diplomacy and persuasive and coercive abilities to remove bottlenecks in the management process.[49] It is this role of a "political *tolkach*" that the Party official frequently plays.

Like the typical project manager, the Party official is also fundamentally a generalist-integrator. The coordinating responsibilities of the Party official require widened horizons, interests, and outlook. Functionally oriented individuals, like those working in Soviet economic ministries and departments, often become narrow in their vision, skills, and loyalties. The tasks of the project manager are to see that the parochial interest of one organizational element does not distort and undermine the overall performance and to overcome the forces that are resisting change, thereby pushing the level of effectiveness upward. At the same time, however, the project manager/Party functionary must not be so close to the project as to lose perspective and forget to see beyond it. As a matter of good administration and necessity, details and decisions that others can handle must be delegated.[50]

In carrying out his responsibilities, the project manager encounters many of the difficulties that beset the Communist Party official. The overriding aim of both is "to get the job done." This objective leads them to focus on performance and results and to counter deviations that inevitably develop from unforeseen circumstances and unplanned behavior. Project control becomes, in effect, their main function. They have the task of mobilizing a project team and welding it together to act as a dedicated and disciplined team rather than a fragmented and indifferent group of functional experts. Like the Party apparatchik, the project manager who ordinarily enjoys no formal authority over line organizations, accomplishes the goal primarily by "pushing, persuading, and ordering." The qualities of a good project manager include management balance, manipulative and collaborative finesse, high motivation, and skill at applying a myriad of control techniques. Needless to say, these are also the essential assets of the successful Party functionary.[51] It is also important to point out that the success of the project manager depends heavily on how clearly the manager can portray to all project personnel general management's objectives and its expectations of the organizations that implement those objectives. Without this clarity of purpose and a strong, decisive management posture, the project manager is incapable of exacting the discipline and dedication required to overcome functional organizational inertia and to accomplish project needs.[52] This situation applies equally to the Soviet system and to the functioning of the Party bureaucracy within it.

If these basic similarities between the Soviet system and the matrix form of industrial organization and management are taken into account, then the dynamics and dilemmas of the Party-state duality acquire new meaning. A dominant tendency among Western writers on the USSR has been to see the role ambiguity and conflict, the fear and mistrust, that envelop the system as peculiarly Soviet irrationalities and atypical aberrations. However, it is important to stress that these phenomena are universally found in matrix organizations. Everywhere, this is an "uneasy form" of organization. The discomfort of dual authority permeates the matrix structure and both poses grave organizational dilemmas and occasions severe personal stress.[53]

The complex organizational dynamics of matrix structures are best explained by the different purposes of project and functional management. The function of the project structure is the reduction of uncertainty, while its purpose is the transformation of a turbulent environment. The task of the functional structure, on the other hand, is the assessment and containment of risk, while its purpose is the achievement of stability within the transformed environment.[54] One concentrates on the lateral process of integration; the other focuses on the vertical process of differentiation and technical specialization. Each requires a very different kind of organizational behavior and management philosophy. The concepts of traditional and project, or systems, management complement each other; they are not two distinct approaches to the executive function. Each form has certain advantages, but neither can be considered best for all situations. By incorporating both design principles, the matrix organization tries to capture the best features of each in order to maximize organizational capacity. At best, the result has been an uneasy compromise and synthesis. In this dual management process, deliberate or purposeful conflict is recognized and required as a mechanism for achieving good trade-offs. The basic issue becomes how to deal with conflict in order to promote resolution rather than division. These difficulties and tensions notwithstanding, the matrix organization is considered in modern Western management literature as an "active adaptation to complexity" that expresses more clearly than a traditional hierarchy the reality of what takes place within a complex organization.[55] Can we not approach and appraise the Soviet system of dual Party and state administration in a similar vein?

¶ The Legacy of a Unique Institutional Experiment: The Limits of Rationality and Primacy of Politics

The experience of the Central Control Commission and Rabkrin in the area of administrative rationalization has left a lasting imprint across the pages of Soviet history and a political lesson not lost, to this day, on the ruling elite. Khrushchev's Party-State Control Committee (PSCC) notwithstanding, this is the only example in the life of the Soviet regime where a Party organ has been amalgamated with a government agency.[56] Significantly, this fusion had fatal consequences, in the end, for both the mission and the survival of the control commission as a Party institution. Having merged itself with the RKI, the CCC became more and more submerged in the latter's affairs and began gradually to lose its Party face and identity. Preoccupied with rationalizing the cumbersome bureaucratic machinery of the Soviet government and taking an extremely mechanistic view of administration, the CCC-RKI became swamped in administrative detail and abstract model building. It increasingly succumbed to a kind of narrow technicism. As a result, it committed the cardinal sin of tending to confuse the lines between the technical and the political; it tended to forget the limits of rationality and the primacy of politics.

When the underlying dimensions and distinctive characteristics of the Soviet political system, as described above, are taken into account, the full import of the legacy of the CCC-RKI begins to emerge. Given the manifold problems and tremendous difficulties that have long beset

Russia's rulers in their drive to build Communism, it is not surprising that the CCC-RKI ultimately broke down and was scrapped. At bottom, the amalgamation of the CCC with the RKI was an attempt to create and rely principally on just one agency, one developmental arm, to affect the transformation of backward Russia. It represented a novel and ultimately unique experiment that tried to combine in a single joint Party-state organization both political and technical tasks and channels of authority. Throughout its existence, however, the CCC-RKI experienced difficulty reconciling and demarcating its diverse functions and contradictory roles. In devising their administrative schemes, the rationalizers in the CCC-RKI failed to take into account both people and politics. By the early thirties the whole control establishment succumbed to a quest for tranquility, a desire to live peacefully, to give up the class struggle, and to avoid conflicts. Becoming very much a regularized institution, it proved incapable of combatting routine, of coping with changing political policies, and of adapting to the new demands and emergent conditions of Stalinist totalitarianism. Its very failure, in fact, seems to vindicate the necessity of a dual system of development administration and to refute the efficacy of a monistic model of organization and monocratic bureaucracy, at least for the purposes and pace of Soviet-style totalitarian social engineering.

In another sense, the legacy of the Central Control Commission and Rabkrin portends the danger that can befall the Party as a whole if it becomes preoccupied with strictly administrative matters and too absorbed in the pathways of rationalization and technical management. The underlying threat of technocratic rationalization is that it tends to erode the primacy of politics and to imply the supremacy of production efficiency and technological progress over political values. Fear of the dangers of technicism reinforces in the mind of the Party elite the need to preserve the preeminently political role and ethos of the Party. The latter are seen as best served by the separation of Party and government functions and institutions. Indeed, it was largely the welling up of these abiding fears in the Party, especially in its apparat, that led to the ouster of Khrushchev. In the eyes of the Party oligarchs, the efforts of the first secretary to transform the Party into a more managerial type of party—not to mention his creation and use of the PSCC—posed a fundamental threat not only to their own jobs and skins but also to the very basis and essence of Party rule.

On the other hand, the CCC-RKI also exemplifies the danger that can result if the Party allows rationalization and the administrative machinery to develop spontaneously and unchecked. Again, the threat posed by rationalization is that "mechanization takes command," in

Mumford's phrase, and displaces "politics in command." Consequently, in this case, fear of the dangers of technicism pushes the Party onto the path of intervening in administrative affairs and of trying to control both the course and the content of technocratic rationalization. The quest for effective Party control, in turn, often leads to a usurpation of technical functions by Party organs and even to a direct fusion of Party and government machinery. Indeed, a major reason behind the move to merge the Party control commission with the RKI in the first place was the growing fear in top Party circles of an autonomous and unchecked industrial machine and managerial bureaucracy. To be sure, the relaxed conditions of NEP and the fact that the nascent Soviet bureaucracy was staffed predominantly by bourgeois specialists and chinovniki from the tsarist regime gave substance to these fears and sparked the felt need to enhance Party control of the "commanding heights" of the economy and government. But the amalgamation also belied a basic distrust of technical specialists and a deep fear of administrative power free of Party control that persist to this day, long after the making over of the economy and machinery of government with a Communist lining and with Soviet specialists and bureaucrats. It also underlies the policies of Khrushchev's successors. While recognizing the need to turn a more technocratic screw in the machinery of power, they have also reaffirmed strongly the necessity of the leading role of the Party in the age of the scientific and technological revolution.

Significantly, therefore, in the search for the proper boundaries between Party and state, between the political and the technical, the problem of administration becomes inseparably linked with the problem of power. Similarly, the need to maintain the primacy of politics becomes integrally connected with the need to preserve the supremacy of the Party over the government. In a sense, the Party bureaucracy can be seen as fulfilling much the same kind of supervisory role over the governmental machinery that the control commission inside the Party ostensibly exercises over the Party apparat. That is, if the task of the commission is to check abuses of power by Party officialdom within the Party, then the function of the Party apparat is to check the misuse of administrative power by the managerial elite in the government. Just as the development of intra-Party control organs has revolved essentially around the question how to make and keep them subordinate to the Party bureaucracy, so has the evolution of governmental agencies turned largely on the issue of how to maintain their subordination and subservience to the Party and its political command.

Moreover, the persistent denial of autonomy by the latter to both the control commission and the administrative machinery of state is rooted in a common fear. In both cases there is an unending fear that autonomy can result in "dual centers" of authority and administration, both inside and outside the Party, which can effectively check the power and possibly challenge the supremacy of the Party command. To protect its monopoly of power and to prevent the possible threat of autonomous systems of intra-Party control and state administration, the Party leadership, therefore, continues to impose limits on administrative rationality.

Part II

Practice and Policy

Erik P. Hoffmann

Information Processing in the Party: Recent Theory and Experience

The purpose of this study is to learn more about the impact of technological change on Soviet policymaking and administration in the 1960s and 1970s. Specifically, what has been the impact of new information processing technology on the chief policymaking and administrative procedures, or "metapolicies," [1] of the CPSU? Most important, if greater information is being sought and accumulated in many policy areas, as seems to be the case, how is this information being *used?* How are Soviet theorists suggesting that this information be used? And what are some of the implications for the fundamental policymaking procedures and substantive policies of the CPSU and for the Party's relationships to other Soviet institutions in an era of rapid scientific, technological, and social change?

¶ Theory

Purposes and types of information: "inner-Party information—an instrument of leadership, a means of education and supervision" Since the fall of Khrushchev, Soviet political leaders and social theorists have repeatedly stressed the importance for policymaking of gathering and utilizing more and better information. The improvement of "political information" and "Party information" has recently been deemed a necessary condition for furthering "the scientific management of society" (*nauchnoe upravlenie obshchestvom*), "the scientific organization of labor" (*nauchnaia organizatsiia truda*), "democratic centralism," "intra-Party democracy," "the unity of action of all Party organizations," and "the effectiveness of Party work." [2]

Soviet authors usually view political information as an important type of social information. "Phenomena, facts, and developments in the po-

This is a revised and updated version of the author's "Soviet Information Processing: Recent Theory and Experience," *Soviet Union* 2, no. 1 (1975): 22–49.

litical sphere of social life" (such as relations among classes and nations) and "politically significant" information about other spheres of human activity (such as economics and culture) are considered political information.[3] "Political information" is thus very broadly and flexibly defined. It may consist of descriptive reporting of events; of interpretation, evaluation, and explanation of individual occurrences and trends; and of normative inducements and prescriptive calls for action based on theoretical generalizations.[4] What is or is not political information varies over time, depending on how political leaders distinguish between the polity and society and on how they ascribe meaning to data. "Party information" refers to information about the substantive activities of the numerous organizations and departments of the CPSU and about their relations with other bureaucracies and social strata, at home and abroad. Party information is a subcategory of political information; "inner-Party information" is in turn a subcategory of Party information and refers chiefly to data about the metapolicies and internal management of the CPSU (for example, information about cadres, the implementation of decisions, or Party meetings).

Some Soviet authors minimize the importance of experience and observation and place heavy emphasis on the allegedly special cognitive powers of dialectical and historical materialism. They stress the continuing relevance of Marxist-Leninist theory as a guide to policy choices, and they reaffirm the traditional goals of the Communist Party—establishment of "Communism" in the Soviet Union, support of "socialist construction" in other countries, and assistance to "antiimperialist forces" throughout the world. They also emphasize the systematic and scientific character of, and the unity of public support for, the basic goals, values, and norms of Soviet socialism.[5]

Other authors, while accepting these fundamental but general tenets, emphasize that Party and state organs must obtain many kinds of information to formulate and carry out specific policies that best express these basic purposes and that spur the fastest progress objectively and subjectively possible toward the attainment of these goals. Thus, political information is considered a vital component of political leadership (*rukovodstvo*) and societal management (*upravlenie*). Together with CPSU leaders' experience, intuition, and knowledge of historical and social "laws," empirical information about the environment is viewed as an essential, although not a sufficient, condition for developing and implementing effective public policies and for maintaining efficient policy-making procedures. Indeed, the lack of policy-relevant information (about resources, capabilities, and contextual conditions, for instance) and insufficient feedback about the consequences of prior policies have been branded as elements of "subjectivism"—the antithesis of scientific, rational, and effective policy formulation.[6]

These two orientations differ in degree, not in kind, for both presume that one will generate and interpret data through a Soviet Marxist-Leninist world outlook. However, in recent directives from the Communist Party and in public statements by top CPSU leaders, there is clear evidence of increasing support for the second of these orientations. At the Twenty-fourth Party Congress in 1971, General Secretary Leonid Brezhnev declared and the Congress resolved, "It is necessary further to improve inner-Party information, to increase its effectiveness, and to make fuller use of it as an important instrument of leadership (*rukovodstvo*), a means of education (*vospitanie*) and supervision (*kontrol*)." [7] This formulation is new, and it seems clearly intended to promote the increased utilization of empirical data in policymaking and administration. Particular emphasis is placed on the Communist Party's leadership and supervisory activities, and it is in precisely these areas that improved upward and horizontal intra-Party communications are expected to play a greater part.

In an authoritative elaboration of this theme, the editors of *Partiinaya zhizn* affirmed that every CPSU committee must strive to obtain and utilize fuller, better-synthesized, and more reliable and timely information to improve the quality of its economic and social-political decisions and to increase its capacity to make effective decisions (for example, through better selection and deployment of personnel). Monitoring to ensure that policies are implemented and taking corrective action to overcome unforeseen problems are Party supervisory functions that are also said to demand a constant flow of significant, trustworthy, selective, and practically applicable feedback and primary information.[8] L. A. Slepov, one of the Party's most insightful senior political analysts, concludes that objective, reliable, and timely information is essential to "facilitate the adoption of well-grounded decisions on various questions, . . . and to check the appropriateness of decisions taken to meet the pressing demands of life." [9] In brief, important Soviet officials seem to consider information a crucial ingredient at different phases of the policymaking process.

To the extent that CPSU leaders have developed an official theory of the policymaking process and various decisionmaking stages and levels, it is the theory of "democratic centralism." But the theory and practice of democratic centralism raise many questions about the ways in which policies are revised, refined, or rejected. The Rules of the Communist Party stress the importance of "regular" and "systematic" intra-Party communication and stipulate the conditions under which "the free and businesslike discussion of questions of Party policy" must take place. A familiar but important dictum in the Party Rules obligates Communists to discuss policy alternatives freely in CPSU meetings and in the press, but only *until* "the organization concerned has adopted a decision." [10] Occasionally one finds an authoritative statement acknowledging that it is sometimes necessary "*critically to review* (peresmatrivat) *various decisions*." [11] Nonetheless, there is no well-developed official Soviet theory about the different types of information needed to accomplish specific purposes at different stages and levels of the policymaking process. In particular, there has been little public discussion about the kind of information that political leaders might or should use to modify existing policies or policymaking procedures.

Yet the recent Soviet literature in the fields of information theory, macrosociological analysis, economic management, and "Party construction" all demonstrates a keen awareness of the adaptive implications of information flows and of the dynamic, sequential, incremental, interdependent, and complex nature of most policymaking and decisionmaking. It is not surprising, then, that important pioneering efforts are being made to categorize different types of information, to identify functions they perform, and to prescribe uses to which they may be put under various circumstances.

Information theory On the most abstract level, Soviet cybernetic theorists such as N. I. Zhukov differentiate among three basic types of information: technical, biological, social. Each kind of information is said to circulate within a distinct dynamic "system"—for example, a machine, a living organism, a society. Particular attention is paid to control (*upravlenie*) and feedback (*obratnaia sviaz'*) mechanisms and behavior. Technological and social systems are believed to operate according to the physical laws of nature and "the laws of social development," respectively, and both types of laws are considered to have cybernetic characteristics, as distinguished from philosophical laws of thought. Important areas of research in social cybernetics include refinement of the concepts of "system," "control," and "feedback"; analysis of relations between a system and its subsystems and among subsystems; and exploration of reciprocal influences among social, technological, and biological systems in theory and practice.[12]

But Soviet scholars disagree with one another about the nature and meaning of the concept of "information." There are at least three major schools of thought: the first emphasizes the material properties of information; the second, its logical and semantic elements; and the third, its pragmatic and instrumental characteristics.[13] An important consequence of these conceptual differences is that each group is developing its own theory of information. This is usually perceived as a problem, and it is frequently lamented in public competition among the various interpretations.

A significant aspect of this competition at present is the effort to distinguish between cybernetics and other branches of information theory and to debunk the frequently unattributed idea of a "cybernetic utopia." "Information" is not merely a cybernetic concept, it is argued, because certain kinds of information have noncybernetic properties and assume different characteristics and perform different functions in various contexts. For example, all social information allegedly possesses a "class" content, and its nature and appropriate uses are said to be determined by the creative application of Marxist-Leninist theory and methodology, not by any inherent or programmed systemic needs. Thus, the goals and tasks of social systems are thought to be determined largely by human actors, not by functional or developmental requisites of the system. Also, it is aptly noted that human, animal, and machine memories (or electronic, organizational, and social feedback) differ considerably from one another. Technologies of communication and automation are contrasted, too. And, perhaps most significant, it is argued that cybernetic analysis overstresses the importance of information relative to other political, economic, social, psychological, and material resources and capabilities, and that pertinent information is a vital, but by no means a sufficient, condition for the judicious choice of societal goals and for effective societal management.[14] Accordingly, A. D. Ursul and other major Soviet information theorists recommend that more research be devoted to the development of a new kind of systems theory that takes into account more fully the distinctive characteristics of *social* and *political* information and systems and that is firmly based on the fundamental principles of Marxism-Leninism.

Macrosociological analysis Among contemporary Soviet social theorists, V. G. Afanasyev has devoted perhaps the closest attention to the role of information in policymaking and administration. Afanasyev, editor-in-chief of *Pravda,* identifies five basic types of information: economic, social, political, ideological, and scientific-technical. He then identifies ten other kinds of information: directive, administrative-legal, organizational, normative, supervisory, accounting (*uchetnyi*), reporting (*otchetnyi*), reference, inquiry, and response. He seems to be offering a complex fifty-item typology, since fifty combinations are logically possible. At the very least, he has presented a thoughtful list of fifteen possibly discrete types of information.[15] Afanasyev has written a major book on social information, which he divides into two broad categories: information about present conditions and information about the future, the latter consisting of "prognostic" and "planning" information.[16]

Afanasyev and others have also undertaken the more important task of analyzing the behavioral characteristics of different types of information. Efforts are being made to identify the functions that various kinds of information perform most efficiently or "optimally"; conversely, decisionmaking stages are being identified that seem to necessitate certain kinds of information for optimal problem-solving in the interests of the system as a whole, not merely of its component parts or subsystems. In short, Soviet social and organization theorists are attempting to study the relationships among various *purposes, types,* and *sources* of information.

Afanasyev has long stressed the importance of a "unified" but *"differentiated"* approach to information work, whereby separate administrative units would process information "in accordance with a specific management objective." [17] He has also noted that different types of information have very different properties, forms, and patterns of behavior, for example, noise and distortion levels, capacity for quantification or coding, and ease of transmission through various channels.[18]

G. T. Zhuravlyev, like Afanasyev, attempts to classify different types of decisions (such as broad and specific, serial and nonrecurring) and to relate various kinds of political information to specific policy purposes. Significantly, Zhuravlyev is keenly aware of the varying nature of decisions at different hierarchical levels of an organization and of the numerous "spheres" and "contours of management" (*kontury upravleniia*). A management "sphere" is an aspect of a broad policy area (ideological work, for instance) toward which the leadership is pursuing a similar goal. A "contour" is viewed as the cluster of relationships between an executive organ and the object of management at a given level. Zhuravlyev concludes that the level, sphere, and contour of management significantly influence political-administrative goals and procedures.[19]

Most important, Afanasyev, Zhuravlyev, and others have recently outlined the major stages of a decisionmaking process and have stressed the need for different kinds of information at every phase and in various contexts. Afanasyev's stages are:

1. determination of the task (goal);
2. determination of the quantity and quality of information needed to make the decision;
3. collection and processing (systematization) of information;
4. creation of information models;
5. determination of alternative methods of fulfilling the task, attaining the goal;
6. selection of the criterion (or criteria) for evaluating alternatives;

7. evaluation of alternatives;
8. selection of one of the alternatives and the making of a decision;
9. adjustment (*korregirovanie*) of a decision in the course of its implementation.[20]

Zhuravlyev identifies five substages in the "preparation" of a decision and four substages in the making and implementation of the decision. The former are all policies on how to make policies, for example, devising a strategy and tactics for resolving the problem at hand.[21] One of the four latter substages is the formulation of programs that express the basic intentions of the decision.

Afanasyev emphasizes that "the primary function of management is the formulation and making of a decision," such as a plan, directive, or law. To reach effective and efficient decisions, he argues, one needs to obtain pertinent information about the nature of the problem and to study thoroughly the opportunities for resolving it, the available resources, and the preparedness of the people who will implement or be affected by the decision.[22]

Afanasyev is well aware of the multiplicity of societal and organizational goals and of the importance of estimating and constantly reevaluating the compatibility and feasibility of different objectives. But he does not squarely confront the central fact that societal and organizational goals are often, indeed usually, in dispute. His analysis of the politics of the feedback process and of the reformulation and adjustment of basic policies is cautious and not very specific. Moreover, he consistently, and perhaps deliberately, blurs the distinction between the politics of principles and the politics of details. Yet he apparently believes that diverse primary and feedback information are highly useful to "responsible" Communist Party officials at all stages and levels of the policymaking process. Even more important, he seems to think that the chief purpose of this information is to help CPSU leaders formulate more realistic goals, implement them effectively and efficiently, *and* adapt all but the most fundamental, centrally prescribed goals, policies, and metapolicies to changing conditions and opportunities. "Only on the basis of profound study of initial data can a well-grounded and, therefore, feasible decision be made. . . . [Also, political leaders] need information about the results of a management decision, so that an old decision can be adjusted or a new one made." [23]

What is most striking about Afanasyev's recent writings is his sensitivity to the *limitations,* both quantitative and qualitative, of even the best policy-relevant data. He seems to be increasingly aware of political leaders' inability to measure most social policy outcomes and interrelationships; to calculate noneconomic (or economic versus noneconomic) costs, benefits, and trade-offs; and to predict the consequences of alternative courses of action. He rightly emphasizes that almost all political and social decisions are made under conditions of considerable "uncertainty" and "risk" (his terms). Hence, he distinguishes between the "ascertainable" and "prescriptive" aspects of a decision and of its informational components. That is, he considers a decision to consist of two basic parts—determination of existing conditions and selection of optimal means to attain desired conditions—and thus he contends that empirical information about the current situation and "prognostic" information about the future are the two main types of social information.[24] Prognostic information is said to help identify the resources, means, and preconditions for achieving gradual progress toward an ideal order and to anticipate choices, trade-offs, and difficulties in moving from present to desired conditions.

Afanasyev recognizes that information about the present state of domestic and international affairs is very important, too. Political leaders may pursue any utopian or general goals, but accurate knowledge of existing conditions can help them to formulate more effective subgoals and to select more efficient ways of achieving these goals. Afanasyev often stresses the policy-relevance of statistics and quantitative sociological data and the importance of electronic data processing. But he insists that all data must be generated and interpreted within the framework of Soviet Marxist-Leninist theory, and he clearly recognizes that they will be presented within the context of bureaucratic and particularistic interests and competition. Hence, he also places heavy emphasis on nonquantitative sociological research and experimentation and on information derived from the first-hand observations and experience of "responsible" political and economic officials.

Briefly stated, he strongly advocates the use of scientific and technological expertise and of the more verifiable kinds of information, such as demographic data, in policymaking. But he appears to be giving increasing weight to informed projections; to very subjective information, such as the intuitive judgments of senior Party officials; and to creative speculation about political ends and means. Furthermore, he has been playing down the importance of cybernetics, as noted earlier, and he is now stressing that contextual conditions and normative communication play a vital role in shaping the nature and accomplishments of society.[25]

What one is witnessing may be the emergence of a fascinating synthesis. Afanasyev, as a modern organization theorist, rightly emphasizes the constraints on rational choice and the importance of coping with uncertainty. As a major Party spokesman he offers many suggestions on how to make these difficult choices and to compensate for, say, the lack of multifaceted political information. And as a contemporary social theorist, he sensibly stresses the complexity and interdependence of social life, the importance of thoughtfully determining enlightened and feasible national goals, and of careful long- and short-range planning to attain these goals. Finally, as an insightful Soviet Marxist theorist of "the scientific-technological revolution," he can provide criteria and standards for selecting among alternative aims and methods and for confronting diverse new situations and problems.

In short, Soviet social theorists are seriously examining the types of information that can and should be used for various purposes at specific stages and levels of policymaking and administration, and these investigations raise an extraordinarily complex set of questions whose theoretical and practical implications have only begun to be clarified.[26]

Economic management The recent Soviet literature on economic management, planning, and automated management systems also reflects a keen awareness of the key role of information in decisionmaking. Because economic goals are clearer and more susceptible to norms of technical rationality, economic analyses are more specific about the types and uses of information than are macrosociological studies. One finds exceptionally detailed discussions about the practical applications of economic, technical, and scientific information in specific branches of the economy.[27] The need for numerous kinds of data (statistical, planning, financial, technical, supply, capital construction) and for data of various degrees of complexity at different levels of economic decisionmaking are well recognized. Furthermore, since these data are almost always said to be used for purposes determined by higher Party and state authorities, feedback and primary information are reportedly solicited to clarify the technical, material, or legal aspects of a directive, but not to adjust the economic goal or target itself.[28]

Some writers, notably G. G. Vorobyev, focus on the "information culture" of economic decisionmaking at the factory level. Managers and administrators are exhorted to establish and maintain efficient technical *and* sociopsychological conditions for obtaining, systematizing, and utilizing vast quantities of scientific-technical information. Economic officials are strongly urged to improve the mechanization of information processing (such as the handling of documents); but they are also charged with creating and sustaining harmonious interpersonal relationships and satisfying job conditions that promote the generation and communication of pertinent, timely feedback from workers and supervisory personnel.[29]

The writings of D. M. Gvishiani, deputy head of the State Committee on Science and Technology, clearly illustrate the concern of top-level government officials with the informational aspects of economic decisionmaking and scientific and technological change. Gvishiani contends: "Of major importance in present-day conditions is comprehensive technical re-equipment, specifically the overall mechanization and automation of the processes of obtaining, storing, processing, and using different types of information, which is one of the basic elements of the management system at all its levels and in all its functional branches. Here a special part is played by automated and computerized management systems . . . , creating . . . a basis for a genuinely scientific approach to solving management problems. . . ." [30]

"Party construction" The Soviet literature on the CPSU has always contained some discussion of the purposes and types of Party information. The Brezhnev administration's interest in improving organizational communication is reflected in the increased number of writings on the topic and in the inclusion of chapters on inner-Party information in the standard texts on CPSU work.[31] Party officials have often made a simple three-fold distinction between downward, upward, and horizontal communication. There has also been a tendency to classify information by sources (such as personal observations of Party apparatchiki, critical remarks and suggestions of primary Party organization secretaries and state and economic officials, and letters from private citizens to Party organs and the press), or by form (such as memoranda from CPSU cadres, statistical economic data, sociological research findings, and public opinion surveys). In addition, there have been occasional efforts to classify information according to the Party's major activities—economic, political, organizational, ideological, cultural, international.

In much of the current CPSU literature, considerable attention is paid to communication from lower to higher Party organs. Three kinds of such upward communication are frequently discussed: information of a general political character, information about Party guidance of economic and cultural development, and information about intra-Party activities.[32] Generally speaking, the most important types of intelligence that CPSU officials seek are information about whether a situation has changed, comparisons of performance with aim (especially progress toward the fulfillment of Party and state decrees), proposals for implementing or adjusting current directives, evaluations of the work of provincial cadres, studies of available resources, systematic assembly of information to cope with an immediate problem, estimates of public moods (domestic and foreign), and data to help forecast trends and future needs.

Interestingly, the Party press contains a growing number of simple systems analyses of policymaking stages. Authors stress the importance of carefully formulating goals, of devising optimal methods of implementing policies, of verifying the fulfillment of programs, and of utilizing feedback about the effectiveness, efficiency, and consequences of prior decisions "as new data for working out the next decisions." [33] Soviet writers sometimes emphasize that primary information is equally essential to policymaking and administration.[34]

Today the officially proclaimed purposes of all inner-Party information are to help the Party to lead, supervise, and educate. This is essentially a call to improve downward, upward, and horizontal communication of diverse kinds. In practice it means that Party bureaus and senior apparatchiki are once again being exhorted to increase downward communication for the purposes of furthering the implementation and legitimation of central policies and of influencing the decisionmaking procedures of lower-level CPSU committees (through talks by national officials at regional Party meetings, for example).

More significant, the new Brezhnev guidelines also seem to mean that CPSU cadres at all levels are expected to utilize additional upward-flowing information for three crucial purposes: to formulate more effective substantive policies and decisions; to implement policies and decisions more efficiently; and to improve the policymaking system itself, that is, "to perfect the style and method of leadership." [35] To be sure, top CPSU officials still emphasize that the chief purpose of improving upward communication is to fulfill centrally determined goals. But the increasing, albeit cautious, appeals to use better primary and feedback information in policy formulation—and in the monitoring of prior decisions, in current and long-range planning, and in other metapolicy areas—bear careful watching.

¶ Experience

Uses of information: "to lead, it is necessary to know" Turning now from theory to experience, let us examine some aspects of the day-to-day collection, processing, and utilization of different kinds of information in the Party. Are important changes currently taking place? If so, why? And what are some of the consequences?

Official assessments First, it must be emphasized that numerous executive Party officials have unequivocally stated that more and better information *is* reaching key decisionmaking points and *is* being used in policymaking and administration at all levels of the CPSU. Moreover, central Party leaders have made it clear that increasing numbers of people are *expected* to participate in, have the *opportunity* to participate in, and *have* participated in different aspects of decisionmaking on various substantive issues at the national, regional, and local levels.

To illustrate:

The information that goes from the bottom to the top, up to the Central Committee, has become more effective and more trenchant. This information helps us to improve our bearings in any given situation, and to take the experience and opinion of the Party organizations and the working people more fully into account in deciding questions. (Leonid Brezhnev, 1971 [36])

The conclusions and data derived from the analysis of upward communication are being used more and more in preparing different measures, formulating decisions and short- and long-term plans, determining the basic directions of ideological activities, the concrete tasks of Communist upbringing, the activization of inner-Party life. . . . Despite some unresolved questions, there have been fundamental, qualitative changes in all aspects of inner-Party information in recent years, which have helped to master the tasks of Communist construction. (I. A. Shvets, 1972 [37])

Decrees based on the reports and accounts of Party committees convincingly reflect the striving of the CPSU Central Committee to analyze in a Leninist spirit the real facts of a situation, . . . to uncover possible mistakes and shortcomings and devise concrete measures to eliminate them, to disseminate the best forms of Party work. It is not accidental that local initiative, local innovation, have been receiving more and more of a hearing throughout the Party (*obshchepartiinoe zvuchanie*) in recent years. . . . (A. F. Kadashev, 1972 [38])

At present increasingly detailed, increasingly valuable comprehensive information reaches the Central Committee. From it the leadership of the Central Committee obtains generalized and timely information of profound substance, not only on many questions of inner-Party life, but also on the attitudes of Soviet people toward the most important decisions of the Party and government, and toward their international actions. (N. A. Zolotarev and P. I. Kotelnikov, 1973 [39])

A smooth-running [*stroinaya*] system of information has now been created which embraces all links of the Party from top to bottom. This enables leading Party organs to know and evaluate the situation more precisely, and to accumulate collective experience. (P. A. Rodionov, 1975 [40])

Statements of this kind do not by themselves prove that the conditions described exist. But if one considers the source, audience, context, and in some cases the specificity of these assertions, they certainly suggest that many top CPSU officials desire improved intra-Party communication and that some progress has probably been made toward this end in recent years. In a word, there may be increasing validity to the claim that "valuable proposals and patriotic undertakings from below find support in the decisions of Party committees" [41]—especially if these initiatives come from apparatchiki, scientific and technical specialists, and Communists, and if they concern the details, rather than the principles, of policies.

Metapolicy and organizational changes Second, the CPSU leadership seems to have made major metapolicy decisions between 1966 and 1969 to improve information work in the central and regional Party apparatuses.[42] The interest of the Brezhnev administration in systematizing "inner-Party information" is reflected in certain organizational changes and administrative measures. For example, a new Party Information Sector was established in the Organizational-Party Work Department of the CPSU Central Committee shortly after the Twenty-third Congress in 1966. Similar sections were then formed in all republic Party committee apparatuses and in many provincial CPSU organizations. After 1968 "all" republic, krai, and oblast CPSU committees, "the overwhelming majority" of city and district committees, and "many" of the larger primary Party organizations discussed in detail specific measures to improve intra-Party communication at their Party bureau meetings, plenary sessions, and special zonal conferences. Particular attention was reportedly devoted to plans for introducing new information-processing and -transmitting technology (such as punchcard systems, teletype machines, and dictaphones), for training staff and part-time specialists to conduct information work, for increasing downward and horizontal intra-Party communication, for reducing distortion in upward communication, for improving the atmosphere for frank, businesslike discussions at Party meetings, and for increasing the quality and quantity of information used to reach and implement decisions.[43]

Some of these new information sectors perform important activities. In the Lithuanian Central Committee, for example, an "information group" collects and generalizes information materials from the district and city Party committees, departments of the Union Republic Central Committee, and ministries and other republic organizations. This group reports to the CPSU Central Committee and Union Republic Central Committee on the moods, questions, suggestions, and statements of different strata of the population and on negative phenomena and unusual incidents. Most important perhaps, this information unit prepares reviews (*obzory*) of the major economic, cultural, and political education activities of the local Party and mass organizations. Also, it has been charged with improving the "Party-political" information work of the lower CPSU committees and ordered to establish mechanized information-referencing systems on the growth of the republic's cities and districts and on the development of the economy and society.[44] The Omsk *obkom* information sector performs similarly important functions.[45]

However, the role and activities of these regional information groups vary considerably. Many are primarily composed of "nonstaff" (*vneshtatnye*) workers or of cadres from only one CPSU department, usually the organizational-Party work or propaganda department. Lacking broad-based support and assistance from its Party bureau, an information sector of this kind is almost inevitably limited to "housekeeping" responsibilities (clipping newspaper articles or registering payment of Party dues, for example). One receives the distinct impression that the Lithuanian and Omsk experiences are exceptional and that information work elsewhere has a long way to go before reaching, if indeed it is intended to reach, this level of importance.

A small, little-known information group was formed in the Central Committee Department of Science in 1956, became a sector in December 1962, and began to serve the departments of both Propaganda and Science in February 1966. The significant functions of this Information Sector, as described by a former "instructor" in it, were to analyze and to generalize "the information received through the traditional channels. However, it also collected information itself. We organized studies of public opinion inside the Party organizations, tried to evaluate the effectiveness of Party propaganda and advanced forms of Party work, and elucidated the optimum forms of ideological pressure. In 1968 the sector's functions were extended to provide analytical material directly to the advisers' sector of the Secretariat of the Central Committee. This served as primary material for reports, the speeches of leading Party figures, etc." [46] These latter responsibilities are of obvious relevance for policy. However, the powers of this Information Sector—especially its consultative activities and its opportunities to conduct its own concrete sociological investigations—were sharply curtailed in the early 1970s. An unpublished CPSU decree entitled "On the Mistakes in the Analysis and Collection of Facts by the Information Sector" was reportedly passed in November 1971. Thereafter, the officials of this sector are said to have worked primarily with information materials from the traditional channels, and the unit has allegedly fulfilled a chiefly symbolic function.[47] By now, it may have been disbanded.

Sociological research in Party work, however, is currently on the increase. To be sure, there were significant upheavals in Soviet sociology and in the major academic sociological research institutes in the early 1970s. At issue was nothing less than the appropriate relationship between concrete sociological research and Marxist-Leninist theory, and the proper role of empirical research (and researchers) in Soviet policymaking and administration. While the lessons of these struggles have surely not been lost on the researchers who conduct opinion surveys and other empirical investigations for the Party, the fact remains that CPSU organizations at all levels are sponsoring a considerable amount of social research. Primary and feedback information from this source is likely to have an increasingly important impact on the details and implementation of various policies, perhaps especially in the local Party organs.[48]

One discerns, then, a somewhat cautious and perhaps ambivalent official Soviet attitude toward information specialists and empirical sociological research in the 1970s. The Brezhnev administration has placed heavy emphasis on improving communication within *existing* channels—among Party and state agencies and departments at the center and in official CPSU meetings at the regional and local levels, for example.[49] The impact of these efforts is difficult to evaluate, because they are apparently intended to promote cooperative problem-solving through increased *private* communication within and among major bureaucracies, or, as one Party spokesman put it, through "debates among like-minded people." [50] But Party and government officials are well aware of the bureaucratic power that accrues to the "debaters" who can gather and interpret fresh data for their own purposes, and this awareness may help to explain the guarded attitude of many Soviet officials toward information specialists and empirical social investigations.

In brief, the recent Soviet metapolicies concerning information sectors, concrete sociological research, and private communication through existing bureaucratic channels—and the modest but growing amount of time, effort, and money expended in pursuing these activities—suggest that most Politburo and Secretariat members perceive a clear need to improve the quality of information used in decisionmaking at different stages and levels and to take cautious, incremental, but serious and well-thought-out practical measures to do so.

Modern information technology Third, and perhaps most portentous, new information technology is being gradually introduced into the Party, in an effort to improve the scientific character and style of Party work. The advent of electronic data processing, together with modern telecommunications equipment, creates the possibility of significant changes in Soviet policymaking and administration. The nature of these changes to date and, in particular, the *uses* to which new and newly processed types of information are being put are the subject of this discussion.

The central facts of the matter are that until recently virtually all Party documents were processed by hand, that few computers are now being used in the internal management of the CPSU, and that mechanized punchcard systems have proliferated rapidly in the regional Party apparatus since the late 1960s. Edgecut punchcards (*perfokarty s kraevoi perforatsiei*) may well be the most important technical development in intra-Party communication since the introduction of the telephone. It is not surprising that the impact of modern information-processing technology on policymaking does not seem to have been very great so far. Although some of the data currently processed by new methods clearly have policy implications, many of them are only indirectly related to the principles or details of policy and are of a primarily "housekeeping" nature.

What is striking about the present situation is the greater mechanization of information processing *outside* the Party. The economy and the military are the most important examples, but even in fields such as law and education, there is evidence of prior and perhaps considerable use of advanced information technology. One of the reasons we know something about the punchcard systems recently introduced into the regional Party apparatus is that identical equipment, techniques, and even codes have been used in the economy and other fields for years. In fact, the chief new Party systems are among the least complicated, although the secrecy surrounding them is, of course, greater than in most other bureaucracies.[51] What is also notable is that the computerization of decision processes seems to be taking place primarily at the *primary Party organization level* and that the mechanization of information processing may be slowly working its way *up* the CPSU hierarchy.[52] But very little is known about the use of new information technology in the departments of the Central Committee apparatus.

Active Party officials and theorists of "the scientific management of society" have contrasting views about information technology, and responsible CPSU apparatchiki have important differences among themselves, which are clearly influencing the practical application of the new technologies. On the most general level, all seem to agree that the growing number of Party and state organs, their increasing structural differentiation and specialization, and, above all, the rapidly increasing volume and complexity of the interrelated problems they must resolve and the new kinds of information and cooperation needed to do so place tremendous strains on the traditional methods of gathering, processing, and communicating different types of information. But social theorists think in longer-range terms, and some are impatient—Afanasyev, for one, writes chiefly about computers and minimizes, even belittles, the importance of nonelectronic punchcard systems that merely classify, rather than analyze, data. Central and regional Party cadres, in contrast, take a more pragmatic and cautious attitude. They acknowledge the existence of many "primitive" (*kustarnye*) information-processing methods within the Party, but they contend that the introduction of even unsophisticated (that is, manual) data-retrieval systems is an important step forward.[53]

Although CPSU officials sometimes express considerable enthusiasm for modern organizational technology (*orgtekhnika*), more common are appraisals tempered by an appreciation of the limitations and shortcomings of available computer hardware and software and other information referencing, retrieval, and transmitting systems and equipment. Also, some CPSU cadres cautiously express skepticism about the mechanization of intra-Party communication, and, in turn, other apparatchiki criticize these attitudes. On occasion, CPSU spokesmen pointedly berate one another for exaggerating the differences between the present-day scientific approach to Party work and that of previous Soviet administrations, especially Lenin's.[54]

Some CPSU spokesmen stress that the core of the scientific approach to Party work is the improvement of cadre selection, *kontrol,* and ideological training, and that the mechanization of information processing has not altered and must not alter the Party's basic activities and style of work. Others argue that the new technology and methods have already enhanced traditional activities and can and should be used to produce further improvements. And still others suggest, albeit cautiously, that both the form and substance of Party work must be adjusted to cope with the changing nature and the increasing volume, complexity, and interdependence of the problems and opportunities created by the "scientific-technological revolution." [55]

It would appear that computer and punchcard technology has only begun to alter the procedures of Party policymaking and administration. It is not clear that computers are now used extensively even in the major internal management units of the Central Committee apparatus, such as the Organizational-Party Work and Administration of Affairs departments. Also, there seems to have been surprisingly little central planning and organization of the campaign to introduce new information-processing technology into the regional Party committees. Individual CPSU units have been given considerable leeway in selecting and procuring modern communications technology, in determining the *uses* of available technology, in establishing and maintaining (for example, staffing) mechanized data-processing systems, in shaping the role of the newly formed information sectors, and in recruiting and training information specialists. Thus, the impact of the new technology has surely varied considerably from Party committee to Party committee, and from department to department.

Better monitoring of the implementation of decisions and systematization and retrieval of information have probably been the most important accomplishments to date. In the city of Serpukhov, for instance, cadres are recording five major kinds of information on edge-cut punchcards: information about Party meetings, personnel, mass-political work, progress toward the fulfillment of decisions, and criticisms and suggestions from various sources.[56] In Novomoskovsk, data are being accumulated and coded about sixteen different aspects of Party meetings (including the type of meeting, speakers, selected questions discussed, action taken), and various kinds of edge-cut punchcards are being used for similar purposes in other city, provincial, and republic CPSU committees. In the Rostov-on-Don obkom, approximately five hundred kinds of data have been extracted from Party documents such as the minutes of CPSU meetings and recorded on punchcards.[57] Broad categories of information include the type of Party work, the nature of the document, its substantive themes, the branch of production, and the sender and receiver. A major category, such as "Organization Work," is subdivided into many topics: intra-Party democracy, Party discipline, Party assignments, meetings, new personnel, work with young Communists, and so on. "Ideological Work" includes subcategories for mass-political activities, Party education, and public lectures.

While it is fairly easy to learn about some of the kinds of information being recorded on punchcards, it is much more difficult to ascertain the actual uses to which this information is being put. Party spokesmen cite instances where this newly processed information is utilized to make decisions and recommendations, to implement decisions, to improve the "style and methods" of Party work, to prevent abuses, to assess public opinion, to disseminate valuable experience, and to broaden understanding of a situation or problem.[58]

Information from the minutes and stenographic reports of Party meetings is especially important, because it is used for all seven of the above purposes. When recorded on punchcards, this information enables Party apparatchiki to supervise more closely the activities of lower-level CPSU committees, in particular the content and conduct of Party meetings. With the aid of punchcards, for example, a gorkom instructor can quickly learn which topics were discussed at raikom meetings, who reported what kind of progress toward the fulfillment of certain decisions, or what criticisms or suggestions were directed to the Party bureau and to higher Party organs. In at least some cases, the availability of this information has led to prompt action, such as rendering political assistance and technical advice to lower CPSU committees and ensuring that they hold regular bureau, plenum, and aktiv meetings and systematically report their activities to higher organs, as required by the Party Rules. "Studying punchcards, the [Serpukhov] gorkom workers have become able to give more effective help to secretaries of Party organizations." [59] As a result of this new technology, more information about the proceedings of CPSU meetings is being recorded, and in a form that can be easily retrieved, generalized, and transmitted to other Party and state officials.

This is a potentially significant development for at least two reasons: first, because current CPSU leaders have been making an effort to encourage freer discussion of the details of policy at official meetings in the regional Party apparatus;[60] and, second, because central Party officials inform us that "in recent years, the obkomy, kraikomy, and union republic Communist Parties have conducted more frequent and systematic analysis of the minutes of bureau and plenary meetings of Party committees." [61] Thorough analysis of these reports, especially over time, is said to reveal many important trends in the work of the local Party organs. In the Azerbaidzhani Central Committee, for example, cadres have recently studied meticulously the minutes of city and district Party committees and have discovered some disquieting facts—in particular, evidence of excessive attention to "secondary, unplanned matters" and insufficient preparation of important questions discussed at these meetings, both of which deficiencies were reported to have had a negative effect on the quality of their decisions.[62] Republic-level officials, applying this information, came to specific conclusions about how to improve the substantive activities and decisionmaking procedures of subordinate CPSU organizations. Needless to say, the Union Republic Central Committee communicated its findings and expectations to the lower Party committees through private and public channels, in an effort to exert greater influence over local decisions, decisionmaking and administrative practices, and policy outcomes.

But the impact of new information technology varies from one policy and metapolicy area to another. For example, the Zhuravlyev book discussed earlier describes the CPSU's daily activities in the field of ideological work and concludes that the diverse information currently being used to make and administer decisions is gathered from at least seven sources: personal observations of apparatchiki; official Party documents (for example, stenographic accounts of Party meetings); written reports (such as memoranda on the fulfillment of directives); sociological research; criticisms and suggestions of Communists; oral information (such as that received from citizens who visit their obkom headquarters); and letters. Significantly, information from all of these sources is being recorded on punchcards and is being utilized to make, implement, and evaluate decisions in the ideological sphere.[63]

Different kinds of information, of course, can be used for different purposes. The most important of the uses frequently discussed in the Party press, and the most important type of data recorded on punchcards, is the monitoring of progress toward the fulfillment of national, regional, and local CPSU and state directives. Party officials have long been well aware of the importance of feedback in helping to control and to verify the implementation of policies and decisions. With the aid of punchcards, however, this work is taking new forms. In the Novomoskovsk gorkom, for example, punchcards are analyzed monthly to evaluate the agenda, proceedings, and decisions of the meetings of district committees and primary Party organizations. Particularly noteworthy are the special punchcard sections to record critical statements by Communists and other information from Party meetings pertaining to the implementation of local decisions or directives from above. "If some organizations forget to supervise the fulfillment of decisions, we remind them of this at the monthly meetings and seminars for Party secretaries." [64]

Systematic collection and utilization of these kinds of data are quite significant, then, because they make possible better-informed and continuous evaluation of policy outcomes and generate pertinent data from various sources, which can be compared in countless ways and which can be and are being used by CPSU committees at different levels for the periodic adjustment of Party policies, metapolicies, and administrative practices and personnel.[65] In short, the new punchcard systems are promoting several important changes: improved collection, organization, and storage of information on substantive political, economic, and social policy questions; more thorough and speedier retrieval of information useful for decisionmaking and administration at various levels of the CPSU; more continuous monitoring of progress toward the fulfillment of Party and state decrees; more accurate personnel information to facilitate recruitment and deployment of cadres; more efficient categorization and communication of criticism and recommendations by Communists and non-Communists; and others.

But it must be remembered that only in the late 1960s and early 1970s were punchcard systems introduced into *some* departments of *some* Union Republic, provincial, and city Party committees. Also, much of the information initially recorded on punchcards—the speakers and attendance at meetings, the source and location of documents, financial data about personnel, for instance—is clearly of a "Party management" (*partynoe khozyaistvo*) or "housekeeping" nature.

Briefly stated, electronic and manual punchcard systems have not replaced and are not intended to replace traditional and informal methods of processing and communicating information, especially at the highest levels of the CPSU. Rather, punchcards are helping to sort out some of the pertinent from the less important intra-Party communication and to speed considerably the retrieval and synthesis of significant information. Thus, punchcard systems have begun to perform two important functions: to help transmit more and better policy, metapolicy, and administrative information to key decisionmaking points at the national, regional, and local levels (as discussed above); and to free responsible officials and other communication channels (such as the telephone) for more meaningful communication on more important questions. Better processing of routine and quantifiable data enables Party workers to seek out more valuable information through on-site inspection trips, for example. Better-processed information also helps CPSU officials to cope with the problems of information overload—that is, the abundance of marginally useful information in Party committees—and the lack of accurate, timely information on many fundamental substantive and metapolicy issues. Inadequate information clearly limits the Party's ability to influence events and wastes considerable organizational resources. Even simple information-retrieval systems can achieve a thirty- to fifty-fold reduction in the time and effort needed to find and to synthesize desired information.

This second function has surely been the more important to date, but the first—the mechanization of policy-relevant data—is likely to become increasingly prominent in the future, especially if more "operative" and secondary decisions on the principles as well as the details of policy are delegated to the republic, provincial, and local Party organizations. In any case, both developments are undramatic but significant manifestations of the current "scientific approach" to Party work.[66]

¶ Conclusion

Important changes have taken place in the Soviet policymaking process under the successive leadership of Lenin, Stalin, Khrushchev, and Brezhnev. These changes have occurred in relations among the Soviet political elite, between the Communist Party and other major bureaucracies, and between the political and bureaucratic elites and Soviet society. It is not surprising, then, that the meaning and use of the concept "political information," and the nature of "Party information" work, have varied from one historical period to the next.

The present Soviet leaders are living under different domestic, international, and scientific-technological conditions than their predecessors. They are also more locked into past political, economic, social, military, and international commitments. Not only do their policy choices seem to be more circumscribed, but the volume of their decisions has greatly increased and their decisions are much more complex, interdependent, and interrelated (with one another and with the decisions and fortunes of other socialist and major nonsocialist nations). Thus, the possibility of significant changes in Party goals and policies is perhaps more limited now than in any other period of Soviet history. Change seems even less likely when one takes into consideration current Soviet policymaking procedures (such as "collective leadership," major compromises before new policies are enunciated, prior consolidation of bureaucratic support for policy implementation, avoidance of "subjectivism," and clear preference for incremental change in institutional arrangements).

What these developments suggest is that the politics of details were more important than the politics of principles in the early 1970s and that the difference between feasible (that is, acceptable, potentially influential) goal-changing feedback and goal-seeking feedback was not extremely great in most policy areas. Proposals for integral or fundamental policy changes came from dissidents of various kinds, but these demands were deemed illegitimate because of their origin and content and the unofficial ways in which they were made.

Some suggestions for far-reaching change were expressed in the official Soviet press in the mid- and late 1960s, and others (solicited and unsolicited) may have been transmitted through the Party, ministerial, and scientific-educational bureaucracies. But by 1970 the Party leadership seems to have formulated and reached a general consensus on a new "grand design" or overall set of coordinated domestic and foreign policy objectives. A key element of this program was the call *"to combine organically the achievements of the scientific-technological revolution with the advantages of the socialist economic system."* [67] Detente with the United States and greater technological borrowing through trade with the West (including Japan) were crucial parts of this broad cluster of policies. At home, information and expertise were actively solicited at all levels of the CPSU—in particular, primary and feedback data and specific ideas for developing more effective economic and social programs and for improving the planning and organizational work needed to implement the general Party line, which was further elaborated upon and legitimized at the Twenty-fourth and Twenty-fifth Party Congresses. Only in the second half of 1974 was there increasing evidence of serious disagreements within the Politburo over basic elements of the new "grand design."

But perhaps more important than any substantive policy change is the

Brezhnev administration's establishment and legitimization of certain policymaking procedures—notably, the use of more and better information in policy formation and implementation. This metapolicy is quite important, because, explicitly or implicitly, political and social information and feedback contain proposals for adjustments in policies, priorities, and resource allocation, and, intentionally or not, they may shape or influence the thinking of Soviet political leaders (for example, by helping to define problems, by posing feasible policy alternatives, or by suggesting criteria, standards, and methods to evaluate perceived options). Clearly, top Party leaders and leadership factions want better goal-seeking feedback, but they may also want limited goal-*changing* feedback of certain kinds, even when the basic short-term and possibly long-term policy objectives are set. And they may want still more goal-changing feedback, if there is mounting disagreement about key short-term and long-term policy objectives. For Marxist-Leninist theory is probably of less practical value today in formulating and implementing substantive policies, domestic and foreign, than ever before. Moreover, the distinction between politics and administration, on both the national and regional levels, seems to be more blurred than formerly.

Thus, significantly, the Brezhnev administration may be attempting to reduce the metapolicy impact of the vital Party Rule (I/3/b) that proscribes free discussion of policy alternatives in CPSU meetings and in the press *after* a Party organization has reached a decision. That is, Party leaders may be trying to push this maxim from the realm of practical ideology to that of pure ideology. Reasons for this effort to adjust the policymaking system might include the apparently broad leadership support for the current "grand design" (from 1970 to 1974, at least); the changing nature of the decisions that have to be made; the growing need for creativity, innovation, risk-taking, and "within system" constructive criticism, especially on economic and technical questions; and the increasing indistinguishability of ends and means, of goal-adjusting and goal-seeking feedback.

Hence, it is not surprising that the present Soviet leadership has placed renewed emphasis on the concepts of Party information and *glasnost*—greater intra-Party publicity, openness, and frankness—and on the "democratic" side of the "democratic centralism" formula. Party theoreticians have by no means abandoned the "centralism" side, which includes "discipline," "unity of ideas and action," and so on. Indeed, it is often argued that while Party democracy is developing, Party discipline must not be slackened and may actually have to be increased. In any case, present-day objective conditions are said to warrant significantly broader and deeper participation in different stages and levels of policymaking and administration, especially from cadres in the regional Party organizations, from officials in the ministerial, scientific-educational, soviet, and public bureaucracies, and from members of the Communist Party.

The current CPSU leaders have demonstrated a clear preference for private rather than open communication of policy-relevant information, and they are relying heavily on the departments of the central and local Party committee apparatuses to study and evaluate policy alternatives and personnel and to coordinate and supervise the implementation of decisions taken. Although plenary sessions of the national Central Committee may be playing a reduced role in debating policy and administrative choices, and the publication of stenographic reports of plenum proceedings has been suspended, these developments do not necessarily mean that significant intra-Party communication is on the wane.[68] For example, Politburo member V. V. Shcherbitsky, describing a plenum of the Ukrainian Central Committee, asserts: "The members of the Ukrainian Central Committee had the opportunity to express their attitudes toward the work of the Politburo of the Ukrainian Communist Party Central Committee, to voice critical remarks and recommendations directed toward the improvement of *all* of our activities." [69] Moreover, as we have discussed, the present national Politburo and Secretariat are making serious and apparently modestly successful efforts to encourage the systematization, processing, and utilization of inner-Party information and to develop their distinctly non-Khrushchevian interpretation of "democratic centralism."

In summary, the present Party leadership apparently believes that accurate political information is essential for effective policymaking and administration on the national, regional, and local levels. Together with Soviet cyberneticists, social theorists, and economists, many important Party officials seem to be acutely aware of the changing nature of policymaking and societal management and of the vital role that innumerable kinds of information and communication play in these processes. Moreover, it seems that central, republic, and provincial CPSU organs *are* currently seeking, receiving, and weighing fuller, better-synthesized, and more accurate and practically relevant information from various sources —notably, from lower Party committees, economic production units, and the ministerial, soviet, educational-scientific, and other bureaucracies. The "scientific-technological revolution" does not yet appear to have had a considerable impact on the CPSU's policymaking procedures or on the management of its internal affairs, but, especially with the increased use of computers, important changes are possible in the not very distant future. The *nature* and *extent* of these changes, and their impact on the Soviet policy process, will depend on the interaction of many political, cultural, and technological factors.[70] But Communist Party leaders are keenly aware of the importance of controlling the adaptation of organizational procedures to new technology and problems, and their capacity to do so is of the utmost significance for the future development of the Soviet political system.

Donald R. Kelley

Environmental Problems as a New Policy Issue

¶ Adaptation and Environmental Problems as Issue Generation

A tentative definition of adaptation suggests at least partial criteria for answering the fundamental question whether the Soviet leadership has managed to cope with the institutional and social imperatives of a complex industrial society or has instead deteriorated into an unimaginative "regime of clerks." In his *Framework for Political Analysis,* David Easton offers us a rough working definition by broadly defining adaptation as responsiveness to internal or external environmental stresses.[1] The responsive potential of a political system refers not only to its ability to mobilize social resources but also to its ability to recognize new problem areas and to channel demands for political action into acceptable patterns of behavior.

Students of Soviet politics have long been concerned with identifying adaptive behavior in the USSR. The extensive literature on elite change and selective recruitment has been at least tacitly based on the notion that the recruitment of specialists and the selection to higher Party bodies of the representatives of important functional elites have been attempts both to secure the services of and to coopt increasingly important elements of the society.[2] Studies of the changing work style of Party and state officials have also assumed that the introduction of the principles of "scientific management" has been an attempt to cope with the increasing complexity of managerial tasks.[3] In similar fashion, the rapidly growing body of literature on interest group and specialist influence in policymaking has been based on the assumption that consultation with such specialized elites is a rational pattern of adaptive behavior to follow in an increasingly complex social order confronted with a range of problems requiring technologically sophisticated responses.[4]

One area in Soviet politics that has thus far not received much attention is the question how new problems are recognized and translated into public policy issues. While there is a convincing body of literature demonstrating that certain issues have been closed to discussion by Party fiat, little has been done on the question of the recognition and legitimation of new issue areas as an index of responsive potential. Soviet genetics under Lysenko and the field of cybernetics during Stalin's rule were taboo, and many critical themes in literature and art have always been proscribed, even during the so-called thaws. But studies of the reverse side of the process—that is, how new issues are raised and acquire legitimacy as public policy concerns—are relatively scarce. Yet this is clearly one aspect of Easton's concept of responsive potential: a system's ability to recognize a new area of strain within its social and institutional environment, to channel demands for public policy raised by the elements of society that are first concerned with the issue, and ultimately to institutionalize the information-gathering and decisionmaking processes in this area. Jerry Hough has convincingly made the case for an examination of policy content, as well as elite recruitment and decisionmaking style, as an index of change, concluding that "ultimately the test of the direction in which the Soviet political system is evolving must be the nature of the policies that emerge from the system." [5]

A study of the emergence of environmental quality as an issue of public policy provides an instructive example of the process through which new issues are created. Three interlocking, although not necessarily sequential, phases can be identified. The first was the initial recognition of the issue by a handful of scientists and conservationists, long before the public or government leaders took note of a deteriorating environment. The second was the legitimation and eventual politicization of the issue, which was accomplished both as the body of scientific evidence about the threat of pollution grew and was simplified into terms that attracted a widespread elite audience, and as demands for better environmental protection were increasingly pressed by concerned state agencies and environmentalists. The process of legitimation and politicization was completed as high-ranking Party and state officials publicly took note of the need for stricter policy, especially in certain crisis situations, such as Lake Baikal, and as the battle over emission standards and other environmental concerns took the form of bureaucratic politics characteristic among competing state agencies. The third stage has been marked by the institutionalization of environmental concern through strengthening the hands of heretofore ineffective state agencies, the creation of ad hoc environmental lobbies, and the passage of new environmental regulations.

No claim is made, of course, that the studies of Lake Baikal and the Desna River will paint a picture of complete reversal of national priorities or of extensive institutional change. Protection of the environment remains only one of many competing national priorities, and the USSR has not moved as quickly as most other major industrial powers in the creation of a centralized environmental protection agency. The point is, however, that the system has manifested at least some evidence of adaptive behavior through its recognition of a new policy area and through its tolerance of extensive and frequently bitter public and interbureaucratic disputes over environmental quality.

¶ The Recognition of a New Issue

The recognition of environmental problems in the Soviet Union was delayed by a set of attitudes toward nature nurtured early in the Soviet experience and by economic and political institutions that proved initially insensitive to environmental concerns. In contrast to such nineteenth-century thinkers as Tolstoy, who saw man and nature existing in interdependent harmony, contemporary Soviet thinking reflects an anthropocentric view of the world. Man is the central focus of the universe; it is for his interests that nature is to be conquered and manipulated.[6] This ecological arrogance was enhanced by the conscious voluntarism inherent in Lenin's concept of an elitist, vanguard Party, which easily modulated into the view that nature could be conquered through discipline and unstinting effort.

Soviet attitudes toward economic growth also proved inhospitable to the recognition of environmental difficulties. Concerned with the rapid creation of an industrial state, Bolshevik leaders raised the creation of a heavy industrial base to a fundamental touchstone of national policy, single-mindedly channeling virtually all available capital into industry and ignoring the environmental consequences of their actions. Although the primitive technology utilized at first had relatively low pollution potential, compared with the more sophisticated technologies of the West, this mixed blessing is rapidly being lost through technological modernization. Even today, Soviet leaders still regard the prospects for future growth as virtually limitless, although a few economists and scientists have begun to look seriously at the limits-to-growth debate popularized in the West by the Club of Rome.[7]

The system of measuring both ministerial and enterprise performance also worked against the emergence of ecologically sound decisions. For decades the only really important criterion was total output; so long as quotas were met or exceeded, environmental impact was discounted. Even recent profit-oriented reforms have done little to change the situation, since the accounting system does not classify pollution-control expenditures as productive investments except in a few experimental programs in the Russian Republic.[8] The limited fines provided by anti-pollution laws have not affected the financial incentives to pollute; they are simply budgeted in advance and in the past have found their way into local government coffers, making town officials understandably more willing to look the other way.[9] Since scarcity prices are not charged for such key resources as water and land, there has been little incentive to guard them from pollution so long as supplies have been thought to be inexhaustible. While some attempts have recently been made to impose steeper fees for use of land and water and other basic raw materials potentially in short supply, the reforms have accomplished little, primarily because the new fee structure does not permit the determination of the true value of these resources in alternate uses.[10]

With these factors restricting the emergence of environmental awareness, it is not surprising that there was no widespread awakening about the deteriorating state of the environment until well into the 1960s. A few concerned scientists had perceived the problem as early as the 1930s, but their warnings fell on deaf ears because of the importance attached to industrialization and the scientists' inability to find a receptive elite audience. Scientists' gradual success in building a wider following is itself closely related not only to their own growing competence to understand and explain the long-term consequences of pollution but also to their increasing skill in utilizing heretofore powerless environmental protection agencies, scientific commissions, and the media to politicize the issue.

As early as the first five-year plan, scientists were already charting the deterioration of air quality in major industrial centers and the pollution of rivers and streams.[11] Medical and biological scientists played the most important initial role. The last decade has witnessed the increasing involvement of other scientists and technicians and of the personnel of state pollution-control and conservation agencies. Pollution-related research is now underway in a small number of institutes subordinated to the Ministry of Public Health, the Academy of Sciences, the Academy of Medical Sciences, the Chief Administration of the Hydrometeorological Service, and the State Committee on Science and Technology. Recognizing a lack, Soviet leaders in January 1973 called upon the State Committee to join with the USSR Academy of Sciences in the creation of an interdepartmental council on environmental problems.[12]

Geographers have also played an active role in spreading the level of environmental awareness beyond the physical sciences. Having fallen on hard times in the intellectual community because of their orientation toward purely physical geography, they are asking for a revitalization of the discipline through the introduction of a biospheric approach to the relationship between man and nature. This perspective inevitably places greater attention on environmental considerations, and some attempts have been made at ecosystem modeling.[13]

On the whole, social scientists have contributed very little to raising the level of environmental awareness, although a few bold (and mostly dissident) historians and economists have condemned environmental decay. For the most part, the problem has been ignored by all but a handful of economists who have called for industry to pay for cleanup measures; urged the revision of the price system for raw materials, land, and water; or advocated the creation of a new economic accounting system better able to measure what one has termed "bioeconomic" costs.[14] Legal scholars have made a limited contribution through a growing body of literature on the legal and administrative aspects of pollution abatement.

The literary intelligentsia has also been a latecomer to the discussion of environmental problems, but it has made an important contribution since the mid-1960s. It was then, when the pollution of Lake Baikal and other important waterways was first discussed in the general media, that both officially accepted writers, such as Mikhail Sholokhov, and dissident authors joined in the call for abatement measures.[15]

An important role in raising the level of environmental awareness in the 1960s was played by state environmental protection and conservation agencies, such as the Ministry of Land Reclamation and Water Resources, the Sanitary Epidemiological Service of the USSR Ministry of Health, and more recently, the Hydrometeorological Service. Long given the formal authority to protect the land, water resources, and atmosphere from contamination, they have historically found their powers circumscribed by political and economic realities that brought Party and industrial forces into close collusion to circumvent environmental protection regulations. Their elevation during the 1960s to active (but no means always successful) participation in the struggle for the protection of the environment was the result of a number of interrelated developments. First was the increasingly undeniable presence of the problem itself; the number of polluted waterways and cities with serious air pollution problems grew to a point where awareness was no longer confined to a small number of concerned scientists. A few dramatic instances of pollution problems emerged to catalyze elite awareness of the issue. There was, additionally, a body of scientific evidence on the causes and long-term consequences of pollution, which provided an increasingly firm backdrop of facts demonstrating the delicate vulnerability of the environment.

No less important was the discovery by state conservation and environmental protection agencies of the tactical value of establishing de facto alliances with other groups and prominent individuals concerned with environmental quality. Whether it was the state agency that sought the support of others or whether worried scientists, writers, or local conservationists turned to them for help—the Baikal and Desna cases discussed below suggest that it has been a two-way street—the result was the same. There arose a mutually beneficial relationship in which the two elements supplemented each other to enlarge their concerned political and institutional constituencies and to provide a broader range of strategies against recalcitrant polluters and unconcerned higher officials. The emergence of such coalitions marked a significant departure from the isolation and departmental fragmentation that had weakened environmental forces in the past.

The media was also an important source of environmental awareness and of institutional and elite mobilization. Discussion of the issue has been remarkably wide-ranging in the otherwise controlled press, although Soviet authorities have on occasion attempted to suppress certain questions. In September 1970, for example, the Party imposed a temporary ban on the discussion of environmental problems, and *Izvestia* was forced to cancel a series on the pollution of the Volga. By early 1971 the ban had been lifted, apparently after discussion among top leaders.[16] A survey of the tone and scope of the coverage accorded the environment over the past decade quickly reveals that the role of the media in expanding environmental awareness has passed through two clearly articulated stages.

The first, dating roughly from the 1950s to the mid-1960s, was essentially concerned with spreading an awareness of growing environmental problems among scientists, naturalists, and other concerned members of the intelligentsia. (It is difficult to attach a precise date to the beginning of this phase, because a small body of poorly circulated scientific studies was in existence well before the 1950s.) The role of the media at this time was largely didactic; journalistic accounts of deteriorating rivers, soil pollution, and a number of other problems reached a much larger audience than the limited readership of the few scientific journals that had previously concerned themselves with the environment. Newspapers such as *Literaturnaya Gazeta* and *Komsomolskaya Pravda* either carried investigative reports prepared by their own staff or opened their pages to articles written by concerned scientists and naturalists. That these newspapers and journals are directed toward essentially elitist and/or youth audiences does much to explain the sociological profile of the ad hoc environmental lobbies that emerged in the mid-1960s. In this first phase, the media also played an important role in establishing an environmental frame of reference and in promoting a more sophisticated understanding of the interrelationship between an industrial economy and the surrounding environment. A subject of considerable discussion and evolution among scientists themselves, this growing sophistication was filtered down through the media, in simplified form, to larger, although essentially still elitist, audiences.[17]

The second phase began roughly in the mid-1960s. At this time, the media became the linchpin linking together the various elements of the environmental lobby and connecting that lobby with a broader constituency. This phase was marked both by the increasingly strident tone with which investigative reporters and guest authors indicted industry and demanded better protection measures and by the eventual spread of the discussion to the general media, such as *Pravda* and *Izvestia.* In the first instance, the primary *cause célèbre* to emerge at the national level was the case of Lake Baikal in Siberia, although localized problems also occupied the attention of the local media. As the intensity of the Baikal debate increased, a new and more politically significant role for the media became evident—that of advocate, gadfly, and potential court of appeal. As in the discussion of the Baikal case below, the media became an important tactical weapon in the hands of a coalition of scientists, intellectuals, and environmentalists who had seen earlier attempts at reform ignored or blunted by ministry personnel and local officials. No longer was the media's function purely didactic (although its role did still include a conscious effort to discuss the technical features of environmental problems and focus public attention on as yet poorly recognized difficulties or threats); it was clearly functioning in a political capacity to articulate the demands of the coalition and to mobilize support for those demands among even wider circles.[18]

The spread of the discussion of environmental problems to the mass circulation media and to television and films marked another important change in the role of the media. Heretofore, the debate had been essentially confined to scientific journals or media directed to elite strata; now it became the common property of all who cared to look on. While in the short run this change was perhaps of little political significance, in the long run it may prove to have had much greater importance, inasmuch as the average Russian knew little, at least in scientific and economic terms, about the likely impact on daily life of further environmental deterioration. In the long run, the careful preparation of public opinion to recognize environmental dangers and to accept the need of economic trade-offs may be an important step in insuring the continued political viability of the environment as an issue; like their Western and Japanese counterparts, Russians have shown a distinct affinity for a host of environmentally destructive consumer goods and services. Unless aware of the long-term implications, they might well be inclined to choose the rewards of refrigerators or new autos in preference to the less immediate pleasures of a clean environment. Since the Soviet Union is only in the beginning stages of building a consumer society, many problems that have occurred in the United States and Japan can be avoided if certain problems can be dealt with in their initial phases and public attitudes groomed early to accept certain environmental imperatives.

Undoubtedly, another important factor in strengthening the hands of environmentalists has been their increasingly sophisticated scientific analysis of the consequences of continued pollution. Moving away from a simplistic conservationist and preservationist focus, in the late 1950s and early 1960s they began to describe the man-nature relationship from what Robert Clawson and William Kolarik have termed the "rational-functional" point of view.[19] This premise holds that man's exploitation of nature is compatible with the preservation of environmental quality insofar as he rationally limits both his consumption of resources and the potency of the pollutants cast into the environment. Stress was placed on the discovery of technological solutions to environmental problems. As awareness of the interlocking nature of complex ecosystems spread throughout the scientific community, a more sophisticated "biosphere" approach developed to stress the importance of considering the total environmental impact of human activity. In addition to underlining the delicacy of the ecological balance on which biosystems depend (and thus implicitly stressing the dangers of dealing with pollution on a piecemeal basis), this approach also helped spread awareness of the problem beyond the relatively few scientists, naturalists, and intellectuals who had previously become involved.

A seeming paradox obscures the level of environmental awareness among top Soviet officials. Even a cursory examination of environment-related legislation passed since the revolution would suggest that officials have not been totally unconcerned with the issue; well-meaning regulations on air and water pollution have been on the books since the 1930s or 1940s, and comprehensive conservation and antipollution laws were passed at the republic level in the late 1950s and early 1960s. This apparent concern with the environment is easily belied by a record of poor enforcement and the unwillingness of top officials to back characteristically weak enforcement agencies against more powerful industrial ministries.

The first meaningful commitment to environmental protection came only in the 1960s and was signaled by the occasional willingness of Party officials to intervene on the side of proenvironmental forces and to foster limited institutional changes to facilitate better monitoring of the environment. With increasing frequency, joint Party-state resolutions on critical environmental problems such as Lake Baikal or the Volga-Ural basins have been issued under the dual imprimatur of the Central Committee and the Council of Ministers. Both houses of the USSR Supreme Soviet now have committees concerned with environmental and conservation questions, and in September 1972 an entire session was devoted to the environment. Similar legislative review and oversight activity have also been noted at the republic level.[20] But no major Soviet leader has personally identified with the cause of environmental protection. Leaders have limited themselves to occasional intervention when disputes spill out beyond the boundaries of other agencies. In such instances, their frame of reference has seemed closer to that of the "rational-functional" school of thought than to the more scientifically sophisticated "biosphere" approach, and the policy decisions handed down in such cases clearly reflect a desire to find compromises that permit the alleviation of the worst visible instances of pollution without incurring the trauma of an extensive reordering of national priorities, especially in the economic sphere.

¶ The Emergence of an Environmental Lobby

There have always been state agencies and mass organizations to speak for environmental protection and conservation. The emergence of an effective environmental lobby is the story not so much of institutional change or the creation of new agencies (although there have been minor adjustments, as we shall note) as of the growing cooperation between the formal state agencies and a looser coalition of proenvironmental forces drawn from other segments of the society.[21]

In the formal sense, responsibility for environmental protection and conservation has been spread among a number of agencies.[22] In many instances, the task of conserving natural resources or limiting emissions is put in the hands of the relevant production agencies themselves; it is not then surprising that those agencies charged with meeting increasing production quotas are little concerned with the environmental consequences of their actions. In other cases, the lines of formal authority are confusingly drawn to involve several agencies and levels of government.

The setting of standards for water pollution is a typical example. The primary responsibility for protecting and conserving water resources initially belonged to the USSR Ministry of Land Reclamation and Water Resources and its republic counterparts. In practice, however, other agencies, such as the ministries of Power and Electrification, Fisheries, Agriculture, Inland Water Transport, and Public Health, also become involved in a less than clearly defined process of consultation. General questions of pollution-control standards are handled by the USSR Ministry of Public Health and its local counterparts, including the Sanitary Epidemiological Service, which supposedly enforces these regulations. In addition, both the national and republic-level state planning agencies become involved, usually through the creation of oversight and policy committees, and regional water basin commissions also play a role.[23] In practice, the formulation of water pollution control standards has usually involved a wide range of agencies, including the water consumers themselves. The emission of harmful pollutants is licensed by state authorities, a process usually involving the local soviet, the Sanitary Epidemiological Service, the Ministry of Land Reclamation and Water Resources, and a host of water users. Effective coordination is rare, and the tone of the proceedings is frequently that of an adversary process, marked by conflicting technical and economic feasibility claims and appeals to higher authorities.[24]

In 1974, Gosplan began to play a more aggressive role in environmental matters through the creation of a Division for the Protection of Nature. Representing an attempt to provide more centralized direction for environmental protection, it was assigned the task of working out environmental guidelines for both the annual and the five-year plans, which then began to articulate environmental as well as production goals. Perhaps of greater consequence, it provided a high-level forum in which demands for water quality protection could be given equal voice with the interests of industrial ministries. According to Thane Gustafson's description of the planning process, draft proposals for water quality goals now originate through two channels: the water basin inspectorates and, at a higher level, the Ministry of Land Reclamation and Water Resources on the one hand and the industrial ministries and their corresponding Gosplan departments on the other. Not surprisingly, the environmental goals and investment levels requested by the production ministries lag far behind the demands of the Ministry of Land Reclamation and Water Resources. Unfortunately for environmental concerns, the Division for the Protection of Nature cannot directly arbitrate these differences; instead, it must act as a lobby for environmental interests to the branch divisions of Gosplan, which are given far greater latitude in determining the actual mix of investment priorities. Thus, an informal bargaining system emerges between the industrial ministries and the branch departments of Gosplan on the one side and the Ministry of Land Reclamation and Water Resources and the Division for the Protection of Natural Resources of Gosplan on the other. It is hardly surprising that in such a setting the industrial ministries and their Gosplan allies most often emerge with the lion's share of scarce investment capital.[25]

The USSR Ministry of Health sets air pollution emission standards and enforces their implementation through the Sanitary Epidemiological Service. However, the power of the sanitary inspectors is limited by inescapable political and bureaucratic realities. Few in number, saddled with literally dozens of public-health-related tasks in addition to environmental concerns, and with few contacts among influential higher leaders, the sanitary inspectors frequently find themselves ignored, outmaneuvered, and outlobbied.[26]

The Chief Administration of the Hydrometeorological Service of the USSR Council of Ministers has recently acquired a strengthened environmental role. It was instructed in January 1973 to monitor harmful emissions on a nationwide scale and to set pollution-control guidelines. The exact powers given it remain vague, however, since the same enactment also instructed other agencies and ministries also having environment-related functions to strengthen their efforts; it is likely that the service will concentrate, much as in the past, on research and the setting of norms.[27]

On the whole, these agencies have enjoyed only limited success in pressing for better environmental protection. Working alone within their own respective bailiwicks, as they have most often done in the past, they have been consistently outlobbied or simply ignored by industrial interests. Their inherent weakness stems primarily from their low standing in the ministerial pecking order. Lodged within a hierarchical and highly competitive bureaucratic policymaking milieu, they possess few of the resources of the more powerful industrial ministries. Most importantly, they lack the close and symbiotic relationship with higher Party and state leaders that has always linked Party and industrial interests. Operating from limited organizational bases, they have been easily overcome in most instances by industrial ministries with large professional staffs, legitimacy in a society concerned with official standing, and a close relationship with equally growth-oriented Party bureaucrats, maintained through the interlocking ties between the functional and branch departments of the CPSU Secretariat and virtually all industrial and commercial agencies.[28] In such a setting, it is not surprising that routine policymaking channels alone have often proved an unproductive forum in which to argue the case for environmental protection. This is not to say that these agencies have not been aggressive advocates of the cause; it is rather to point out that the cards are simply stacked against them so long as environmental disputes remain essentially within intra- and interbureaucratic policymaking channels.

Little help in counteracting these weaknesses has been forthcoming from the mass organizations concerned with conservation and environmental matters. The most visible of these is the All-Russian Society for the Conservation of Nature, which concerns itself with virtually all aspects of environmental and conservation policy. It numbers some nineteen million members in the Russian Republic, six million in the Ukraine, and lesser numbers in other republics. The numbers are deceptive, however, since most members are enrolled through the schools and are personally involved only as the targets of the society's educational programs. It maintains a low profile even in such spectacular cases as Lake Baikal; its only real active role has been at the local level, as in the formation of the Committee on the Desna River (discussed below) and in the less sensitive area of wildlife conservation.[29]

Informal, ad hoc coalitions of environmental interests have also formed in recent years. Most evident has been the coalition of naturalists, conservation officials, scientists, writers, and academicians who have come to the defense of Lake Baikal. The thread that has linked them together has been their concern with the fate of the lake, rather than any common organizational or institutional base. Having no such base of operations, they have been compelled to rely on existing scientific commissions, state-related environmental protection agencies, the receptivity of certain segments of the media, and the personal prestige of leading scientists and intellectuals who have joined their cause. The relationship between the environmental protection agencies and the more diverse coalitions has been a symbiotic one; the former have certainly continued to play a central role. But it has been the latter—the scientific commissions, the intellectuals and academicians from a diverse assortment of fields, and the investigative reporters—who have succeeded in politicizing the question of environmental protection and in shifting the arena of decisionmaking from routine bureaucratic channels.

John Kramer paints a general portrait of such a coalition.[30] The most active single category of the participants he studied included scientists and members of the academic community usually only tangentially involved with the question of the environment; they together contributed nearly twice as many demands for pollution abatement and conservation as the next largest group. Second and third in activism were deputies of local, republic, and the all-union soviets and members of state environmental protection enforcement and inspection agencies. In the former case, demands came primarily from the rank-and-file deputies and not from the top-level political or administrative personnel; it is likely, therefore, that they were intended essentially to register local complaints. Much the same motivation was undoubtedly at work for the representatives of the state environmental protection agencies, who complained of continued violations and attempts to avoid legislative controls. Economists (but not managerial personnel) ranked fourth. Next in line were the administrative officials of various ministries and state committees. There was a striking absence of the representatives of agencies concerned with various aspects of heavy industry or other high-pollution activities; only one such ministry was heard from in the period of time Kramer surveyed. Surprisingly inactive were the members of all-union or republic societies for the conservation of nature and the representatives of state agencies concerned with purely conservationist activities. This unresponsiveness underlines the continued narrow focus and self-imposed passivity of both groups, further indicating that the driving force for such broad coalitions has come from individuals concerned primarily with pollution-related rather than traditional conservationist goals. Also conspicuously absent were enterprise directors, who have traditionally shown little interest in strengthened environmental protection.

Considering the apparent weaknesses of these ad hoc coalitions, it is somewhat surprising that they have had any impact at all. Judged by the traditional indicators of power in the Soviet context, the environmental lobby should not have constituted an important political force, especially on an important question like Lake Baikal. The degree of success it has enjoyed—and it is at best only a qualified success—can be attributed to its ability to politicize the question of the lake's fate and its scientific legitimacy in challenging the views of industrial leaders. Perhaps equally important has been its growing skill in using the prestige of its limited organizational base, the media, and key individuals to build an active following and to mount appeals to higher authorities outside the regular policymaking channels. Therein also lies its primary weakness: such dramatic appeals can be successful only in a limited number of cases. In a case as striking as that of Lake Baikal, enough people will become sufficiently mobilized to make this a viable strategy; but for less dramatic, routine cases of pollution violations, such highly motivated coalitions are unlikely to form, although the unique Committee on the Desna River has proved an exception.

¶ Recognition and Response: Lake Baikal and the Desna River

Two case studies have been chosen to illustrate how specific environmental problems have been recognized and translated into issues of public policy. The first is the well-known case of Lake Baikal, which shows a clear picture of a newly formed environmental lobby raising the issue of water quality in the lake and then successfully challenging decisions reached within routine channels, without fundamentally altering the basic institutional structure. The second concerns the Desna River and serves to illustrate the activities of the Committee on the Desna, which formed in response to continued complaints about the deteriorating state of the river. Both cases are unique situations, as would be any study of the recognition of and response to newly perceived issues. What is important about them is not whether they paint a picture of extensive institutional change or dramatic reversals of national priorities, but rather that they suggest the outlines of the subtle interaction of industrial and environmental interests both within and outside routine policymaking channels.

Lake Baikal The battle over the protection of Lake Baikal clearly illustrates the process by which new issues are generated.[31] Two major groupings of protagonists have emerged. On the side of those favoring the industrial use of the lake have been the Ministry of Timber, Paper, and Woodworking (now the Ministry of the Pulp and Paper Industry), whose cellulose mills represent a major threat to the lake; a number of other industries that have developed along the shore of the lake and on its tributaries; and municipal governments that have dumped their wastes into Baikal. On the other side have been grouped the Ministry of Land Reclamation and Water Resources, which bears primary responsibility for the purity of the lake's water; the Ministry of Public Health and its Sanitary Epidemiological Service; the Hydrometeorological Service; and a diverse coalition of members of the academic community, scientists, writers, and other intellectuals who have come to the lake's defense.

While the growth of industry has been constant since the 1930s, the first really serious threat to the lake's ecological balance to be perceived by local environmentalists was the planned construction in the late 1950s of two cellulose mills, one at the southern tip of the lake at Baikalsk and the other on the Selenga River, which flows into the lake from the southwest. The first public outcry came in 1960 in an essay published in nearby Ulan Ude, which warned that the mills would damage the lake. A year later the question was again raised by two local writers, but to little avail.[32] The first warning to reach a national audience came two years later from G. I. Galazii, the director of the Limnological Institute of the Siberian branch of the Academy of Sciences, who warned that the mills' discharge would destroy the lake and endanger the water supply of Irkutsk.[33] Construction continued at the mill sites, however, and gradually the debate between ministry spokesmen and environmentalists intensified. As the discussion reached its most intensive phase in the mid-1960s, an investigative reporter for *Literaturnaya Gazeta* took up the cause and bitterly condemned the Ministry of Timber, Paper, and Woodworking for its destruction of the lake's purity.[34] Ministry spokesmen responded that the new mills required the exceptionally pure water of

Lake Baikal to produce high-quality cellulose cord needed for national defense. This argument did little to quell the increasingly vocal opposition of the Ministry of Land Reclamation and Water Resources, various public health and pollution inspection agencies, and the growing coalition of scientists and other concerned intellectuals. The public efforts of the latter reached their high point in May of 1966 in an outspoken letter in *Komsomolskaya Pravda* signed by over thirty distinguished scientists, writers, and creative artists, including several members of the USSR Academy of Sciences.[35]

The public debate was paralleled by a second battle between conflicting state agencies. Two issues arose: the initial certification of the Baikalsk plant, which was scheduled to begin production first, and the determination of proper emission standards. In its testimony before the State Acceptance Commission, which must approve such building projects, the Ministry of Land Reclamation and Water Resources opposed the construction of the Baikalsk plant because of inadequate purification facilities. Twice the commission refused to sanction the plant's construction, changing its position only when the Ministry of Timber, Paper, and Woodworking obtained the appointment to the commission of one of its former consultants, in order to end the stalemate.[36] The second confrontation came over the setting of emission standards for the mill. Plant officials had begun operation before the completion of the purification facilities, itself a clear violation of law. Breakdowns were frequent, and it soon became clear that the original facilities were simply inadequate.[37] Under pressure to stop operations (a step legally required under such circumstances) pending the construction of new facilities, mill officials requested that the emission standards be "temporarily" lowered, until new purification equipment could be installed. The Ministry of Health and the Sanitary Epidemiological Service gave their approval, since it was determined that human health was not endangered, and the Ministry of Fishing also raised no objections. The Hydrometeorological Service vigorously objected, and the Ministry of Land Reclamation and Water Resources, which had been in the forefront of the struggle against certification, was not even consulted, although legally entitled to have a say in the proceedings. The "temporary" standards were easily approved and remain in effect to this day.[38]

It is evident that the fate of Lake Baikal had also come to occupy the attention of top-level Soviet leaders by 1967 or 1968. In February 1969 the USSR Council of Ministers made the first of several authoritative pronouncements on the lake. Acknowledging the need for stricter pollution abatement and conservation measures, it created a special water conservation zone of some twenty thousand square miles. Within the zone, restrictions were placed on lumbering, also a major cause of pollution.

The enactment ordered the enlargement of the purification facilities at the Baikalsk mill, and the Selenga mill was instructed not to begin production until its purification facilities were completed. Other industries on the lake's tributaries were also ordered to improve their purification operations, and cities such as Ulan Ude were ordered to purify their municipal wastes.[39]

But the battle was far from won. Despite the seeming importance attached to the new regulations, de facto violations continued. Facilities at the Baikalsk plant continued to be inadequate. A report published in *Komsomolskaya Pravda* in the summer of 1970 indicated that pollution levels had actually gotten worse since the 1969 enactment, and little progress was made on the control of logging operations or in purifying municipal wastes.[40]

Continued ministerial evasion prompted the passage of a new enactment in September 1971, this time under the dual imprimatur of the USSR Council of Ministers and the CPSU Central Committee, signaling even greater concern among top officials.[41] Like the earlier enactment, it ordered that the Baikalsk purification plant be completed by the end of the year, a deadline not met. In October 1972, however, sufficient progress had been made to permit Russell Train, then chairman of the U.S. Council on Environmental Quality, to visit the mill and report that the discharged wastes seemed fit for human consumption, although they might still endanger some of the more delicate of the lake's inhabitants. A similar report came a year later from a team of American pollution-control experts, who found the purification equipment to be as good or better than similar systems in the West.[42] The 1971 enactment also ordered that purification facilities at the Selenga mill be completed before the end of 1972; however, when the mill began production behind schedule in July 1973, mill officials were conspicuously silent on the status of the treatment facilities.[43]

The 1971 enactment also instructed other industrial enterprises and municipalities in the area to have improved sewerage systems in operation by the end of 1972, although Ulan Ude, the area's urban complex, was given an extra year. A report from the area in April 1972 indicated that construction delays were numerous and that the deadlines would be missed.[44] Evidence that the systems were not in operation was provided a little more than a year later, when local officials did not permit a group of visiting American environmentalists and waste-control experts to visit Ulan Ude's worst-polluting factories; water samples taken later by the group near the delta of the Selenga River, which carries the city's wastes to the lake, indicated high pollution levels, further confirming that problems remained.[45]

Instructions to the logging industry to improve its performance and to clear sunken logs from stream and river beds were also repeated in the 1971 enactment. Evidence from the scene indicates that some progress has been made in this area and that the catch of commercial fish, once the victim of both logging and industry, has begun to increase.[46]

Late in 1974, Soviet authorities issued a more comprehensive set of regulations governing the water quality of the lake and the further industrial development of the region. According to these new regulations, the product of several years of consultation and bargaining among environmental protection agencies and the major industries and municipalities, new emission standards are to be set in accordance with a current study by the Academy of Sciences of acceptable contamination levels in the unique Baikal basin. The future industrial growth of the region is also subject to new guidelines, as is the recreational use of the lake. Commenting on the plan, I. I. Borodavchenko, USSR deputy minister of Land Reclamation and Water Resources, noted that high-pollution industries are to be banned from the entire Baikal basin, although plans for the extensive development of the entire region will undoubtedly make this regulation difficult to enforce in practice. The pulp mills will be permitted to continue operations, providing that their wastes are effectively treated. The ban will prohibit the construction of any industries directly on the lake shore or on the major tributaries, another provision that will prove difficult to enforce. Instructions are also given to speed the construction of other municipal and industrial waste-purification facilities, and Borodavchenko makes it clear that much still needs to be done.[47]

Reports from the region since 1974 indicate that plans for regional economic development have hardly been altered to reflect new environmental priorities. Much of the regime's hope for the further economic exploitation of the region hinges on the Baikal-Amur railway, which will facilitate the development of local industry and the extraction of the region's considerable natural resources. But the railway itself has for several years suffered from long construction delays, and it has been the subject of numerous warnings from local environmentalists concerning ite deleterious impact on the virgin tundra. Frustrated by these long delays, Soviet developers are likely to shift environmental concerns even further into the background, despite the regime's promises to limit the development of the Baikal basin.[48]

Another concern has also emerged in the last few years—Soviet tourists, who, in the words of one concerned official, "behave as if they owned the place." [49] While their environmental impact on the lake is certainly limited in comparison with the effluents of industry, they apparently take an enormous toll of the local wildlife, much of which is unique to the Baikal basin. Despite the pledge of the 1974 pronouncements to limit recreational use of the lake, there is apparently little done in actual fact to control tourist access.

The Committee on the Desna River Another successful example of the activities of an ad hoc environmental lobby at the local level is to be found in the experience of the Committee on the Desna River, the left tributary of the Dnieper. The primary threat to the river in the mid-1960s, when the problem was first perceived, was the diminishing quantity of water that reached the river from its tributaries. The destruction of a network of both natural and manmade small dams on the tributaries had upset the river basin's ability to control runoff and therefore to dilute wastes. Pollution from industrial and municipal sources was a less serious concern, although committee members were aware that the problem existed and that a reduction of stream flow would concentrate existing wastes.[50]

The events resulting in the creation of the committee were triggered by the publication in the local newspaper, *Bryansky Rabochy*, of a letter from a collective farmer living along the Sev River, a major tributary, which began the public discussion of the river's deteriorating condition. An exchange of views in the press and the deliberations of several scientific meetings further refined the issue. Conflicting proposals were submitted to the Bryansk Conservation Society, which finally recommended the construction of a large number of small dams on the Desna's tributaries as a way of restoring the river's self-regulatory capacity. The society also became the moving force in the creation of the Committee on the Desna River, composed of representatives from the conservation society, local collective and state farm directors, economic administrators, factory directors, scientists, and members of the academic community. In a unique departure from the Baikal case, local Party and soviet officials also became involved, and the committee was initially chaired by the Bryansk oblast Party secretary.

Initially, the committee's prospects did not look bright. Working without funds in an area where little precedent had been established, the committee was compelled to fall back upon the resources of its members—perhaps not an insubstantial factor, if one assumes that the local Party secretary was sincerely committed to their goals—and on their ability to devise programs widely acceptable to collective farm and industrial leaders. As its first action, the committee adopted an earlier recommendation, drawn up by the conservation society, that 264 small dams be constructed to control stream flow in the Desna's tributaries. Each separate project was recommended to the appropriate agency or collective farm according to the advantages created for the builder himself; for the collective and state farms, which built the vast majority of the dams, benefits accrued in the form of increased agricultural productivity, livestock increases, and the creation of lakes and reservoirs. By the beginning of 1974, some six years after the committee had been formed, 182 dams had been completed, with the remaining ones reportedly under construction. All projects had been locally financed by the builders themselves, making requests for funding unnecessary from higher authorities.

The committee has also concerned itself more recently with the construction of waste purification systems for local industries and municipalities. Again the emphasis was placed upon the construction of small-scale purification units to handle the effluents of individual enterprises, alhough city-wide units have been put into operation in a few cases.

The committee's evident success suggests that many of the factors characterizing the ad hoc coalition of environmentalists formed on the question of Lake Baikal have also been operative in the Desna case. Most obvious is the nature of the coalition itself, a diverse assortment of concerned individuals deriving momentum from a press campaign and the activities of relatively weak conservation organizations. Two additional advantages have been present in the Desna case. First, the committee has had the visible support of local Party officials from the very beginning; and the committee has also reportedly secured "a great deal of assistance" from Kiev Party officials concerned with preserving the city's access to the Desna's relatively clean waters. Second, local industrial forces apparently did not initially see the committee as a direct threat, because the problem facing the river was essentially tied to the disruption of the tributaries. Indeed, industry was itself a clear victim of the dropping level of the river, since it too needed considerable quantities of fresh water for industrial consumption.

There is also a lesson on the importance of institution-building to be learned from a comparison of the Baikal and Desna cases. In the former, the ad hoc coalition of environmentalists has not yet built an independent institutional base from which to argue its case. Although it has found willing allies in state environmental protection agencies and within the forums dominated by scientists and intellectuals, it has not taken control of or created any ongoing body that has played an effective role in making policy concerning the lake's protection. Its activities, while dramatic, have always been sporadic and cast in the form of appeals to higher authority, outside normal channels. Quite the opposite is the case with the Committee on the Desna. It appears to be regularly consulted on matters concerning the river and has shown its own initiative and institutional muscle in moving independently to protect the river. It has also apparently emerged as a major clearinghouse and coordinating body for the environment-related activities of other organizations, so much so that an official of the Russian Republic Ministry of Land Reclamation and Water Resources has bitterly complained that the committee has taken over its functions and arrogated too much authority to itself. He called for the termination of the committee's activities in the area of dam construction and pollution abatement on the grounds that these topics fall under the authority of his agency. Apparently, time-honored "departmental barriers" are difficult to overcome even among environmentalists.

Admittedly, the Baikal and Desna cases are different in many major respects: the scope and nature of the immediate threat, the backing of Party and industrial leaders, and the ability of the Desna committee to suggest corrective measures that were also in the economic interests of the local collective and state farms. But the importance of institutionalization remains evident. As an investigative reporter for *Literaturnaya Gazeta* put it, "Just think: if there had been a similar committee on the Ural, how much easier it would have been to carry out the 1972 government resolution [concerning pollution-abatement measures in the Volga and Ural basins]." To those who have studied the attempts to preserve the more uniquely pure waters of Lake Baikal, a similar observation comes easily to mind.

Sanford R. Lieberman

The Party under Stress: The Experience of World War II

How well an organization is able to adapt and change under stress and pressure may provide the most accurate yardstick for measuring its strength and effectiveness as well as providing significant insights into its nature and that of the system of which it is a part. This essay attempts to judge the Communist Party of the Soviet Union by such a yardstick and asks how well the Party functioned during one period of great stress: the Second World War. To understand both the impact of the war upon the Party and the Party's role in the war effort, however, something first needs to be said about the position of the Party in the general Stalinist system on the eve of the war and about the system of wartime administration and control.

¶ The Prewar Stalinist System and Crisis Management

Although the Communist Party on the eve of World War II continued to be officially depicted as the leading and directing force in Soviet society, Stalin's victory over the opposition some years earlier had in reality reduced the Party's position to that of one (albeit a very important one) of the regime's several regular instruments of administration and control. Stalin himself, rather than the Party or any other organization, had become the central element in this system. And what Stalin wanted more than anything else was a system of rule that would protect and enhance his personal power position. Accordingly, as Merle Fainsod has noted, the dictator's totalitarian formula was based upon a system of institutionalized mutual suspicion in which "the Party and the secret police guarded the loyalty of army and administration . . . [and] the competing hierarchies of Party, police, army and administration were kept in purposeful conflict and provided with no point of final resolution short of Stalin and his trusted henchmen in the Politburo. The concentration of power in Stalin's hands rested on the dispersal of power among his subordinates." [1]

The instability resulting from this system contributed to the seemingly perpetual atmosphere of crisis politics that was a hallmark of the Stalinist era. Crises, domestic and/or foreign, real or manufactured, were almost the rule rather than the exception in this period. But whatever their cause or nature, such crises compelled the regime to take rapid, all-out action in response. In administrative terms, this means that the Stalinist regime during crisis situations had to circumvent the rigidities of formal bureaucratic institutions and procedures and to rely to a large extent on extraordinary forms and methods of administration and control. In particular, considerable use was made of the principle of personalization of power.

Personalization of Power The administrative concept of personalization of power implies not only the personalized exercise of authority by a specific individual but also (and more significantly) the *delegation* of large amounts of power to specially appointed individuals who, acting more in their personal than in their organization capacities, are relied on to carry out extremely important assignments. That personalization of power was a key aspect of the Stalinist administrative system was, at least in part, the result of the dictator's personality. In fact, the Soviets themselves, recognizing the extent to which one man, Stalin, dominated the entire period, aptly refer to it as "the era of the cult of personality."

What we know about Stalin's personality—in particular, his megalomania, his apparent paranoia, and his seemingly perpetual restlessness[2] —suggests a nature that would favor extraordinary forms of administration and control over standard bureaucratic institutions and procedures, that would seek to imprint itself firmly and fully upon the regime's system of administration and control. And, indeed, Stalin did precisely that: his nocturnal work schedule became the schedule for much of the country's bureaucracy; his ruthlessness and arbitrariness provided subordinates at all levels with a standard of behavior to emulate. The system had not only its Stalin but also its countless "little Stalins."

Personalization of power, especially in an institutionalized form, also offered Stalin a mechanism for achieving the closest possible approximation of personal exercise of total power. From this vantage point, the ideal system would have been one that permitted him to be everywhere and to do everything at once himself. Since this was impossible, the next best thing was to grant selected individuals broad mandates—even near-total authority—to deal with particular problems. In this way, he was able to bring great power to bear on particular situations while keeping responsibility focused on specific individuals. In a sense, Stalin was not giving up any power at all, because such plenipotentiaries were acting as his eyes, ears, and fists in the field. This system, arbitrary, forceful, and ruthless in its operation, was not only what Stalin desired—indeed, what he demanded—but also what the Soviet regime would need in time of crisis.

¶ The Wartime System of Administration and Control

Caught off-guard by the German invasion of 22 June 1941, the Soviet Union was confronted with the increasingly grim prospect of defeat. If it was to survive, the regime had to mobilize the country's human and material resources rapidly and fully. Such mobilization, however, required the creation of a special wartime system of administration and control, one that would facilitate decisionmaking and policy implementation while at the same time permitting Stalin and his associates to retain centralized control over the war effort. Thus, a great expansion of extraordinary forms and methods of administration and control, including personalization of power, took place. One major aspect of this expansion was a considerably increased use of the plenipotentiary system. At the same time, new extraordinary organs and institutions were created. Of particular importance was the establishment on 30 June 1941 of the State Defense Committee (GKO)—a kind of inner Politburo with Stalin as chairman and Molotov, Malenkov, Beria, and Voroshilov as its other original members—which was accorded "the entire plenitude of power in the country." [3] More specifically, the State Defense Committee "issued resolutions that had the force of law in wartime. All citizens, all Party, soviet, Komsomol, and military organizations were obliged unconditionally to fulfill the decisions and orders of the GKO. It exercised general leadership of the national economy in the interests of war production, led the build-up of the armed forces and their administration, took measures for guaranteeing social order and security, and created, when necessary, special committees and administrations on matters pertaining to the military-economic and defense effort." [4]

Here, as in so many other aspects of the war effort, the Soviet regime was to draw heavily upon its past experience in dealing with crisis situations—above all, upon that experience dating from the periods of the Civil War and Intervention and the collectivization of agriculture. In the face of all-out war, not only particular traditions and techniques but also specific organizational forms for crisis management were revived. The State Defense Committee, for example, in certain respects was modeled after the Council of Workers' and Peasants' Defense, which had functioned during the years of the Civil War and Intervention. That significant use was made of forms and techniques, especially those of an extraordinary nature that had worked successfully in earlier crises was owing to the dictator's personal preference and to the regime's correct perception that this was not the time for experimentation and innovation.

¶ The Party and the War Effort: An Introduction

The Party continued to function within the wartime system as one of the regime's main regular instruments of administration and control. For example, on the second day of the war, the Central Committee of the Party and the Council of People's Commissars, in a joint resolution directed to local Party and soviet organizations, demanded that they "take full responsibility for the work entrusted to them . . . [including] the operative and concrete leadership of all aspects of the military, economic, and political life of the country."[5] The Party accordingly became directly involved in such diverse activities as the mobilization and training of manpower for military and paramilitary organizations, the reorganization of the economy (especially the evacuation of industry to the East), and the development of war-oriented agitation and propaganda.

In addition, throughout the entire war, in line with wartime priorities, the Party was concerned particularly with the maintenance of loyalty and discipline in the armed forces and with the development and proper functioning of the war economy.

That the Party was accorded such a significant role in the war effort was to a large extent because of its long-standing position as one of the regime's leading regular instruments—and in the pre-Stalin period, its leading instrument—of control. The Party also embodied certain important traits that proved of great significance in helping the Soviet leadership cope with the wartime crisis. Above all, the Party's familiarity with the exercise of authority, its mobilizational tradition, and its campaign-style approach to problem-solving were to fit in well with the regime's wartime requirements.

¶ The Vanguard under Fire

For all that has just been said, however, the role of the Party during the war was not as great as it has been depicted in retrospect by Soviet historians. Indeed, during the first period of the war, the vanguard of Soviet society itself was under fire. The Party in the prewar period had been given credit for the successes—especially the economic successes—that the country had achieved. Now, in time of crisis, it was to be blamed for the serious setbacks suffered by the regime in the initial period of the war. That it laid claim to infallibility only served, in the face of apparent failure, to weaken further its popular position. The result was a somewhat paradoxical situation: while the Party continued to function as one of the regime's main instruments of control, its inability to engender popular enthusiasm caused the leadership to play down its role, both in the press and in official statements. Thus, in the first months of the war, those relatively few articles about the Party that appeared in the press were usually limited to such general topics as the wisdom and importance of the Party's prewar policies of industrialization and collectivization, and the loyalty of the Soviet peoples to the "Party of Lenin-Stalin" in time of war. The decline in the Party's prestige also caused the regime to push Marxist-Leninist themes into the background. Indeed, in those first disastrous months of the war, references in the press to principles of Marxism-Leninism were virtually nonexistent. In their place, there was a heightened emphasis on nationalistic and patriotic themes. This emphasis would remain at least until the end of the war, although the regime would make an effort, after the tide of battle had decisively turned, to redress the balance somewhat between such themes and those of a Marxist-Leninist nature. Meanwhile, the Party, once the initial, extremely critical phase of the war was past, would be depicted as the leader of this great patriotic struggle.

The impact of the war, however, did more than affect the image of the Party. It also caused significant—and, in some instances, profound—changes in its organizational structure, composition, allocation of personnel, functions, modus operandi, and position in relation to the regime's other instruments of administration and control.

¶ The Impact of War on the Organizational Structure of the Party

Although certain modifications were introduced into the organizational structure of the Party's apparatus, below the level of the Central Committee, at the Eighteenth Conference in February 1941—modifications that implied a partial retreat from the functional pattern of organization[6] —the basic functional scheme reintroduced at the Eighteenth Congress in 1939 remained in effect.[7] Indeed, at the level of the Central Committee, this pattern of administrative organization, with one possible exception, remained in effect throughout the war. The 1939 reorganization of the CC Secretariat is shown in table 1.

The apparent stability throughout the war years of the formal administrative structure of the Party apparatus at the center resulted, at least in part, from the critical situation that confronted the regime during this period. As has been noted, it was not the time for major administrative innovation or reorganization; stability, not reform, was needed.

The stress on functionalism at the center was well suited not only to the regime's need to maintain strict centralization of control over vital resources, including Party cadres, but also to its desire to maintain at least a modicum of centralized control over all aspects of Party activity. On the other hand, the Party's greatly increased involvement in economic affairs during the war (and the vital importance of such affairs to the war effort) militated in favor of the reestablishment, at the local level, of a system of Party administration more in line with the production-branch pattern of administration. Accordingly, at the outbreak of the war the reemphasis on production-branch departments (*otdels*)—first noted at the time of the Eighteenth Conference—was extended much further in the territorial Party organizations. Many new production-branch otdels were set up to deal with particular sectors of the economy. Whereas, for example, in the Chelyabinsk obkom "prior to July 1941 there were nine production-branch departments (ferrous, nonferrous metallurgy, coal industry, etc.) . . . seven new departments were organized (tank industry, electrical industry, electric power stations, etc.) during the period July–September 1941,"[8] bringing the total to sixteen.

The reemphasis on production-branch otdels produced considerable strain—especially vertical strain—in the sphere of Party administration. That it did so is not surprising, in view of the previous history of Party administration. The prewar years had shown not only that both the production-branch and the functional patterns of administration had

Table 1. Central Committee Secretariat as Reorganized in 1939

Secretariat						
Cadres Administration	Propaganda and Agitation Administration	Organization-Instruction Otdel	Agricultural Otdel	School Otdel	Special Section	Administration of Affairs

Source: Fainsod, *How Russia Is Ruled*, p. 197.

their own peculiar strengths and weaknesses, but also that the two organizational principles frequently worked at cross-purposes.[9]

In light of such administrative history, it seems quite likely that the interjection of a rather sizable number of lower-level production-branch otdels into what had previously been basically a functional pattern of administration produced considerable intraorganizational tension. This tension seems to have become so intense that certain administrative changes were introduced at the level of the Central Committee. The strongest evidence of such changes appears in the final issue of *Partiinoe Stroitel'stvo* for 1944, where the author of an article is listed as the manager of the railroad sector of the *transportation* department of the CC.[10] Such departments had previously been introduced *below* the Central Committee level in 1941. Although it is possible that this author was part of the railroad sector of the Cadres Administration, the reference also suggested that the Party leadership may have decided that a separate CC department was needed to alleviate the tremendous amount of strain and confusion that existed, both in the transport sector of the economy and in the Party's control over transport affairs. If so, the creation of a transportation otdel at the CC level may be regarded both as a sign that all was not well in the sphere of Party administration and as a harbinger of the 1948 reversion to the production-branch pattern of administration.[11]

¶ Party Cadres and the War Effort

As Stalin once said, "Cadres decide everything," [12] and judging from the massive redistribution of Party personnel that took place in the initial, most critical stage of the war, the Soviet leader's statement was not just a matter of words. Because the most important aspect of the war effort was the military front, the flow of both apparatchiki and rank-and-file members was from the civilian to the military Party organizations. In the first six months of the war, over 1,100,000 Communists were called for military service[13]—expanding the ranks of the military Party organizations during this period from 654,000 (or 16.5 percent of the Party's prewar membership) to approximately 1,300,000 (42.4 percent of the Party's total membership at the start of 1942).[14] Included in this number were approximately 60,000 specially mobilized "political soldiers," [15] whose function it became "to strengthen the Party influence in the ranks." [16]

The mobilization of Party members for military service (and for work in the military Party organizations) was entirely in line with the general tendency of the regime to fall back on its past experiences with crisis management, especially those of the period of the Civil War and Intervention. In the earlier military struggle, "Trotsky . . . [had] relied heavily on the Party to infuse spirit and resolution into the Red Army." [17] "Many . . . army Communists were transferred from one front to another during the civil war and were always to be found at the most critical points." [18] Indeed, the combat efficiency of the Red Army units had been measured by the percentage of Communists in the ranks. Now once again, in time of crisis, it was hoped that these Party activists, whose loyalty to the regime (or at least whose vested interest in the system) was the greatest and who, moreover, had assimilated the Party's mobilizational approach to problem-solving, would be able to produce similarly positive results.

In addition to those Communists entering military service through the regular and special mobilizations, a considerable number of new members and candidates were recruited by the military Party organizations themselves. In the last six months of 1941, these organizations accepted 49,931 members and 126,625 candidates.[19] These figures represented an increase in membership of 184 percent and 318 percent, respectively, over the first half of 1941. At first glance, these percentages are very impressive. Yet, in light of the national peril, a much greater rallying to the cause might have been expected. However, the precipitous decline in the Party's prestige at the beginning of the war, along with stringent admissions requirements, militated against a more rapid increase in military Party organization membership in the early months of the conflict. Although there was very little that the Party could do about the former problem, it could and did facilitate the expansion of its ranks in the armed forces by lowering admission standards, as it had done in the earlier crises of Civil War and Intervention. This move was accomplished by two Central Committee decrees, dated 19 August 1941 and December 1941.[20]

The increase in the membership of the military Party organizations was, of course, offset to a certain extent by an extremely high casualty rate. In the first six months of the war, over 500,000 members and candidates lost their lives.[21] On balance, however, the membership gains registered by these organizations were quite substantial. During the war years, military Party organizations recruited 2,667,823 members and 4,084,344 candidates.[22] These recruits represented 73.8 percent of all members and 76.7 percent of all candidates enrolled by the Party during the war. Viewed from a somewhat different angle, the number of Communists in the armed forces increased from 654,000 on 1 July 1941 to a peak of 3,031,000 on 1 January 1945, and to a high of 55 percent of total Party membership in December 1943.[23]

The distribution of Party membership in the armed forces was considerably higher in field units than in units located in rear areas and also significantly higher in the special branches of the service than in infantry units.[24] In addition, reflecting the importance that the regime attached to intertwining the interests and fate of the officers' corps with that of the Party, a rather high percentage of the members and candidates accepted by the military Party organizations was drawn from the relatively small officers' corps.[25]

The tremendous flow of Party members into the armed forces put a serious train on the nonmilitary Party organizations. In the first six months of the war, 91,000 of the Moscow organization's 236,000 members departed for the front.[26] The situation was even worse in Leningrad, where Party ranks during this same period declined by 70 percent. Some front-line cities, such as Odessa, lost more than 90 percent of their membership to the military. Even Party organizations in the rear were hard hit. Typical was the case of the Sverdlovsk organization, which in the period June–October 1941 declined in membership by 50 percent.[27]

Local Party organizations also felt the strain. In addition to the normal short-term problems that such losses might have been expected to produce, "attempts to make good . . . [on] depleted membership [of these organizations] . . . proved for some time to be a labor of Sisyphus, since new members continued to depart for the front almost as fast as new ones were admitted." [28]

The extent to which the territorial Party organizations were able to rebuild their membership ranks during the war years was to vary considerably. Most drastically affected were those organizations in areas occupied at one time or another by the Germans. Many of these organizations, especially in the rural non-Russian areas of the western borderlands, had been weak even in the prewar period. However, in time of war, under the combined impact of large-scale military mobilization, civilian evacuation, civilian and partisan casualties, and the established German practice of exterminating all known or suspected Communists, membership in these Party organizations was reduced to a minute fraction of its former size. For example, in October 1943, the entire Communist Party of the Ukraine had only 5,615 members, or approximately 1 percent of its prewar membership.[29] Those Party organizations located in front-line areas that escaped German occupation were somewhat better off. The Moscow and Leningrad organizations, for example, although losing a great portion of their membership, especially in the initial phase of the war, both attained a certain measure of success in rebuilding their ranks before the war's end.[30] Still better off were Party organizations located in the Soviet rear.

In composition, it was a considerably different Party that emerged from the war. Under the combined impact of the tremendous Communist losses and the massive recruitment of new members, the Party's ranks were substantially renewed during the war years: two-thirds of the membership on 1 January 1946 had joined the Party during the war.[31]

It also was a younger Party that emerged from the war. Whereas at the start of the war, only 345,000 Communists, or 8.9 percent of the Party's total membership, were under 24, by the end of the war this group totaled 1,002,000, or 18.3 percent, of the membership.[32] And perhaps because of the Party's increased emphasis on youthful recruits drawn from the best-educated generation up to that point in Soviet history, its educational profile underwent a substantial improvement during the war years. For example, the number of Communists with a higher, secondary, or incomplete secondary education increased in time of war from 39.8 percent to 57.4 percent.[33]

At the same time, in line with the regime's desire in time of crisis to strengthen its ties with the Soviet masses, the Party's social base was broadened. Whereas the relative weight of workers and peasant recruits into the Party in the period 1939–41 was approximately 20 percent and 10 percent, respectively,[34] during World War II, "in the Party as a whole, . . . 32.1 percent of all . . . admissions were classified as workers, 25.3 percent as peasants, and 42.6 percent as white-collar workers or intelligentsia." [35]

It was also a Party in which female representation, at least in the territorial organizations, rose substantially throughout the Soviet Union[36] in time of war, reflecting both the mass mobilization of men into the armed forces and the more prominent role of women in the national economy. By the war's end, women composed 41.3 percent of the territorial Party organization's membership; they had made up somewhat less than 14.4 percent at the start of the war.[37]

Finally, it was a Party with an even stronger degree of overrepresentation of Great Russians than it had had in the past.[38] Of the approximately 1,680,000 new members entering the Party in 1941–44, according to a Soviet authority who lists them by nationality, 1,545,230, or roughly 92 percent, were Great Russians.[39]

It would appear that Party wartime membership policy, even though it was subordinated to the pursuit of the war, was, on the whole, successful. However, the long-range effects of Party membership policy were rather negative, since new shortcomings were created and the old ones intensified. In particular, the lowering of admission standards, while admittedly facilitating the mass recruitment of new members and candidates, enabled a great many people who were politically unsophisticated and/or inert to gain entry into the Party. In time of war, such problems and shortcomings could be—or at least had to be—overlooked. Once victory had been won, however, the regime, relying on intensified indoctrination and widespread purges, would move quickly to correct this situation.

Nor was the problem limited to the Party's rank-and-file membership. Of even greater importance was the fact that a similar state of affairs prevailed among the apparatchiki. All levels of Party administration were to some degree affected by the problem.

¶ The Impact of War on the Party's Central Apparatus

Although the picture of the wartime situation of the Party's central apparatus must necessarily remain incomplete, some light can be shed upon personnel turnover and intra-elite relationships by piecing together the limited biographical information available on a number of leading cadres in the Central Committee's Secretariat during the war years.

At the top level, that of the CC Secretaries, no changes (except for the death of A. S. Shcherbakov in the spring of 1945) occurred during the war. Throughout this period, five men served as Party Secretaries: Shcherbakov, A. A. Andreev, G. Malenkov, A. Zhdanov, and, of course, Stalin himself. With the exception of Stalin, each seems to have been charged with oversight of—or, in the case of Malenkov, formal responsibility for—a particular sector of Party affairs. Malenkov thus, among other things, served as head of the CC's Cadres Administration,[40] and Andreev and Zhdanov, in fact, if not in name, held positions of similar responsibility in the spheres of agriculture[41] and agit-prop work,[42] respectively. Finally, Shcherbakov, as head of the Main Political Administration (MPA) of the Red Army for the greater part of the war, served as the Party's chief watchdog over the military.[43]

Direct involvement in the war effort, however, severely limited the amount of attention the Party Secretaries could devote to their particular areas of concern, or, for that matter, to any aspect of Party work. Malenkov was occupied, in addition to his other wartime assignments, with his various duties as a member of the State Defense Committee, and Zhdanov spent nearly all of the war away from Moscow, in Leningrad, where he was occupied almost completely with the defense and the subsequent reconstruction of the city. Involvement of CC Secretaries in work that had no direct relation to their activities as Secretaries was not something new to the war years: Zhdanov, for example, had been both a Party Secretary and the leader of the Leningrad organization for several years prior to the war. What was new was the scope and magnitude of this outside involvement. Thus, Malenkov and Zhdanov, the most important Secretaries after Stalin, were so removed from the affairs of the Central Committee during the war years as to reduce their Secretaryships almost to titular positions. It is probable that this absence of leadership contributed to the problems and shortcomings in the work of the apparat during the war years.

At the next lower levels of command in the Secretariat, there also appears to have been a fair degree of personnel stability during the war years. Men such as N. N. Shatalin[44] (an assistant head of the Cadres Administration), G. F. Aleksandrov[45] (head of the Propaganda and Agitation Administration), M. I. Iovchuk[46] (assistant head of the Propaganda and Agitation Administration), and A. I. Kozlov[47] (assistant manager of the Agriculture Department), to name only a few, seem to have occupied their posts for most, and in some cases for all, of the war. The low turnover rate among such leading cadres was due, at least in part, to the client-patron relationship that appears to have existed between such officials and the individual Party Secretaries[48]—between Malenkov and Shatalin, for example. Stability in the ranks of the Secretaries thus tended to engender a similar stability among these lower-level (though still very important) cadres and was an indication of the importance of these cadres for the proper functioning of the CC apparat.

At still lower levels of the CC's apparat, the situation appears to have been somewhat different. The personnel turnover among the lower-ranking apparatchiki of the CC seems to have occurred at a somewhat higher rate because of the mobilization of such cadres, along with great numbers of apparatchiki from the territorial Party organizations, for political work in the armed forces. Undoubtedly, the great majority of the 270 Central Committee apparatchiki mobilized for such work were drawn from the ranks of the Secretariat's lower-level cadres.[49] How many or what proportion of the Secretariat's lower-level cadres were so mobilized, however, is impossible to ascertain even approximately.

¶ War and the Personnel of the Territorial Party Organizations

The war's impact on the personnel of the territorial Party organization is much easier to document. All levels of local Party administration were plagued by personnel problems. During the first year of the war, for example, 120 obkom, kraikom, and union republic Secretaries from the rear areas (not counting Central Committee members and candidates) were directed to work in the Red Army.[50]

The lowest level of Party administration, the primary Party organizations, were also hard hit. In Leningrad 98.5 percent of the primary Party organization Secretaries came to their posts at the start of the war.[51] Similarly, in the first period of the war, 70 percent of the primary Party organizations in Moscow received new secretaries.[52]

The turnover of intermediate-level apparat workers was almost as serious. The Omsk oblast Party organization, for example, lost over 700 apparatchiki to the armed forces in the first three months of the war alone,[53] and "an analogous situation . . . prevailed in almost all Party organizations." [54] Moreover, the problem of restaffing all levels of the local Party apparatus was to continue to trouble the Party throughout the war. Thus, the apparat of the Moscow gorkom was renewed by 38 percent in 1942–43.[55] Similarly, in Irkutsk oblast 277 out of 630 Party workers were replaced in 1943 alone.[56] In Leningrad 88.5 percent of the gorkom and raikom workers were advanced to their posts during the war.[57] In Irkutsk oblast, 71.7 percent of Party secretaries were replaced in the course of the war. Much of this fluidity resulted from large-scale military mobilizations in the first period of the war; however, once the initial phase of the war was over, mobilizations accounted for only a very small portion of the turnover. The Moscow city Party organization in 1943, for example, replaced 282 cadres, or 32.5 percent of the capital's entire district-level apparat: of these cadres only 10 were called into the army.[58] Soviet sources maintain that this nonmilitary turnover of cadres in the Moscow organization was produced by unjustified replacements of leading cadres by the gorkom and raikoms.[59] In other instances, local Party organizations were criticized for "a lack of organizational and ideological-political work . . . with newly advanced cadres." [60] These shortcomings were both apparent and real and did place serious constraints on the operational effectiveness of the local Party organizations. At the same time, the task confronting these organizations, of rebuilding their apparats, was much more difficult and complex than the criticism suggests.

To say the least, personnel losses, especially those caused by military mobilizations in the first period of the war, temporarily handicapped the everyday operational activities of the local Party organizations quite severely. New cadres not only had to be found and trained to perform their various administrative duties but also had to be initiated into the equally laborious (and perhaps even more important) work of learning the informal aspects of the system, the personal "know-how and know-who" needed for the successful execution of their functions.

The restaffing of the apparats was even further complicated by other serious problems. The first was the general manpower shortage; in some instances, it was simply impossible to find the requisite number of cadres. Second, there was the question of the qualifications of the replacements. Many had little or no experience in Party administration and had joined the Party only recently. Many apparatchiki thus had not developed the habits and skills of Party work, especially those relating to the exercise of Party control. Nor did many of the new cadres receive much assistance from the more experienced members of the apparat, who themselves were overburdened with the vital problems of day-to-day administration. Finally, it appears that many of these new cadres, especially those assigned to the various economic otdels, lacked the technical expertise to cope with their assignments.

All these personnel problems could not but affect the operational ability of the local Party organs. However, in line with wartime priorities, the economic functions of these organs were least affected.

¶ The Party and the War Economy: The Role of the Local Party Organs in Industry

In the words of a leading Soviet authority on local Party organs: "During the period of the Great Patriotic War, conditions of wartime placed new tasks pertaining to the leadership of the economy before Party committees. The situation, at that time, was complicated by the fact that Party organs were forced to [involve themselves in] . . . the operative work of governing the economy, . . . [and to take on] functions [having to do with] . . . the direct leadership of the economy." [61]

Despite the existence of a number of factors, above all the increased centralization of certain aspects of economic decisionmaking and administration, which placed definite limits on the local Party organs' activities in industrial affairs, the statement quoted here appears to be a reasonably accurate description of the local Party organs' involvement in industry during the war years.[62] That they were accorded such a significant role in industry during the period under consideration was due, in large measure, to the Party's familiarity with the exercise of authority, its mobilizational tradition, and its campaign-style approach to problem solving.[63] In addition, the role of the territorial Party organizations in overseeing and coordinating the economic affairs of their areas was to take on even greater importance because of the disruption in time of war of the commissariats' lines of communication with their enterprises. Frequently, decisions had to be made and actions taken quickly and effectively, and it was quite natural for the local Party organs to do these things. Moreover, even when the local Party organs could not resolve such problems themselves, they could often facilitate solutions by providing a powerful alternate channel for communicating high-priority appeals to higher-standing organs and officials.[64]

The foregoing discussion should not be taken to mean that the work of the local Party organs in industry was not afflicted by serious problems and shortcomings. Weaknesses in production-verification work, for example, tended to place certain limits on the local Party organs' actual involvement in industrial decisionmaking and administration. Local party officials sent to check on production at particular factories and enterprises frequently were criticized as passive or superficial observers.[65] For example, the Trud factory in the Oktyabirsk district in Novosibirsk was visited on one day by

> an obkom inspector, a gorkom inspector, the raikom's second secretary, and the managers of the organization-instruction and the propaganda department. . . . What do these facts indicate? They are indicative of the fact that many Party workers go to enterprises without concrete goals and tasks and that their visits not only do not bear any results, but also divert the attention of the leaders of the enterprises and the Party organizations from their work. . . . Besides that, it is evident that in the Party apparat there still are the kind of worker-"investigators," "guests," who superficially and irresponsibly tour around the enterprises.[66]

But not all factories and enterprises received this much attention. Since time and Party cadres were limited, the local Party organs concentrated their attention upon the major defense plants in their areas.[67]

The higher-standing territorial Party organs themselves were often lax in their conduct of industrial performance-verification work. The Tadjik Party organization, for example, was criticized in 1942 for limiting its contact with enterprises in many instances to the receipt of the monthly report on plan fulfillment.[68] The lower-level Party organizations frequently made a bad situation even worse by failing to inform the higher-standing Party organs of the state of industrial affairs in their locales. In 1942 the Chkalovsk obkom, for example, did not receive even one such report from a number of its raikoms.[69] Such shortcomings, however, although they undoubtedly decreased the effectiveness of the local Party organs' involvement in industry, were not so great as to have prevented the local Party organs from playing an important role in industrial affairs during the war years.

¶ The Impact of War on the Staff Functions of the Territorial Party Organizations

The increased emphasis on economic affairs by the territorial Party organizations, especially in the face of substantial cadres problems, meant that certain of the regular functions of these organizations had to be given short shrift. According to John Armstrong, what suffered was the work of the Party's "staff" agencies, that is, organization-instruction, agitation and propaganda, and cadres selection and assignment, whose function it was "not to direct the substantive operations of the Party and subordinate spheres of Soviet life, but to see that these operations proceeded efficiently in accordance with the will of the central authorities. . . . The entry of the Soviet Union into the war apparently destroyed the primacy of the staff agencies, although most of the 1939 organization was to be retained until 1948."[70]

Armstrong certainly is correct, at least as far as agit-prop and organization-instruction work is concerned. However, the situation he describes was not entirely a wartime phenomenon. In many cases one has the impression that the new problems and shortcomings connected with such work differed from those of the prewar period more in degree (albeit, at times, a significant degree) than in kind. In addition, it is quite possible in light of what has been said that the Party could have done very little in either period (but especially during the war) to have improved the situation greatly and that therefore criticisms of the Party's work must be viewed more as expressions of concern and hope than as realizable demands. Still, an examination of such criticism provides some insight into the war's actual impact on these Party functions. However, since many of the problems connected with agit-prop work were essentially of an organizational-instructional nature, discussion here will focus on the problems and shortcomings of organizational-instruction work during the war.

The key problem, judging from the frequency and strength of criticisms of organizational-instructional work voiced in the Soviet press during the war years, was that of leadership. Party organs and officials were frequently accused of leading in a superficial, formalistic manner or of using "incorrect" methods of leadership. More specifically, it was frequently asserted that too many "paper" decisions were being made—that is, resolutions were passed, but often no one would see to it that they were implemented.[71] Also, officials, especially leading officials, in many instances never bothered to go out to the locales to meet with people and view particular situations at first hand.[72] At the other end of the decisionmaking process, local Party organizations and officials frequently failed to pay attention to decisions taken by higher Party organs and, in addition, were lax in informing higher organs about the state of affairs in the local organizations.[73] Moreover, it was charged that leading officials, at all levels of Party administration, contributed to the further deterioration of intra-Party work by their frequent failure to call Party plenums and aktiv meetings for the exchange of views and information.[74] Rather than involving themselves in such activities, many of these leading cadres tended to rely upon campaign-style methods of administration, or "storming": problems would often be neglected until the situation became critical, and then all of the given Party organization's resources would be put into motion.[75] Moreover, in their dealings with lower-ranking cadres, many leading Party officials at all levels of administration often chose to rely on compulsion rather than taking the time and effort to train well-meaning but inexperienced apparatchiki.[76] On balance, this style of leadership appears to have had quite negative results, including high rates of personnel turnover (and hence the continued existence of a rather inexperienced Party apparat) and the stifling of initiative among lower-level apparatchiki. Furthermore, though such methods of Party leadership might have enhanced the personal power positions of the leading officials in question, they led also to a decline in the activities (and hence in the relative position) of the organization-instruction departments.

Although it was extremely difficult, and probably impossible, to eliminate such problems and shortcomings in time of war, the Party made it quite clear, especially as the fortunes of war began to improve, that the organization-instruction departments were supposed to play an extremely important role in Party affairs. This position was emphasized in a CC resolution of 21 September 1943, "On the Tasks and Structure of the Organization-Instruction Department of the CC VKP(b)." [77] As it turned out, this resolution did not effect any important changes in either the structure or the functions of the department. Yet the rather detailed description of the department's structure and broad functions may have been intended to stress the importance the Party attached to the work of the department.[78] Despite the Party's intentions, serious problems and shortcomings continued to plague its organization-instruction work throughout the war and afterward. In the postwar period more drastic attempts would be made to correct this situation.[79]

The situation with respect to the cadres work of the territorial Party organizations was somewhat different. Here the problems seem to have been primarily problems of commission rather than omission—of local Party organizations (and, in particular, their cadres departments) trying to do too much rather than too little. Some Party organizations failed to limit their activities to such important tasks as the selection of cadres for the most important Party, soviet, and economic posts; the provision of training and administrative assistance to other non-Party organizations; and the maintenance of overall control over both Party and non-Party cadres policy. Rather, they "squander their talents on trifles, attempting to select cadres for any and all posts. Frequently, instead of putting right the work of the cadres departments of [non-Party organizations], . . . they themselves are occupied [only with the task of fulfilling] . . . numerous requests for people. . . ." [80] The same situation prevailed within the Party organizations, themselves. [81] The result was a considerable expansion of personnel work and an informal assumption of power by the cadres departments. At the same time, however, a sizable expansion of the nomenklatura of some Party organizations was brought about: "In the North-Kazakhstan obkom, for example, . . . there are more than 2600 posts on the obkom's nomenklatura, . . . [and] about 700 posts in the nomenklatura of Danilov raikom of Yaroslav oblast." [82] This superfluous expansion of nomenklatura, it was asserted, was characteristic of many raikoms and gorkoms and led to a lowering of the other Party and non-Party departments' responsibilities in matters relating to the selection and placement of cadres.[83]

Many of these complaints about superfluity in nomenklatura and the failure of agencies other than the Party's cadres departments to do their proper share of personnel work were not unique to the war years. The crisis of war, however, accentuated both the problems and the complaints. Nevertheless, it can be argued that the established position of the cadres departments, together with the clear line of communication with the center afforded by the existence of a CC Cadres Administration, gave these departments a great advantage over the local production-branch otdels. This advantage undoubtedly was reinforced both by the basic importance of personnel questions to the Party and to the war effort and by the inability of the production-branch departments to handle such questions effectively. In time of crisis, therefore, both reason and force of habit dictated that the Party's cadres departments continue to exercise authority over personnel affairs.

¶ The Impact of War on the Party's Modus Operandi

Personalization of power and the territorial first Party secretaries One effect of the war was the further enhancement of the power positions of key local Party officials and, in particular, the first secretaries of territorial Party organizations. John Armstrong notes that, before the war, "with relatively few first-rate men available, the central authorities probably considered it more effective in the long run to let a single vigorous Party leader be 'on a small scale God and Tsar in the oblast,' judging him on overall results." [84] This state of affairs came to be even more prevalent in time of war, when the personnel problems confronting the territorial Party organizations became even more severe than those of the immediate prewar period.

Use of extraordinary forms and methods of administration and control by the Party Over and above the enhancement of the personal power positions of local Party officials, the Party itself, mirroring the regime's general system of wartime administration, made considerable use during the war of extraordinary forms and methods of administration and control, including institutionalized forms of personalization of power, such as the plenipotentiary system. Extraordinary forms and methods were used by the Party not only in its attempt to deal with critical problems, such as the evacuation and relocation of industry, but also in major sectors of the war effort, such as agriculture, where the mass mobilization of Party and Komsomol members into the armed forces in the initial stages of the war further weakened the regime's already none-too-strong control over the countryside.[85]

Once again the machine tractor station and sovkhoz politotdels One major aspect of the extraordinary wartime system of administration and control in the countryside was the reinstitution of machine tractor station (MTS) and sovkhoz politotdels as vital components of the regime's struggle to secure its minimum agricultural needs and to maintain a degree of political oversight over the countryside.[86]

According to the Central Committee resolution of 7 November 1941 that reestablished the politotdels, the basis of their tasks was "political work not only among the workers and employees of the MTS and sovkhozes but also of kolkhozes, in order to guarantee the timely fulfillment of state assignments and plans of agricultural work." [87]

They, like their predecessors of the 1930s, were supposed to exercise direct control over Party-political work in the areas served by the MTS. Political oversight, of course, was intertwined with economic oversight. The politotdels thus were to be actively concerned with questions of work discipline, to ensure not only that all the kolkhozniki participated in kolkhoz work but also that the quantity and quality of their work met the regime's established standards. In addition, the selection, training, and distribution of agricultural cadres, as well as the organization, payment, and recording of work, fell within their purview. In sum, the politotdels were to be the eyes of the Party and to control all aspects of work in the MTS and the kolkhozes.

Just how much importance the regime attached to the politotdels is indicated by the mobilization of more than 13,000 Party, soviet, and Komsomol workers for work in the politotdels at a time when there was a considerable drain of leading cadres away from the rural areas. A great many of these cadres had previously occupied important posts at the district and, in some instances, the oblast level.[88] Almost half the number of chiefs and their deputies, for example, had been secretaries of raikoms, department managers, and instructors;[89] 80.3 percent of them had been members of the Party for more than seven years, which suggests that they had acquired at least the requisite minimum habits of Party and political work.[90]

The politotdels' work frequently was marred by the same problems and shortcomings that had been in evidence during the earlier existence of the MTS (and sovkhoz) politotdel system. Most serious was the conflict-laden relationship between the politotdels and the regular local Party organs, especially the raikoms.[91] In part, such conflict stemmed from a general lack of precision in the delineation of areas of jurisdiction and from the fact that each body received its orders from a different superior organ.[92] Raikoms and politotdels thus frequently found themselves either working at cross-purposes or both abdicating certain functions. More specifically, they both tended to focus their attention on economic issues and problems while abstaining from such matters as Party-political work.[93]

At the same time, a natural basis for rivalry and conflict between the raikoms and politotdels existed. In the past, Party jurisdiction in a given area had belonged to the raikoms, but now the raikoms were forced to share their authority with the politotdels. Confronted with this new state of affairs, some raikoms tried to maintain their former superiority by subordinating the politotdels to their control.[94] While clearly displeased with this state of affairs, the regime, for the time being, was prepared to tolerate the continued existence of such problems and shortcomings, as long as it was able to meet its minimum agricultural needs and assure the political reliability of the rural population.

The politotdels were abolished in May 1943. Although the official reason given at the time was that they had served their purpose and were no longer needed,[95] the real reason for their abolition was that the ongoing friction and rivalry between them and the raikoms had reached a point at which "the disadvantages of their corrosive effect on the local Party organizations had begun to outweigh the advantages of guaranteed procurements." [96]

The abolition of the politotdels seems, however, to have resulted in a further deterioration of political controls in the countryside. Robert Miller maintains that "paradoxically, it may have been the wholesale involvement of the raion Party officials in the details of agricultural life, after the abolition of wartime politotdels, that brought about the breakdown of discipline in kolkhozes and MTS. . . . [Furthermore,] physically they were in a far less advantageous position to exercise daily overall surveillance in the manner of politotdels and zampolits." [97]

The regime would begin to combat such problems effectively only in the postwar period, with such measures as the formation of the Council on Kolkhoz Affairs and the reestablishment of the MTS zampolit system.

The system of plenipotentiaries in the countryside Like many other extraordinary aspects of Party administration during this period, the use of the plenipotentiary system in the countryside had its origins in the prewar period, when it arose from the need to strengthen the regime's regular system of controls over the agricultural sector of the economy. The system of plenipotentiaries was to gain even greater importance during the war years, as it enabled the regime to achieve some degree of command-control over agriculture with a minimum outlay of personnel.

Essentially, what the system of plenipotentiaries involved was the mobilization of Party and non-Party cadres, especially during various agricultural campaigns, to go out to the individual kolkhozes, MTS, and so on, and to oversee personally and ensure by whatever means necessary that the given agricultural unit fulfilled its obligations to the state. Such work was so important to the regime that, in the face of a serious shortage of cadres, the local Party organizations were frequently prepared to drain the available supply of Party and non-Party apparatchiki to obtain the requisite number of plenipotentiaries. Raikom department managers and instructors, as well as agronomists and state bureaucrats, were thus mobilized for work as plenipotentiaries. Moreover, as a plenipotentiary's assignment often entailed spending a long period (even an entire agricultural season) in a particular kolkhoz, other aspects of Party and state administrative work were sometimes seriously weakened and disorganized: "On one occasion . . . in Pokhvinsk-Nevsk district, the raikom secretary urgently needed the militia to clear up some matter. The head of the district militia office, however, had been serving for a long time as a plenipotentiary in one of the kolkhozes, and there was no one to investigate the urgent matter—and only then did they suddenly realize in the raikom . . . that the organ which was supposed to preserve order, battle with misappropriations, etc., had essentially ceased to work in the district." [98]

The use of the plenipotentiary system also caused some problems for agriculture itself. A considerable number of these officials lacked the technical and administrative expertise to deal effectively with agricultural matters. Indeed, in many instances, the plenipotentiaries made the tasks of both the rank-and-file kolkhozniki and the kolkhoz administrators all the more difficult. Iu. V. Arutunyan, for example, noting that such plenipotentiaries were derisively called "impotentiaries," [99] quotes a secretary of the Altai kraikom, who charged that "they send some plenipotentiary, and he walks behind the chairman or brigadier, like a shadow, with an expression of unconsolable anguish in his gaze and buzzes like a mosquito all sorts of directions into the ears of the local workers. . . . Such plenipotentiaries we do not need; they stifle initiative; they decompose the remains of discipline among local cadres." [100]

In some instances, the situation became so extreme that "people who knew what to do, who knew how to solve a problem most successfully, did not do anything and just sat and waited for the plenipotentiary." [101] The Soviet press regularly reported instances of agricultural plenipotentiaries using "formal-bureaucratic" methods of leadership—that is, force and threats, rather than persuasion—and of their foiling or unjustly firing kolkhoz administrators. However, as was the case with the politotdels, the regime was willing to tolerate the various shortcomings of the plenipotentiary system, as the system contributed to the maintenance of the regime's control over the agricultural sector of the economy.

¶ The Party and the Regime's Other Instruments of Administration and Control in Time of War

Party-military relations The coming of the war, and especially the massive setbacks suffered in the war's early stages and the resulting decline in military morale and discipline, quickly led the Soviet regime to tighten political controls over the armed forces. As part of this move, the regime strengthened existing institutionalized forms of political control, such as the Military Councils.[102] At the same time, here, as in many other aspects of the war effort, it also tended to fall back on past experience. As has been noted, great numbers of Party members were called up for military service through regular and special mobilizations. In addition, on 16 July 1941 another tried, if not always true, form of political control—the system of military commissars—was reintroduced.[103]

Tightening of political controls, especially through the system of military commissars, was not achieved without a considerable amount of friction between political and military authorities. Resentment, fear, and demoralization of the officers' corps were the most common results.[104] The regime, however, was apparently willing to overlook, or at least tolerate, such problems and shortcomings in its quest for the continued maintenance of political controls over the armed forces. But with the passage of time it became increasingly apparent to the regime not only that the armed forces and their command staff were loyal and able, but also that the system of political controls, especially the system of military commissars, was impairing the military's effectiveness. Thus, the armed forces, and especially the officers' corps, whose prestige had begun to skyrocket once the tide of battle started to turn, were showered with ever-increasing honor and praise by the regime,[105] and the system of military commissars was abolished in October 1942.[106] Further than this, generally speaking, the regime, ever wary of the dangers inherent in independent military power, could not go; political controls over the armed forces could be relaxed, but not abolished. In particular, the system of Military Councils was to continue in existence throughout the war.[107] As the war moved into its final stages, the regime attempted to strengthen its control at the lower levels of the military hierarchy.[108] Here, however, efforts by the military Party organizations to strengthen control and to improve their Party-political work ran up against problems resulting from the recruitment into the Party of great numbers of politically illiterate people. No really satisfactory solution to these problems was to be forthcoming before the end of the war. In the meantime, the military, as the instrument first of defense and then of victory, was to make substantial gains in its power position in relation to the Party and the regime's other regular instruments of administration and control.

The role of the NKVD As might have been expected, given the need for heightened vigilance and control in time of war, the NKVD played an important role in the war effort. Indeed, in some respects, the power position of the NKVD was further enhanced during this period: in addition to both its regular control function and its key role in the war economy (the result of its being the master of a massive forced labor empire), the NKVD, through its own military units and its part in the organization and leadership of people's militia units and destruction battalions, was an active participant in the military aspects of the war effort. It was also to play a leading role in the partisan movement (especially in its early stages),[109] in the re-Sovietization of the former enemy-occupied areas of the USSR,[110] and in the procurement of grain and other agricultural products from the countryside, where, in places, the situation seems to have resembled the first years of collectivization of agriculture.[111] Wartime necessity, perhaps reinforced by the regime's preference, in all three cases resulted in the enhancement of the power position of the NKVD. And in all three cases, the enhancement of the NKVD's position appears to have been achieved, in the first instance, at the expense of the Party.

The local Party organs and their economic counterparts Somewhat less clear than the organizational power relationships described above was the power relationship between the territorial Party organizations and their economic counterparts. A quick reading of the wartime situation in the industrial sector might lead one to conclude that the territorial Party organs had improved their position relative to that of the local economic organs and their officials. And it is true, as has been noted, that the Party organs played an important role in industry in this period and that they and their officials frequently took a demanding and dictatorial attitude toward economic administrators in their locales. When their orders failed to achieve the desired results, the element of force was soon forthcoming: reliance on force and arbitrary administrative methods being basic ingredients of Stalin's personal formula of totalitarian rule, it is only natural that the little Stalins sought to emulate their supreme leader.

But for all that has just been said, the real power relationship between the territorial Party organs and local economic administrators may have been somewhat different. It is even possible that the latter gained in strength at the expense of the former during the war. The turnover rate among economic officials seems to have been somewhat lower than the rate for local Party apparatchiki. And, to the extent that local Party officials, as a result of their frequently brief tenure of office, were unable either to develop effective methods of Party work or to become familiar with the problems and personnel of the various enterprises under their jurisdiction, they would not have been able to exercise proper supervision over the concerns and officials in question. More important, they may have had to defer frequently to the views of their economic counterparts on matters of technology, operations, and policy.

Local Party-soviet relations The position of the local soviet organizations in relation to their Party counterparts also appears to have been strengthened somewhat during the war. Once again, the key factor seems to have been personnel. While the mobilization of apparatchiki affected all organizations significantly, it seems to have hit the Party organizations the hardest. It therefore fell to other organizations, especially the local soviets, to pick up the slack whenever possible. The local non-Party organizations were thus often forced to assume functions which in normal times would have been the Party's preserve. This phenomenon appears to have been most pronounced in front-line areas, especially where control was vested in "constricted ispolkoms." Composed of fairly small groups of important Party, governmental, police, and military officials, the "constricted ispolkoms," among other things, helped coordinate the activities of civilian and military authorities and regulate the allocation of vitally needed resources to factories and other enterprises.[112]

The increased importance of the local Soviet organizations, even in areas where "constricted ispolkoms" were established, should not be taken to mean that the local Party organizations underwent a complete collapse during the war. Indeed, generally speaking, the local Party organizations remained considerably stronger and more important than their local soviet counterparts. What took place, thus, was only a relative strengthening of the local soviet organizations in relation to their Party counterparts.

¶ Conclusion

An examination of the wartime course of events in the Soviet Union leads to the conclusion that the role of the Party during this period did not have the scope and magnitude that Soviet historians and propagandists, especially those of the postwar period, have depicted for it. When confronted with some difficult problem or situation, the regime frequently either bypassed Party organizations or used them as auxiliaries of its extraordinary organs and specially empowered officials. This clearly was the case, for example, during the first two stages of the evacuation of industry. That the Party as an organization did not play a more important role in the war effort was the result of a number of factors. First, over and above the exigencies of war, which forced the regime to rely heavily on extraordinary organs and on the concept of personalization of power, the crisis of war had an adverse effect on the Party itself and hence on its ability to cope effectively with the wartime situation. Second, the Party, along with the Soviet government and armed forces, suffered a precipitous decline in prestige at the outset of the war. As it had claimed credit for the regime's successes in the prewar period, it had to shoulder much of the blame for the ever-mounting setbacks and defeats. In time, as the fortunes of war started to improve, the Party's prestige did also. However, undoing the damage to the image of the Party as the infallible organizer and leader of the Soviet peoples was to be both difficult and slow.

What has just been said, however, should not be taken to mean that the Party underwent a complete collapse, even in the countryside, during the war years. In fact, the Soviet regime continued to rely on the Party throughout the war as one of its main instruments of control. More specifically, the Party was involved in, among other things, the maintenance of political controls over the armed forces, the administration and control of the country's economy, and the re-Sovietization of the former enemy-occupied areas of the USSR. The Party's work in these spheres, while not devoid of shortcomings, even serious shortcomings, was a valuable contribution to the Soviet war effort. That it was able to make such a contribution was in large measure because it possessed certain traits—in particular, its long-standing familiarity with the exercise of power and its mobilizational approach to problem solving—that clearly could be of great value to the regime in time of war.

It thus has to be concluded that the Communist Party of the Soviet Union achieved a fair level of success during the crisis of World War II. Moreover, even in those instances in which the Party, as an organization, did not figure significantly in the war effort, Party members, in their individual capacities, did. Not only did they have a near total monopoly on positions of authority, but they also provided the Soviet leadership with a much-needed elite force, prepared to do its bidding. In a sense, then, Communists were the organizers and leaders of the Soviet war effort. Although they were both literally and figuratively under fire throughout the war years, they were in the vanguard of the Soviet Union's march to ultimate victory in the war. And the victorious war effort, a most severe test, in turn proved the organizational and mass-psychological viability of both the Party and the Soviet system itself.

David E. Powell

Alcohol Abuse: The Pattern of Official Response

An old Russian saying holds that "V Rossii, piut i ptitsy" (In Russia, even the birds drink). Drinking has been and remains a major part of the country's culture. Western scholars have noted the existence of a "drinking culture" in the USSR, and Soviet commentators have often expressed dismay at its strength and prevalence. As a Soviet physician once put it: "People drink when they meet, when they take leave of each other; to quiet their hunger when they are hungry, to stimulate their appetite when they are satisfied. They drink to get warm, when it is cold, to cool off when it is hot. They drink when they are drowsy, to wake up, and when they are wakeful, to bring on sleep." [1]

In the USSR, almost everyone drinks. Soviet specialists have estimated that upwards of 90% of the adult population drinks at least once in a while and that many of these people are problem drinkers or alcoholics.[2] To be sure, there is a great deal of regional variation within the USSR, as well as certain striking differences within and between various social groups (male-female, urban-rural, differing socioeconomic strata, and so on). In general, however, a greater proportion of Soviet citizens drink than do their American counterparts. (The most recent authoritative poll in the United States, a series of surveys conducted by Louis Harris in 1972–74, found that one-third of American adults had not consumed *any* alcohol within the previous year. This abstention rate is far higher than the one found in the USSR.) [3]

Although we lack much of the data necessary to construct an accurate picture of Soviet drinking practices, several recent surveys of urban workers in the USSR provide suggestive findings. Thus, a poll conducted at one Moscow factory found that virtually all male workers (99.3%) were drinkers.[4] Only six men in the entire sample declared that they did not drink—and three of these said it was because they were presently being treated in a clinic for alcoholism.[5] Of the entire group employed at the plant, some one-third were said to "misuse" (*zloupotrebit*) alcoholic beverages, and 30% of these individuals (or about 10% of the plant's male work-force) exhibited symptoms of alcoholism. Other studies have yielded similar findings. In general, Soviet researchers estimate that approximately 6% of the drinking-age population can be medically classified as alcoholic.[6]

Moreover, there has been a dramatic increase in alcohol consumption in the USSR. During the period 1940 to 1973, when the country's population increased by only 28%, sales of alcohol beverages (corrected for price changes) increased by 534%.[7] At the present time, the USSR is in or near first place among the countries of the world in consumption of distilled spirits (80 proof or stronger)—although it ranks a good deal lower than others in consumption of all alcoholic beverages. During the period 1968 to 1972, each Soviet citizen fifteen years of age or older consumed 5.12 liters (about 5.4 quarts; 1 liter = 1.06 quarts) of absolute alcohol annually in the form of distilled spirits. Only the citizens of Poland (5.16 liters) and Peru (5.68 liters) drank more than their Soviet counterparts. (The United States ranks fourth, with a per capita figure of 4.25 liters, or about 4.5 quarts.)

In terms of *total* alcohol consumption (distilled spirits, wine, and beer), official Soviet data put the USSR in seventeenth place in the world. The Soviet figure of 8.87 liters of absolute alcohol consumed by each citizen fifteen years of age or older is considerably below that of France (22.13 liters), Portugal (20.95 liters), Belgium, West Germany, and a number of other states. (The United States is in thirteenth place; each American adult consumes 10.16 liters of absolute alcohol annually.)

The Soviet data, it should be emphasized, include only beverages that have been produced and sold through the state retail trade network (stores, restaurants, bars, and vending machines); they do not take into consideration the production and/or sale of illegally distilled *samogon* (home brew). Although it is not possible to ascertain precisely how much of this liquor is produced or consumed, enough information is available—through estimates published by Soviet and Western scholars —to suggest that the volume is considerable. Therefore, Soviet alcohol consumption is greater than official data indicate.

For example, figures provided by the USSR Central Statistical Administration for 1927 and 1928 (when data on the production of legal and illegal alcoholic beverages were more plentiful) indicate that more vodka was made at home in the form of home brew than was produced by the state. Government distilleries produced 446 million liters in 1927, while samogon production was slightly greater—467 million liters. In 1928, the proportion of home brew was somewhat higher.[8] More recent data indicate that the contribution of samogon to total consumption has fallen but that it still represents a large proportion of the total. Thus, a 1960 study of the Dimitrov district of Moscow oblast showed that 12.7 liters of vodka obtained through legal channels were consumed by each citizen fifteen years of age or older, along with 10.4 liters of home brew. In 1974, two leading Soviet scholars, while acknowledging that the gap

Table 1 Consumption of Alcoholic Beverages in Selected Countries (In Liters of Absolute Alcohol per Capita of the Population Aged 15 Years and Over)

	Year	Distilled spirits	All alcoholic
France	1970	4.09	22.13
Portugal	1971	1.47	20.95
Belgium	1972	2.04	15.93
West Germany	1972	3.81	14.97
Austria	1972	3.17	14.08
Italy	1972	1.26	13.73
Switzerland	1966–70	2.46	13.03
Spain	1971	3.24	12.85
Australia	1971–72	1.57	12.72
Hungary	1972	3.80	12.36
New Zealand	1971	1.48	12.22
Czechoslovakia	1970	3.13	11.06
USA	1973	4.25	10.16
Denmark	1971	2.03	9.18
Canada	1971	3.04	9.18
Netherlands	1972	3.13	9.05
United Kingdom	1971	1.31	8.57
Ireland	1973	2.50	8.31
East Germany	1969	3.35	7.71
Poland	1972	5.16	7.68
Peru	1970	5.68	7.27
Sweden	1971	3.11	7.00
Japan	1970	1.50	6.59
Finland	1971	3.10	6.35
Norway	1972	2.20	5.11
Iceland	1971	3.43	4.58
Israel	1972	1.72	3.15
USSR	1968–72		
State-manufactured beverages only		5.17	8.87
Total, including estimated illegally produced samogon		8.07	11.26

Source: Vladimir G. Treml, "Production and Consumption of Alcoholic Beverages in the USSR," *Journal of Studies on Alcohol* 36, no. 3 (March 1975): 297.

between official and illegal vodka had widened still further, concluded that the production of samogon remained at a very high level—approximately 50% as great as the amount of legally distilled vodka.[9]

Estimates prepared by an American economist, Vladimir Treml, are in line with these Soviet figures. Treml estimates annual samogon production today at more than one billion liters (more than twice the 1927 figure) and suggests that it contributes about 25–30% of all alcohol consumed in the country.[10] If we accept Treml's figures and add the volume of home brew to official Soviet data, then it is clear that the USSR is far ahead of all other countries in consumption of distilled spirits (8.07 liters, or about 8.5 quarts, per capita). In overall consumption of alcoholic beverages, the Soviet Union is in twelfth place (11.26 liters, or about 12 quarts). What is more, per capita consumption of alcoholic beverages has been increasing at an extremely rapid rate—5.6% annually over the past decade and a half—one of the highest rates in the world, exceeded by only five countries for which data are presently available.

¶ Urgency of the Problem

This high and continually rising level of drinking cannot help but concern the Party. But alcohol abuse, a form of antisocial behavior in its own right, has also led to significant public health problems; it has undermined the welfare, safety, and economic well-being of the citizenry and threatens the future development of Soviet society. Indeed, a leading Soviet jurist has argued that the destructive force of alcoholism can be compared only with that of nuclear weapons.[11]

More precisely, the major consequences of drinking, all of which have been the subject of animated discussion in the Soviet press, are the following:

1. Alcohol, especially when consumed in large quantities over an extended period of time, is harmful to health. The incidence of diseases of the respiratory and digestive tracts is significantly higher among drinkers than among nondrinkers, and the former also suffer from a variety of other ailments, especially cardiovascular and neurological disorders.[12] Those who overindulge for protracted periods may find their capabilities or even their life expectancies sharply reduced. Alcoholics often develop such serious symptoms that they become incapacitated or totally disabled or die prematurely. In the USSR today, alcoholism and the diseases associated with it are the third leading cause of death, and the death rate from cirrhosis of the liver is ten times greater among alcoholics than

among those who abstain.[13] Indeed alcoholism has been termed "the great killer": the life expectancy of an alcoholic typically is ten to fifteen years less than that of a nondrinker.[14]

2. Heavy drinking has become an increasingly severe threat to the younger generation. On the most obvious level, excessive drinking by adults is omnipresent, and it promotes drinking by curious and/or daring children. Thus, two Soviet physicians, observing that schoolchildren at play often pretend that they are drunk, conclude from this behavior, "The alcoholic serves as a constant and visible negative model for the younger generation."[15] Medical authorities have already begun to speak of a "rejuvenation" of alcoholism; they note the steady increase in recent years in the proportion of young people appearing for treatment at psychoneurological dispensaries and other medical establishments.[16]

3. Soviet analysts are increasingly concerned about the link between alcoholism and birth defects. The rapid rise in alcoholism among women, cited by several observers, is only part of the problem.[17] According to a number of studies, alcohol abuse by either parent increases the likelihood that the children will be born unhealthy. Pregnant women who drink to excess are said to be more likely than nondrinkers to have miscarriages, premature births, and small babies. Moreover, there is a higher incidence of infant mortality among the offspring of heavy drinkers and alcoholics, as well as a higher incidence of mental retardation.[18]

4. Alcohol abuse has a destructive effect on family life. Nearly half of all Soviet divorces are attributed to drinking problems, although it is unclear whether Soviet data refer to instances where drinking is the principal cause of divorce or where overindulgence is only a contributory factor.[19] More important, almost all spouses of alcoholics show neurotic symptoms brought on by the drinker's erratic behavior, and many of them develop serious emotional problems.[20]

5. The demand for alcoholic beverages causes great harm to Soviet agriculture and industry. Legal and illegal production of liquor diverts large quantities of grain, potatoes, sugar, and other produce that might otherwise be used to feed people or livestock. (One liter of home brew, for example, requires more than a kilogram, or over 2.2 pounds of sugar to produce.)[21] In the industrial sphere, the costs are probably greater: they include problems of labor discipline, increased labor turnover, loss of work-time, diminished labor productivity, more frequent on-the-job accidents, and the presence of "parasites," "slackers," "loafers," and others who work poorly or not at all.[22] Soviet specialists estimate that half of all industrial accidents are caused by the carelessness of intoxicated workers, and some officials put the figure as high as 80%.[23] A large proportion (precisely how large is the subject of controversy) of

those who leave jobs "at their own request" are in fact problem drinkers who have been asked by their employers to leave, but who have been allowed to use this euphemistic formulation so as not to endanger their job prospects elsewhere.[24] On Mondays and the days after holidays, labor productivity falls off markedly, and much of what is produced is of poor quality. Along these same lines, one study of industrial enterprises in the city of Gorky found that more than half (56.2%) of all violations of labor discipline—lateness, leaving work without permission, shirking, appearing at work in a drunken state, and so on—could be traced to drunkenness or to hangovers. Others have given estimates for this link that range as high as 90%.[25]

The economic consequences are palpable: the economy is deprived of three billion rubles' worth of output each year because of losses of work-time attributable to worker idleness and absenteeism.[26] Indeed, two leading Soviet specialists (one an economist, the other a jurist) have suggested that the economic costs associated with liquor are so great that they exceed the sum brought in by the state alcohol monopoly.[27]

6. The available evidence suggests that people who have been drinking are also particularly apt to be involved in automobile accidents. Between one-third and one-half of all traffic accidents are said to involve a driver who has overindulged, and one-fourth of the pedestrians who are injured are inebriated at the time of the mishap.[28] The most serious incidents are even more likely to involve alcohol: in the RSFSR, for example, 58% of the auto accidents resulting in fatalities involve one or more persons under the influence of alcohol.[29] In fact, the situation is probably a good deal worse than even these figures would suggest, since a significant (but never specified) number of those involved in motor vehicle accidents manifest the symptoms of a hangover associated with the previous night's drinking.[30]

7. The consumption of alcoholic beverages is also closely associated with crime and delinquency. Approximately half of all crimes are committed by individuals in a state of intoxication, and certain categories of criminal behavior are even more strongly correlated with drunkenness. Thus, 58% of those convicted for theft "systematically use alcohol," while the figure for burglars is even higher, 67%. Those who commit crimes against the person are especially likely to have been drinking: some 80–90% of all instances of murder, rape, assault, and "hooliganism" are committed by people who are under the influence.[31]

¶ The Official Response

Given the magnitude of the USSR's drinking problem, the nature and range of the harmful consequences it has brought, and the steady worsening of the situation with the passage of time, what can we say about the adequacy of the Party's response? Several conclusions seem inescapable.

1. The medical community and the Party apparatus are guided (or perhaps we might say "misguided") by old-fashioned, moralistic attitudes toward problem drinkers. As a rule, neither Party officials nor physicians distinguish between excessive drinking and alcoholism, considering the two phenomena to be essentially the same. "At the present time," a leading medical specialist pointed out several years ago, "subjectivism reigns" among doctors specializing in alcohol studies. Some do no more than distinguish between "those who drink a little" and "those who drink a lot." [32] Moreover, most commentators tend to express irritation with, rather than concern for, those with drinking problems. The Party line still classifies alcoholism as a "vestige of the past" and regards people who drink too much as "malicious" (*zlostnyye*). Medical opinion, too, tends to depict the alcoholic as a person of weak will, someone who behaves badly and merits condemnation. As two leading doctors have put it, alcoholics should first of all be condemned and only thereafter given sympathetic assistance.[33] Fifteen years ago, two Soviet physicians described alcoholics "not as sick people, but as people lacking in self-control, morally unstable [individuals]. . . ." [34] More recently, another doctor has suggested that to speak of someone as "suffering from alcoholism" is no different from saying that one "suffers" from hooliganism, sadism, or the propensity to steal. Overindulgence, he concluded, is the sign of a weak character; it is a harmful habit to be condemned by decent people. Other commentators almost invariably speak in a similar vein.[35]

Articles on alcoholism that appear in medical journals (except for those on very technical subjects) tend to convey the same sense of outrage, the same moralistic fervor, that characterizes discussion in the daily press. Indeed, Soviet physicians warn against "pushing the medical view of alcoholism to extremes," suggesting that if the alcoholic is permitted to think of himself as a sick person, he will thereby be relieved of any feeling of personal responsibility.[36]

Whether such statements express the view actually held by medical practitioners, or instead indicate that Soviet doctors are compliant, bending to the Party line, is not altogether clear. As Walter D. Connor has noted, "It would . . . be extremely difficult for the Soviet medical profession, whatever its collective private conviction, to fly in the face of the state with a definition of the alcoholic as sick when the state is engaged in an attempt to stigmatize him as a deviant deserving of condemnation." [37] Nonetheless, the available evidence, buttressed by private conversations with Soviet psychiatrists, suggests that the medical profession really is expressing its own view.

To be sure, such attitudes are not universal either among Soviet physicians or among Party officials. But it is significant to note that critics of the prevailing wisdom are generally "outsiders," that is, individuals who are neither apparatchiki nor members of the medical community. A Soviet writer, commenting in *Literaturnaya Rossiya,* has urged that alcoholism be "rehabilitated" as a disease, that is, recognized by the authorities as an illness. (If nothing else, he argues, such an approach will make it easier for those who have drinking problems to seek the aid of a doctor and then to profit from treatment.) Similarly a Soviet journalist has dismissed the official characterization of drunkenness (a "vestige of the past") as a prescription for passivity. This orientation, he points out, "weakens our ability to find the cause of this phenomenon and act upon it in a direct manner." [38] Perhaps most important. a few commentators have noted that statements linking people's drinking habits with will power tend to be highly unscientific or mere tautologies. As two doctors have said, "Many years of psychiatric experience indicate that a predilection toward alcohol can develop in practically any person—independent of personality characteristics." [39]

Such statements are highly unrepresentative of the Party's and medical doctors' attitudes. A tendency to overimbibe is far more likely to elicit demands for punishment than expressions of solicitude among physicians. In fact, the notion of moral and legal condemnation is intimately intertwined with the Soviet approach to treatment. The existing system for treating problem drinkers is basically punitive, providing for compulsory hospitalization and "labor reeducation." [40]

A decade ago, during one of the antialcoholism campaigns that periodically seize Soviet society, a psychiatrist wrote: "The usual psychiatric hospitals and dispensaries are not suitable for curing chronic alcoholism. It is necessary to create special medical establishments with special conditions and regime; and they must be set up not in the health system, but in the system for maintenance of public order." [41] Three years later, the authorities introduced the system of "labor-treatment institutions" (*lechebno-trudovyye profilaktorii*). Again, we do not know whether the Party was responding to pressure from below or whether plans for the new network had been laid before the article's publication. In any event, after a period of experimentation in several of the smaller republics, the RSFSR Supreme Soviet adopted a decree in 1967, stipulating that "habitual drunkards (alcoholics) who regularly misuse alcoholic beverages, shun voluntary treatment or continue to drink to excess after treatment and who violate labor discipline, public order and the rules of the socialist community, in spite of public or administrative measures taken against them, are subject to be sent to labor-treatment institutions for compulsory medical treatment and labor reeducation for a period of one to two years." [42]

For many years, the Party relied primarily on programs of voluntary hospitalization or outpatient therapy to treat people addicted to alcohol. Even now, problem drinkers who receive medical assistance generally become associated with an outpatient clinic, rather than receiving treatment in a hospital.[43] But both these sets of institutions are conventional medical facilities of the Ministry of Health. The new labor-treatment centers are something fundamentally different. Not medical units in the usual sense of the term, they are special facilities that apply "measures of an administrative-medical character" (some legal specialists actually claim that they were established more to prevent crime by "socially dangerous alcoholics" than to deal with a public health problem).[44] Chronic alcoholics who refuse to undergo treatment voluntarily, and who violate the law or "the rules of the socialist community," are sent to these centers to be simultaneously punished and cured. "Patients" at these institutions are not considered convicts, since they have not been convicted of a crime. They even receive remuneration for their work, usually several rubles per day. The centers themselves generally receive income from whatever industry they are attached to, and some even make a profit. This is probably one of the principal attractions of the new system: inpatient treatment in a conventional medical facility is very costly to the state, since it requires approximately 100–120 rubles per month to care for a hospitalized alcoholic.

But compulsory treatment programs are beset by numerous problems. The matter of motivation is probably the most significant of these: people compelled to take a cure are generally uncooperative, and treating them is therefore difficult. The available evidence indicates that people who are required to seek medical assistance are far less likely to profit from the experience than those who receive treatment voluntarily.[45]

A second difficulty stems from the shortage of facilities and trained personnel. In 1972, the deputy minister of the interior promised that additional centers would be constructed, but in February of 1975 it was acknowledged that there were still no labor-treatment centers in some republics.[46] Some of those sentenced to compulsory treatment, then, must be placed in other kinds of institutions. Some are sent to conventional hospitals or to alcoholism units within psychiatric hospitals, where they are placed together with patients who have voluntarily admitted themselves, with inevitable disruptions in the therapeutic regime; a variation on Gresham's Law seems to take place, as "bad" patients drive out "good" ones.[47] Others may find themselves sent to the medical section of a corrective-labor colony. There the medical treatment they will receive is thoroughly inadequate, and, of course, the experience is presumably harmful to the "patients" in other ways as well.[48]

Just how well the system of labor-treatment institutions works cannot be ascertained on the basis of published sources. Statements tend to be contradictory, and the results of some studies are acknowledged to be inflated by frustrated, ambitious, or unscrupulous personnel.[49] Certainly the system succeeds in one respect: it keeps a certain unspecified number of problem drinkers off the streets. But there is a good deal of disagreement on another question, whether or not it succeeds in its ostensible task, the transforming of "habitual drunkards" into sober people. Some sources claim that a majority of those who complete the treatment program at a profilaktoriya "are rid of this baneful weakness forever." [50] Other commentators are more critical. For example, one legal scholar, writing in 1973, declared that the effectiveness of these institutions "is still extremely low." Individuals sent to them do not stay long enough to be cured, he added, and most former patients begin to drink again shortly after they are released.[51]

While advocates of both points of view can be found, and it is not at all clear who is more nearly right, the critics' views are probably better grounded. Compulsory treatment is in general ineffective, and given the organizational and administrative problems encountered by the profilaktorii, one suspects that their contribution to the fight against alcoholism is marginal at best.

2. *Contemporary antialcohol propaganda does not provide much evidence of adaptability, responsiveness, or innovation among Party ideologists.* Very little of this propaganda appears sophisticated to a Western observer, and Soviet critics regularly express dismay at its pedestrian character and "formalism." As recently as May 1975, a *Pravda* editorial pointed out that official attention to problem drinkers is, "like any other short-lived campaign," sporadic.[52]

Moreover, propaganda messages seem, for several reasons, to have little effect on those who drink too much. First, alcoholics are simply not exposed to many of the Party's measures; they tend to withdraw from the official information network and are thus less apt than other citizens to encounter the Party's antialcohol messages.[53] This circumstance, familiar to Western students of mass communications, involves the familiar screening devices of selective exposure, selective perception, selective interpretation, and selective retention. Thus, problem drinkers try to avoid mass meetings organized to discuss alcoholism. As a Soviet police official has put it: "Formalism is multifaceted. One can still see meetings on the struggle against drunkenness in which people respected at an enterprise participate, while those who partake of the 'demon drink' never participate. The 'visitors' at a sobering-up station in the city [of Minsk] were once questioned. It turned out that the overwhelming majority of them had never attended meetings which discussed measures to combat drunkenness." [54]

A third reason for questioning the utility of the Party's antialcohol propaganda is its heavy-handedness. Typical slogans, such as Vodka is Poison, are said to be unpersuasive, since they ask too much of the audience. People obviously can see that spirits, unlike poisons, are sold openly in state stores.[55] Moreover, it is difficult for them to link their own pleasure in drinking with difficulties that may or may not materialize some time in the distant future. Similarly, learned arguments about the harmfulness of certain alcoholic beverages are apt to puzzle or amuse the typical reader—if he reads them at all. A farmer who has been brewing and consuming samogon for years is hardly going to be persuaded by a newspaper article on "The Poison of Home Brew" to give up the practice. An even more striking example of clumsy propaganda is an article in *Literaturnaya gazeta* alleging that "in certain countries, alcoholics are castrated." [56]

Perhaps the most powerful reason for challenging the Party's propaganda against alcohol abuse, however, is the failure of ideologists to understand the psychology of alcoholism. Official messages seek to persuade problem drinkers to renounce their "false consciousness," to recognize that they are hurting themselves and others. But logic and reason would appear to be singularly inappropriate here. People do not "choose" to become alcoholics; their drinking is an irrational response to conflicts, a symptom of more deeply rooted concerns, or possibly even the product of habitual unthinking behavior.

To be sure, there is some evidence that propaganda officials are becoming more resourceful in their approach to alcoholism. For example, the Party has begun to assign individual activists to work with one or more problem drinkers; the activist's task is to befriend the "afflicted" person, provide moral support, and try to induce him or her to seek medical counsel.[57] In addition, both medical and legal specialists have become increasingly aware of the desirability of adapting their messages to the distinctive needs of particular audiences. This response suggests a growing appreciation of the basic principles of opinion formation and change, that is, a more scientific approach to propaganda.

For example, a public health journal has recommended arranging lectures relating to alcoholism as follows:

> Why pregnant women and nursing mothers should not drink alcoholic beverages (for an audience of women; the lecturer should be a gynecologist)
>
> Even small quantities of alcohol are harmful to the growing organism (for parents or upper-grade schoolchildren; the lecturer should be a pediatrician or a school doctor)
>
> Alcohol and motor vehicle accidents (for transport workers; the lecturer should be a doctor employed in the first-aid service)
>
> Alcohol and labor productivity (for workers; the lecturer should be a trade union hygienist)
>
> Alcohol and physical culture are irreconcilable (directed at young people; the lecturer should be a physician specializing in physical culture)
>
> Why alcoholic beverages should not be consumed at health resorts (for those taking a cure at a resort or sanitarium)[58]

A comparable array of topics has been recommended for law-enforcement personnel who deliver lectures or lead discussions on the dangers of alcohol.[59]

Despite these indications of innovation among Party ideologists, certain basic questions remain. First, it is not clear whether rank-and-file propagandists are faithful to recommendations such as those outlined above. They may consider their own approaches superior to those presented in authoritative sources, or they may be unable to obtain enough information to speak intelligently on the narrow topics assigned to them. Second, no matter what the themes of their lectures are, they will not necessarily be presented in an interesting manner. The experience of Soviet propaganda directed against other "vestiges of the past" suggests that lectures tend to be highly stereotyped, usually boring the audience.[60] Finally, even the most scintillating lecturer may be unable to reach the problem drinker, since, as noted, such people are unlikely to expose themselves to messages they would find disagreeable. The lecturer, that is, will probably speak to an audience that does not need the message. But this situation in essence means that the Party is not really responding to the problem of alcoholism.

3. The authorities have not been responsive to the increasingly serious problem of motor vehicle accidents caused by intoxicated drivers and pedestrians. The problem of traffic accidents is obviously a matter of concern to Soviet authorities, and it is likely to grow more urgent as time goes by. The number of vehicles in use in the USSR has increased perceptibly in the past decade, and the number of automobiles in private hands has grown especially rapidly. More relevant for our purposes is the fact that the number of traffic accidents has increased faster than the number of vehicles, a circumstance that can be explained only in part by such factors as road defects, faulty road markings, and mechanical defects in the vehicles themselves.[61] A major component of the problem involves the excessive use of alcoholic beverages by drivers, pedestrians, and passengers. Indeed, regardless of the volume of liquor actually ingested, drinking often leads to accidents.

That drinking and driving do not mix is a truth no less valid in the USSR than in the United States. Everywhere, drivers who have been drinking are more likely than their sober counterparts to be involved in accidents. But Soviet data indicate that those with high blood alcohol concentrations are *significantly* more likely than those with low concentrations to be involved in accidents. According to one Soviet estimate, a blood alcohol concentration of 0.6 grams per liter (that is, 0.6 grams of pure alcohol per liter of blood) increases the probability of an accident by a factor of two. Someone with this level of alcohol in his or her blood, that is, is twice as likely as someone who is completely sober to be involved in an accident. What is more, any additional drinking makes it *much* more likely that there will be an accident: concentrations of 1 gram per liter increase the probability by a factor of seven, and a concentration of 1.5 grams per liter increases the probability by a factor of twenty-five.[62]

The various factors involved here are quite clear. Alcohol is a depressant on the central nervous system and causes a general slow-down in perceptions and behavior. Soviet studies suggest that the efficiency of a driver who has consumed as little as 20–30 grams of absolute alcohol (approximately the amount contained in a mug of beer) will be lowered by as much as 16–17% and that this loss will persist for upwards of twenty-four hours. Vision, hearing, and reaction time are impaired after any driver or pedestrian drinks, and judgment may be seriously marred. Someone who has been drinking is less alert, has a diminished capacity for depth perception, and is less likely to be cautious, prudent, and attentive to the environment. Significantly, alcohol consumption often interferes with the ability to distinguish between the colors red and green: objects of both hues appear grey to many intoxicated individuals, especially alcoholics. This inability to discriminate can and sometimes does lead to tragic consequences.[63]

The official response to the growing problem of accidents on the road has been to erect an increasingly comprehensive array of laws and regulations. Furthermore, the penalties available for dealing with violations of traffic safety have been made more severe. To date, however, police, prosecutors, and judges have generally not taken advantage of the harsh legal weapons at their disposal.

The basic law in use today is aimed at those who drive while intoxicated. Anyone found driving while under the influence of alcohol—whether or not an accident occurs—is subject to a fine of ten to fifteen rubles and a suspended driver's license for up to two years. (Some republics, in addition to levying a fine, allow arrest of the offender for a period of up to fifteen days.) A second offense, should it occur within five years of the first, carries another fine of ten to fifteen rubles, but this time the license may be taken away for two to five years. Anyone with a suspended license who drives a motor vehicle while under the influence of alcohol may be punished still more harshly. According to a 1972 law, such persons may be sentenced to deprivation of freedom for up to one year, to corrective labor for the same period, or to fines of up to a hundred rubles with the loss of the right to drive for up to five years.[64]

But these and other laws have not had a very significant impact on the drinking habits of Soviet drivers, passengers, or pedestrians. While more and more people who are inebriated cause damage or destruction on the road, Soviet law enforcement personnel continue to be indulgent toward them. In a very real sense, the police and the courts reflect the citizenry's permissive attitude toward alcohol abuse. There is, for example, a law prohibiting the use of roads by anyone who is inebriated. Violators, even if they are bicyclists or people walking along a road, are supposed to be punished by a ten ruble fine, but the fine is almost never imposed unless a serious accident occurs. Similarly, Soviet law prohibits persons in positions of authority from allowing access to a motor vehicle to someone who is under the influence of alcohol. But violators are liable to a fine of no more than thirty rubles, and even this very mild penalty is applied only on rare occasions. Finally, Soviet law makes it a punishable offense for an intoxicated individual to interfere in any way with traffic, even by falling, in a drunken stupor, under a car or truck. If there is loss of life or "other serious consequences," the offender may be sentenced to a prison term. But this law, like the others, is invoked very infrequently, usually when the negligence is particularly egregious and causes catastrophic loss, or when an antialcohol campaign is under way.[65]

Somewhat more vigorous efforts have been made to curb the drinking of professional drivers employed by local or regional transport administrations. An *Izvestia* editorial, for example, called upon "all trucking agencies" to "wage a resolute, uncompromising struggle against drivers who drink." It demanded that "the most drastic sanctions" be applied "against employees who slide behind the wheel in an inebriated condition," urging that "an atmosphere of intolerance be created around them." [66]

In some areas—though by no means everywhere—trucking officials have been responsive to such recommendations. They have arranged to have daily medical examinations given to all drivers before they are assigned to routes. A driver whose check-up reveals the presence of alcohol in the bloodstream will be prevented from working that day or will be assigned to less remunerative, less attractive tasks within the garage. Although such examinations are said to have led to a sharp reduction both in the number of drivers found with traces of alcohol in their blood and in the number of motor vehicle accidents involving particular fleets,[67] the system has thus far been introduced only in certain parts of the country. Moreover, drivers still can and do drink *after* setting out on a run.

4. Contemporary efforts to combat alcohol abuse include little that is new. Most of the measures adopted in the recent past, generally to the accompaniment of massive self-congratulatory propaganda, are actually variations on older themes. Since the very beginning of the Soviet regime, Party and state authorities have issued numerous decrees and introduced numerous legal, medical, economic, and educational measures aimed at curtailing excessive drinking. Few of the resolutions and laws promulgated—the adoption of compulsory treatment for alcoholics is a striking exception—differ significantly from those that came before. Interestingly enough, while most of the changes have been in the direction of increased harshness, some of the laws today are less strict than their predecessors.

For example, a 1918 statute declared those who produced samogon to be "enemies of the people" and mandated prison terms of not less than ten years for violators. A second decree, issued a year later, deprived moonshiners not only of their freedom but of their property as well. Additional laws, promulgated in 1948, 1960, 1961, and 1972, were designed mainly to bring the accomplices and customers of moonshiners within the reach of the law.[68] It should be pointed out, however, that the penalties for making home brew today are milder than they were in 1918, when the Party began to attack the problem. (The maximum penalty for a first offense is one year in prison; repeated offenses bring a prison term of two years. Manufacturing samogon "with a view to selling it" is punishable by a term of one to three years; repeated offenses can be punished by three to five years in prison and the confiscation of all property.) Moreover, the authorities do not move vigorously against violators. High-ranking officials continue to call attention to the "misguided liberalism" of police, prosecutors, and judges who are reluctant to arrest, bring to court, or punish moonshiners.[69] The result, as we have seen, is a flourishing samogon industry, with more than one billion liters brewed annually.

Other "new" measures, such as restrictions on the sale of alcoholic beverages, also turn out to be merely revised versions of traditional policies. Decrees of 1927 and 1929 established the basic approach—raising prices, reducing the number of retail outlets selling liquor, and encouraging the production of milder beverages (beer and wine) and nonalcoholic drinks. Laws and administrative regulations adopted in 1958 and 1972 added only marginally to the earlier restrictions, by curtailing the time period during which liquor may be sold, limiting the quantities that may be purchased in restaurants and cafes, and so on.[70] But one essential fact remains: the USSR has *not* reduced its production of alcoholic beverages. Indeed, as table 2 indicates, output of vodka, beer, and wine has risen substantially. This trend shows no sign of abating.

Table 2 USSR Production of Alcoholic Beverages (In Millions of Liters)

	Vodka[a]	Grape wine	Fruit wine	Champagne	Brandy	Beer
1957	1,402	552.0	154	23.8	11.04	1,965
58	1,454	618.2	169	26.0	12.25	1,991
59	1,373	669.0	185	28.0	13.64	2,319
60	1,373	776.8	203	29.9	15.02	2,498
61	1,457	847.5	222	32.1	17.80	2,667
62	1,620	1,008.0	243	35.3	20.57	2,818
63	1,689	1,185.5	265	37.4	23.38	2,807
64	1,765	1,270.8	291	40.7	25.23	2,830
65	1,883	1,338.8	318	44.7	26.83	3,169
66	1,972	1,585.9	328	48.6	29.01	3,437
67	2,115	1,800.0	350	53.7	30.13	3,613
68	2,247	1,912.5	410	58.3	32.54	3,830
69	2,361	2,402.1	453	63.4	35.14	3,970
70	2,384	2,680.0	505	68.6	37.95	4,190
71	2,308	2,800.0	562	74.5	40.99	4,410
72	2,178	2,930.0	626	80.8	44.30	4,690

[a] Including, in accordance with the Soviet classification, vodka-based beverages, such as various liqueurs, cordials, and flavored vodkas.

Source: Treml, "Production and Consumption of Alcoholic Beverages," p. 288.

In devising its approach to the problem of alcoholism, then, the Party has not been innovative. In fact, the key organizations active on "the antialcohol front" today seem to be pale reflections of one of the most active and vocal organizations of the 1920s and 1930s. During the earlier period, the All-Union Society for Combatting Alcoholism organized a wide array of propaganda measures and published a good deal of literature. It published the journal *Trezvost i kultura* (*Sobriety and Culture*), while its Ukrainian affiliate published *Za trezvost* (*For Sobriety*).[71]

In 1972, networks of "commissions for combatting alcoholism" were established. According to the statute formally creating them, the fundamental tasks of these commissions are "to coordinate the activities of state organs and social organizations directed at combatting drunkenness" and "to work out and implement measures to prevent and curb manifestations of drunkenness." [72] But the efforts of these commissions seem to be rather modest so far; they have received very little publicity in the Soviet press, do not publish either scientific or popular literature, and apparently have been assigned to play a low-key role. (Most ordinary citizens appear to be unaware of their existence.)

¶ Concluding Remarks

It is clear that the network of legal, medical, economic, and propaganda measures designed to curtail drinking has not been effective. Despite the presence of various incentives, punishments, and treatment and educational programs, Soviet citizens are drinking more and more. It has not proved possible to keep youngsters from contact with alcoholic beverages or to persuade adult drinkers to give up the practice.

One wonders, however, whether the Party really is interested in dealing successfully with the problem of alcohol abuse—not to mention the question whether it is able to do so. A leading Western specialist has concluded that the regime "appears both unable and unwilling to reduce the alcohol consumption of the population." [73] The reasons for official reluctance are powerful indeed. The tax on alcoholic beverages plays such an important role in the state budget that any significant change in the country's drinking habits would require major fiscal readjustments. Introduction of a "dry law" would have the same effect and could also be expected to stimulate the production of home brew.[74] In fact, the Party may well see liquor consumption, and even alcohol abuse, as a kind of safety valve. Drinking provides people with an outlet for their frustrations, one that does not, at least at first glance, endanger the stability of the Soviet system.

But drinking does involve considerable costs, and these may weigh more heavily on the authorities in the future. Before the Party decides on any major new approach to its citizens' drinking problems, however, it will have to be persuaded that the sale of alcoholic beverages is unprofitable. That is, it will have to conclude that the revenue generated by the liquor industry is more than offset by the social and economic costs of drinking. In other countries of Eastern Europe, critics of official policy are increasingly apt to base their views on the *economic* costs of alcohol abuse, rather than citing "mere humanistic considerations." They seek to convince their governments that increases in the production and sale of alcoholic beverages are "only seemingly and at best conditionally" in the national interest.[75] As we have seen, this notion has only begun to make its appearance in Soviet scholarly publications.

Even if the Party were to "declare war" on alcoholism, however, it might find no more success than Lyndon Johnson encountered when he "declared war" on poverty. There are problems afflicting almost all advanced industrial societies—such as crime, delinquency, pollution, inadequate housing and alcoholism—that may well be ineradicable. At the very least, the Soviet leaders have proved no more able than their capitalist counterparts to devise effective strategies to deal with these problems.

The CPSU's policy toward alcohol and alcohol abuse, for example, has not fundamentally changed the attitudes or behaviors of Soviet citizens. At the same time, the growth of the problem has not significantly altered the Party's understanding of and policy toward excessive drinking. The leadership's conception of the drinking problem remains as moralistic as it was at the time of the Revolution, and the system of incentives, threats, and sanctions it uses today does not differ materially from that available in Lenin's day.

To be sure, people who drink to excess do so for their own personal reasons. But political, social, and economic conditions can either promote or inhibit such practices. Government policy can stimulate people to drink or lead them into more fruitful activities. The leaders of the CPSU have not encouraged Soviet medical specialists to focus their attention on alcoholism, and doctors themselves complain that their colleagues are uninterested in and uninformed about the problem. Very little policy-relevant research is published; one critic has referred condescendingly to the "miserly quantity" that is available. Indeed, he goes on to talk about a specialist in this field who has been forced to ask his alcoholic patients to translate foreign sources for him, since official restrictions have denied the medical community access to the latest Western findings.[76]

The evidence, then, strongly suggests that the regime has not been effectively responsive to the serious and growing problem of alcohol abuse. Physicians, legal scholars, economists, and other specialists who study and deal with problem drinkers have shown very little imagination in devising new approaches. Officials responsible for implementing the existing laws and regulations have shown little interest in the task. The Party leadership seems to have acknowledged, however tacitly, that it is powerless in the face of this massive societal problem. It apparently has decided that the cost involved in waging a successful "war against alcoholism" would be prohibitive.

Specialists in Policymaking: Criminal Policy, 1938–1970

Peter H. Solomon, Jr.

A prominent feature of post-Stalin politics in the USSR has been the participation in policymaking of specialists (that is, scholars and professionals regarded as expert on policy subjects). Assessing this participation is of considerable importance, for its nature and impact bear upon the way Soviet leaders choose policies and the probable effectiveness of those policies. Western observers have disagreed about the role and significance of this participation, some regarding it as of inferior quality and low influence, others finding it serious and influential.[1] This essay reappraises Soviet specialist participation by examining the role of criminal law scholars in the formation of criminal policy from the late Stalin years through the first two post-Stalin decades.[2] The broad time span provides an opportunity to discover how the participation and influence of one set of specialists changed during the course of these years and thereby to gain some insight about the evolution of the Soviet policymaking process.

¶ Participation under Stalin

As a rule, Western scholarship has treated Soviet policymaking under Stalin as almost devoid of serious participation by specialists. Either there was little or no participation to be found, or participation was found to consist of attempts at modifying policies in the course of their implementation.[3] This conventional image requires some modification, at least for criminal law scholars and criminal policy. For, although these scholars took part in policymaking neither often nor regularly, they did have opportunities, which they used to introduce and to argue for policy proposals, most importantly during the preparation of a draft USSR criminal code, first in 1938–39 and then in 1946–47.[4] On each of these occasions leading criminal law scholars from Moscow prepared the original draft, and a larger number of scholars discussed and criticized the draft in the legal press and at special conferences. To illustrate the role of scholars in the preparation of a draft criminal code, let us turn to the 1938 code and in particular to one of the proposals introduced by scholars, namely, the removal of the principle of analogy from Soviet criminal law.

The preparation of a USSR criminal code was prompted by the 1936 Stalin Constitution, which shifted the jurisdiction of criminal law from the republican to the All-Union level. Stalin made this project more urgent when in 1937 he denounced the "nihilism" of the radical legal theorists Krylenko and Pashukanis, who had dominated the legal scene since 1930. It was in this setting that in August 1938 the USSR commissar of justice, N. M. Rychkov, instructed the All-Union Institute of Juridical Sciences attached to his commissariat to prepare a draft code. Within the institute a special drafting commission was formed. Headed by Professors A. A. Gertsenzon and B. S. Osherovich, the commission was composed of members of the institute's criminal law sector. These scholars were well qualified for the task, since they represented the best and most experienced of Soviet criminal law scholars.[5] As befitted their status and ability, they were given a broad mandate, which encouraged them not only to repackage existing law but also to scrutinize it and to propose changes where appropriate.[6]

The commission worked under great pressure of time, but by the end of October it completed the third version of the draft code, which it sent for comment to scholars and officials around the country. Some jurists also had a firsthand opportunity to offer criticism at a large national conference, held at the All-Union Institute in early 1939.[7] After the conference the commission reviewed the suggestions, made its final revisions, and in the spring of 1939 submitted to the commissar of justice the draft criminal code and explanatory materials. A meeting of high officials in the Commissariat of Justice reviewed the draft in May 1939 and decided to appoint a new commission to edit it; this second commission included seven representatives of the All-Union Institute of Juridical Sciences. Later that year a version of the draft code was published by the institute, and for the rest of 1939 and the first months of 1940 criminal law scholars discussed it on the pages of the law journals.[8] Early in 1940 the draft code was approved for promulgation and presented to the Supreme Soviet, but the outbreak of war intervened before the legislative organs had time to act.[9]

The most important change in Soviet criminal law proposed by the draft USSR criminal code of 1938 was the elimination of the principle of analogy, which empowered judges to convict persons deemed to have committed socially dangerous acts analogous to those cited in the criminal code. The political context of 1938 facilitated an attack on analogy, but as we shall see, scholars took the initiative in proposing that analogy be removed entirely from Soviet criminal law. Although a part of Soviet criminal law since 1922, analogy took on special significance when E. V. Pashukanis and N. V. Krylenko made it a cornerstone of their political program. Committed to the belief that crime would disappear, these jurists advocated the elimination of the code's list of specific crimes and punishments, so judges would expediently apply general principles of law to individual cases. The Krylenko draft code never became law, but in the early 1930s, when Pashukanis and Krylenko dominated Soviet jurisprudence, they encouraged the wide use of analogy by the courts. In 1937, after Stalin chose to stress the "stability of law" rather than its disappearance, Pashukanis and Krylenko fell from power, and A. Ya. Vyshinsky was entrusted with the task of restoring legal stability.[10]

The implications of this new line on the legal system for the principle of analogy were far from clear. At the Eighth Extraordinary Congress of Soviets in 1936, Stalin had decried "the situation whereby not any one organ but a whole series of organs legislates." [11] In his influential treatise of 1937, Vyshinsky said this did not mean that analogy should be removed from Soviet law. According to Vyshinsky, analogy was still needed because the code could not foresee all possible crimes, and its careful and limited use would enhance rather than harm the stability of Soviet law.[12] Despite Vyshinsky's interpretation, some of the scholars who were drafting the new criminal code sought the repudiation of analogy, and after considerable debate the commission decided by majority vote to adopt the proposal of its co-chairman, Professor A. A. Gertsenzon, and to omit analogy from the draft code.[13] Eventually, Gertsenzon gained the support of a strong patron, I. T. Golyakov, who like Vyshinsky held a triad of important positions in the legal world.[14] But Golyakov did not announce his support for Gertsenzon's proposal until the conference in January 1939.

At the conference, the question of analogy occupied the spotlight. In the opening plenary session before 350 scholars and officials, I. T. Golyakov rehearsed the arguments against analogy, including the claim that "the court often uses analogy to violate the law," a strong statement from the chairman of the USSR Supreme Court.[15] Then, in the session devoted to criminal law, Professor Gertsenzon presented a report on the draft criminal code, where he explained in detail the grounds for the elimination of analogy. Afterward, eleven scholars spoke to the question, five supporting and six opposing analogy's elimination from the code.[16] The argument focused both upon the practical need for analogy and upon the theoretical significance of the principle.

As of the late 1930s, Professor Gertsenzon claimed, analogy was not needed because the Soviet state was no longer young, weak, and infested with class enemies set on destroying it; little likelihood remained that new socially dangerous acts would abound in great number before the Praesidium of the Supreme Soviet had time to issue new edicts proscribing them. Gertsenzon also offered evidence that analogy was often abused, serving as the instrument for convicting offenders of crimes more serious than the ones they had committed. But neither of these arguments convinced analogy's supporters.

The theoretical discussion revolved upon the interpretation of the phrase "stability of law." Gertsenzon claimed that by allowing judges to legislate in individual cases, the principle of analogy placed judges above the law and thus undermined the law's stability.[17] One of analogy's proponents, V. M. Chikhvadze, answered that analogy was inconsistent not with the "stability of law" but only with the slogan of the classical school, the "bourgeois" principle *nullem crimen sine lege,* which, Chikhvadze claimed, had no place in Soviet law. In other words, Chikhvadze believed that, to achieve "stability of law," it was unnecessary to accept the "rule of law." But P. S. Romashkin challenged Chikhvadze's assumption and made explicit what Gertsenzon had only implied—that stability of law did require the adoption of "rule of law." [18] In insisting that the "rule of law" had a place in socialist legality, Romashkin was quietly supporting a change in the relationship of the Soviet legal system to the political order. For a legal system characterized by "rule of law" would have to be relatively autonomous from politics, so that politics determined the rules of its operation, through legislation, but not the details of that operation, through intervention in individual cases.

The effort by Gertsenzon and his colleagues to secure the removal of analogy from Soviet criminal law was almost successful. Despite some dissenting voices, the draft code excluding the principle was approved at the conference and sent to the Commissariat of Justice for examination by the revision commission.[19] During 1939 and 1940 the law journals contained four articles defending the retention of analogy, but the draft code as presented to the highest political organs still excluded the principle.[20] The draft code without analogy was approved for promulgation and sent to the Supreme Soviet in early 1940, but then the war intervened and stopped the momentum.[21] In the draft USSR criminal codes prepared after World War II (in 1946, 1949, and 1952), the principle of analogy continued to be excluded, but none of those draft codes was ever promulgated.[22]

The attempt by A. A. Gertsenzon and his colleagues to secure the removal of analogy illustrates how seriously criminal law scholars could participate in policymaking during the Stalin years. The scholars proposed analogy's removal against powerful opposition and conducted their campaign well enough to convince most leading law enforcement officials of its merit. The scholars were not trying to affect policies already chosen in the course of their implementation, nor were they seeking to mobilize support for decisions taken by politicians, or simply providing legal language for political decisions. In 1938–39, as in most other instances when criminal law scholars entered the policymaking process under Stalin and afterward, their function was to propose, advocate, and assess possible changes in the law.

The campaign against analogy represented only one example of criminal law scholars' participation under Stalin, but, although others might have been described (the cases of parole and laws on theft, for example), it would be misleading to suggest that the scholars' role in policymaking during these years was a large one. Some of the most important decisions taken in criminal policy under Stalin—such as the 1935 law on juvenile crime, the 1947 laws on theft, the 1947 law on rape, and the 1947 abolition of the death penalty—did not involve scholarly participation.[23] Moreover, even when criminal law scholars did take part, they rarely achieved the ends they sought. In short, the scope of their overall participation was narrow and their influence on criminal policy, small.

The narrow scope and low influence of criminal law scholars' participation under Stalin cannot be explained by the scholars' position in the legal community. Throughout the Stalin years, the status and prestige of legal scholars remained high and a number of scholars maintained good working relations with law enforcement officials, at both middle and high levels.[24] The problem was with the relationship of the leading law enforcement officials to the party leaders, especially to Stalin. Normally, in taking policy decisions, leaders consult their top administrators in the area. But Stalin frequently ignored his judicial chiefs, going ahead with such decisions as the abolition of capital punishment and increased penalties for rape without even informing them in advance. Before announcing the new laws on theft of 4 June 1947, Stalin reportedly asked the chairman of the Supreme Court, I. T. Golyakov, to prepare a draft statute increasing penalties for theft; Stalin then discarded Golyakov's carefully worded document and replaced it with his own crude one, which not only raised the penalties drastically but also eliminated most of the traditional distinctions between types of theft and categories of offenders.[25]

There is reason to suspect that law enforcement officials were not alone in this dilemma— that under Stalin other high government officials sometimes found their role in policymaking curtailed. Yet the situation of the law enforcement chiefs was somewhat special. The amassing of power by the NKVD USSR had occurred partly at their expense, as the NKVD had encroached, with Stalin's backing, upon the functions of each of the law enforcement agencies. The Commissariat of Justice had lost to the NKVD control of the administration of penal institutions for non-political offenders; the Supreme Court had lost jurisdiction over that large number of cases which sent citizens to prison after hearings of the NKVD's Special Board; and the Procuracy had lost its capacity to oversee the legality of the administration of justice and of government operations, because the NKVD could not tolerate investigations of its patently illegal activity.[26] The loss of much of the agency leaders' capacity to execute criminal policy seriously inhibited their scope for policy initiative[27] and may have reduced their importance in the eyes of party leaders.

The way Stalin treated the top law enforcement officials made it difficult for criminal law scholars to succeed in influencing criminal policy decisions. The officials represented the scholars' usual line of access to the center of decision, and now that line of access was obstructed. The scholars did not, as far as we can tell, have any special relationship with Stalin that could substitute for normal channels of communication. It was, therefore, unlikely that they would have much influence on criminal policy until after Stalin's death, when the relationship between the party leadership and the legal community improved.

¶ The Expansion of Participation

Even under Stalin the participation of Soviet criminal law scholars was more serious and of better quality than some Western observers thought characteristic of the first decade after his death. As we saw, when criminal law scholars did participate, they initiated and advocated policy proposals more often than they mobilized support for decisions already taken;[28] and in working on the draft criminal codes, they were concerned more with the substance than with the form of the legislation.[29] Nevertheless, their participation was limited in scope and had little influence upon the policies actually adopted. During the course of the 1950s, both the scope and the influence of Soviet criminal law scholars upon decisions in Soviet criminal policy changed. Especially during the second half of the 1950s, their participation underwent a marked expansion, and at the same time they began to exert influence in criminal policymaking.

Although the death of Stalin was a necessary precondition for these developments, the changes in the role of the criminal law scholars did not occur right away. Between 1953 and 1955 the scholars were active in the political process, but in much the same way as when Stalin was alive. What made their participation different in the years 1953–55 was not its extent but the setting in which it took place. Unlike the drafts of 1938 and 1946, the code on which the scholars worked in 1954 was part of a criminal justice reform already initiated by the political leadership.

In its first phase (1953–55), the post-Stalin criminal justice reform had two main components: the restoration of the functions of the law enforcement agencies; and the liberalization of criminal and criminal procedure law. The decision of the leadership to eliminate the Special Board of the NKVD and to curtail the power of the security police paved the way for the strengthening of the other law enforcement agencies, each of which regained functions it had lost under Stalin. Also in 1953 the leaders announced their intention of reducing the severity of the criminal law and ensuring the observance of procedural norms.[30] These changes were introduced partly through a series of edicts and administrative orders issued between 1953 and 1956 and partly through the preparation of new codes of criminal law and procedure. Although the edicts started the reform—by removing criminal responsibility for some offenses, by reintroducing parole, and by reducing the penalties for petty theft and for petty hooliganism—much of the liberalization and rationalization of the criminal law waited for the preparation of the new criminal and criminal procedure codes.

As far as one can tell, Soviet criminal law scholars played no role either in the fundamental decision of 1953 or in the series of edicts reducing the severity of the law. The scholars' opportunity to contribute to the reform came with their participation in the writing of the new codes, which contained a whole series of important changes in the law. Among other things, the draft USSR Criminal Code of 1955 was to reduce the maximum prison term from twenty-five to fifteen years, to raise the minimum age of criminal responsibility from twelve to fourteen, to remove from Soviet criminal law the principle of analogy, and to reintroduce distinctions between grades and types of theft.[31] Preparation of the first version of the new code was carried out by a group of Moscow scholars working under the supervision of the USSR Ministry of Justice and was dominated by members of that ministry's institute, the All-Union Institute of Juridical Sciences: A. A. Pyontkovsky, A. A. Gertsenzon, and B. S. Utevsky. In the course of this work, versions of the draft code were discussed at the All–Union Institute, at the Institute of State and Law, and also in the legal press. At the end of the year a version of the draft code was sent to law faculties and institutes outside Moscow for reactions.[32] By spring 1955 a final version had been completed, and the code was ready for promulgation.

Despite the not-insignificant role played by legal scholars in the preparation of this and other draft codes, some scholars were dissatisfied with the extent of their participation. Their view found forceful expression in an editorial in the leading law journal written two months before the Twentieth Congress of the CPSU. "In spite of a certain degree of activization," the editors opined, "the participation of legal scholars in the development of Soviet legislation and its codification is still completely insufficient and unsatisfactory." [33] Part of the problem lay with the scholars, who, according to the editorial, did not pursue readily enough the kinds of study most useful for the improvement of legislation. But the editorial's list of the potential contributions of scholars made it clear that greater participation did not depend upon them alone. Before many scholars would be willing to "boldly reveal the mistakes" in current legislation and practice and to "give their recommendations" for changes in the law, they had to be convinced that politicians and high officials were ready to hear those criticisms and recommendations.[34]

In advocating greater contributions from criminal law scholars to codification and law reform, the editors could hardly have anticipated how the actions of the new leader, N. S. Khrushchev, would in the succeeding months encourage the expansion of specialist participation in criminal policy as well as in other realms. When Khrushchev urged his countrymen at the Twentieth Party Congress to overcome the negative consequences of the "cult of personality," he called both for the restoration of "Leninist norms" in Party (and state) administration and for the further development of "democratic procedures" in Soviet political life.[35] Each of these tasks lent support to the idea of increased specialist participation in the policymaking process. The "Leninist norms" that Stalin had violated included "collegiality" and the consultation of knowledgeable persons on policy questions. The habit of acting on his own without taking into account the views of fellow politicians or of relevant administrators and specialists was among the clearest signs of Stalin's hubris. Another of Stalin's serious "faults," according to Khrushchev, was disregard of the democratic features of Soviet politics. To strengthen "Soviet democracy," Khrushchev called not only for the revival of the local Soviets but also for a heightened public role in the formation and implementation of policy. In this case, representatives of the public (*obshchestvennost*) meant both ordinary members of society and its more interested and expert members.[36]

The implications of Khrushchev's speech for the participation of legal scholars and officials in the preparation of legislation were clear enough. But to make sure that "Leninist norms" would be observed in the further development of the law reform, a few legal scholars took the trouble to remind their colleagues just how codes had been drafted in the early 1920s, while Lenin was alive.[37] Characteristic of those first codes were "the large role played by collegiality in [their] preparation and adoption" and "the attraction to discussions of the drafts of practical workers, including local ones, from many agencies and also of members of the public; also the wide discussion of questions of codification in the specialized and sometimes in the general press." This "Leninist" pattern of codification, one author concluded, "is useful to remember and to use creatively in carrying out the current codification work." [38]

The observance of "Leninist norms" in the codification of Soviet law might have had little meaning for the participation of criminal law scholars, because new criminal and criminal procedure codes had already been drafted, discussed, and readied for promulgation before Khrushchev spoke. In the summer of 1956 he changed the situation by shifting the jurisdiction of criminal law. By returning criminal law to the competence of the republics (another "Leninist" practice and a gesture to the minorities), Khrushchev provided a vehicle for reopening criminal law reform; for now the draft code had to be set aside and replaced with new draft legislation—a set of Fundamental Principles of Criminal Legislation of the USSR and Union Republics, and separate republican criminal codes.[39] It might have been possible to produce the required new statutes simply by dividing and editing the already prepared draft code. But after Khrushchev's revelations about the terror and his promise to restore fully "socialist legality," jurists were eager to consider changes in criminal and criminal procedure law that had not been incorporated into the 1955 draft code.

During the second phase of the post-Stalin criminal law reform (1956–59), criminal law scholars took part in the preparation of four new pieces of legislation. Here we shall trace the expansion of their participation through the preparation of one of these laws, the Fundamental Principles of Criminal Legislation of the USSR and the Union Republics. The first version of this draft legislation was written by a commission established in the fall of 1956 under the auspices of the Juridical Commission of the USSR Council of Ministers, which had come to perform some of the functions of the recently abolished USSR Ministry of Justice.[40] This drafting commission, headed by Professor B. S. Nikiforov, was composed mainly of scholars from a variety of Moscow institutes and faculties; the commission was larger and more representative of the Moscow community of criminal law scholars than was the commission that had prepared the 1955 draft code. Therefore, more Moscow scholars outside the commission were enabled to contribute to its preparation, since it was common practice for members of such commissions to consult colleagues at their places of work.[41] Scholars from Moscow and some from outside the capital as well had a chance to discuss the new legislation at this early stage through attendance at one of a series of conferences held during the preparation of the first version of the draft Fundamental Principles.[42] Although the draft criminal code had been the subject of one local conference, that conference had been convened at a later stage in the drafting process, after the first version of the draft legislation had been completed, discussed, and revised.

Normally, the second stage of legislative drafting, that of the discussion and revision of an already completed version, attracted broader participation of scholars than did the initial drafting stage; scholars from outside the capital city as well as some middle-level law enforcement officials entered the discussions. Although it was clear that these jurists would get a chance to comment also upon the draft Fundamental Principles of Criminal Legislation during the discussion stage, a number of them believed that the discussion of this legislation and of its companion, the Fundamental Principles of Criminal Procedure, ought to be broader and more open than the discussions of earlier draft legislation. Encouraged by the new political atmosphere and the legitimacy of "democratic" procedures, the legal journal *Sotsialisticheskaya zakonnost* lent its support to this view. Its advocacy of open discussion of the new legislation followed an incident at a conference in the spring of 1957. During a discussion of the Fundamental Principles of Criminal Procedure, the deputy chairman of the Juridical Commission of the USSR Council of Ministers, V. N. Sukhodrev, made an appearance but offended those present with his reluctance to discuss the content of the draft law as it then stood. Noting the bitter feelings among the conference participants, the journal editors berated Sukhodrev and faulted the Juridical Commission itself for failing to include a broader range of scholars and practitioners in the initial preparation of the draft Fundamental Principles of Criminal Procedure. The editors charged that the commission "had carried out its work virtually cut off from the community of legal scholars and the army of practical workers.[43]

The preparation of the draft Fundamental Principles of Criminal Legislation was not so elitist and closed as the preparation of the draft Fundamental Principles of Criminal Procedure apparently was.[44] Nevertheless, most of the work took place behind the scenes, and up to the spring of 1957 the legal journals published only a few articles relating to the draft legislation; therefore, the bulk of both practitioners and scholars outside the capital had little knowledge of the draft legislation. The editors' call for a "businesslike, comprehensive and objective" exchange of opinion "to be organized without the commotion of a parade" was applicable also to the Fundamental Principles of Criminal Legislation.[45]

Following this incident, the Juridical Commission made sure to circulate both draft laws among legal scholars and practitioners around the country. The many responses concerning the draft Fundamental Principles of Criminal Legislation were analyzed by the commission that had prepared it,[46] and before completing its work, the commission composed a list of the changes it was willing to support and passed the original draft, with the proposed revisions, to the Praesidium of the Supreme Soviet. After giving preliminary approval, the Praesidium transferred the draft law and materials to the Supreme Soviet's Commission on Legislative Suggestions for further consideration. As was customary, the commission appointed a subcommission of scholars and officials to edit the draft legislation;[47] in this case, the commission was also authorized to take the additional step of publishing the draft. The appearance in June 1958 of the draft legislation, both in the legal journals and in the journal of the local soviets, opened a second phase of discussion, this one in full public view.[48]

In the five months that followed, each issue of the legal journals carried a special section containing articles, notes, and letters about the draft legislation; more than fifty criminal law scholars from all over the USSR took part in this "public discussion." [49] In authorizing the publication of the draft and encouraging the public discussion, the political leaders had sought to demonstrate the "democratic" way in which this important legislation was being prepared.[50] Despite the fact that it was staged, the discussion represented a genuine exchange of opinion, as scholars responded seriously to the invitation to express their views publicly. For many of them the public discussion provided the chance to reiterate points they had already made in private communications to the drafting commission; for some, the public discussion provided a first chance to offer comment. Most authors followed the editors' instructions to send their comments directly to the Commission on Legislative Suggestions as well as to the journals, so that as a result most suggestions made in the public discussion were made directly available for consideration by the editorial subcommission.[51]

Both in the initial drafting and in the later discussions (private and public), the participation of criminal law scholars in the preparation of the Fundamental Principles of Criminal Legislation was broader than it had been in the preparation of the 1955 draft criminal code. Not only a greater number of scholars, but also a more diverse group, including persons of varying age and geographical location, took part. At the same time, with the larger number of persons involved, the participants tended to offer advice only on those issues for which they had particular expertise. As a result of this specialization, a typical issue would be debated by a discrete set of scholars, varying in number from two or three to five or six.

To determine the nature of the contributions made by criminal law scholars to criminal policymaking in the late 1950s and also the nature of their influence upon policies, it is necessary to consider particular decisions in which the scholars played a part. In the larger work upon which this essay is drawn, I examined in detail the participation of criminal law scholars in the decisions on two issues, the shape of the parole system and the development of special sanctions for recidivists.[52]

As reestablished in Soviet law in 1954, parole could be awarded to any adult prisoner after completion of two-thirds of his court sentence; but in practice corrective-labor officials relied upon an alternative system for releasing prisoners ahead of time, the so-called system of "early release through labor-day counts," according to which a prisoner's successful performance of one full day's work in labor camp gave him two day's credit toward his sentence. The corrective-labor officials preferred this system to parole, because it seemed to help them get the camp's economic plans fulfilled, but the abuses of the system recorded by criminologists made it obvious to most scholars that it ought to be replaced by parole.[53] The parole article in the draft Fundamental Principles of Criminal Legislation, drawn up by Professor B. S. Utevsky, reflected this belief by requiring *actual* serving of half or two-thirds of the term, rather than work credits, as the basis for parole; and this wording was later adopted into law. The parole article in the Fundamental Principles of Criminal Legislation as promulgated in 1958 also contained two important additions not included in the original draft: parole was extended to persons sentenced to corrective work; and the provision was added that parolees who committed new crimes of the same order of seriousness as their original offenses would be returned to confinement to complete their original terms. Both of these provisions had been suggested by various criminal law scholars who had commented upon the draft legislation, and according to members of the drafting commission, the new provisions were a consequence of these scholars' efforts.[54]

The idea of a special punishment for recidivists developed partly as a reaction to the leniency inherent in the criminal law reform and partly because some jurists believed that a special response to recidivists was part of a rational penal policy. Although the initial impetus for the legislation seems to have come from officials in the MVD, it was criminal law scholars there and elsewhere who did the analysis necessary to arrive at coherent proposals. Within the MVD's research section, a group of scholars studied more than one thousand repeat offenders before coming to the conclusion that they were of many types, some far more dangerous than others, and that as a result no single response was appropriate. Prof. B. S. Nikiforov, the head of the commission drafting the Fundamental Principles of Criminal Legislation, agreed with this point and, like his MVD colleagues, tried to elaborate on a set of criteria for distinguishing dangerous recidivists from others. The criteria listed in the RSFSR criminal code were the result of the combined efforts of Nikiforov and of A. M. Yakovlev, a member of the original MVD research team who had become a specialist on recidivism. Likewise, the special sanctions to which "specially dangerous recidivists" became liable—extended sentence, denial of parole rights, confinement in a prison regime—were suggested by scholars.[55]

The examples of the parole and recidivism decisions suggest that, just as in the Stalin period, the participation of Soviet criminal law scholars in the late 1950s related to the substance of decisions, took place before decisions were made, and served as a vehicle for the advocacy of policy proposals. But, in contrast to the 1930s and 1940s, in the 1950s the scholars did sometimes affect the policies chosen and incorporated in legislation.

Soviet criminal law scholars' success in influencing policy decisions in the late 1950s reflected a change in the way Communist Party leaders treated the criminal policy community as a whole, scholars and officials alike. Both had taken part in criminal policymaking in the Stalinist years, but their participation had not been regular and was frequently ignored. Stalin more than once encouraged leading scholars and top officials to devote a great deal of time to the preparation of a new criminal code, and then discarded their work. In contrast, the Khrushchev leadership did not act so presumptuously, and when it solicited the help of scholars and officials in preparing major legislation, it took their work seriously. While reserving for itself the right of final decision, the Khrushchev leadership used that right judiciously. In the cases of the Fundamental Principles of Criminal Legislation and the Fundamental Principles of Criminal Procedure, it did not overrule consensus among officials and scholars but took on the task of making real choices only where that community was seriously divided.[56] Had the political leaders done otherwise they could hardly be said to have effected the promised normalization in the legal realm.

¶ The Institutionalization of Participation

The participation of Soviet criminal law scholars in policy formation during the late 1950s was associated with two conditions that were no longer present in the sixties and seventies: a connection with the preparation of new codes or their equivalent and the presence of a major law reform. By 1961 the new legislation had been promulgated, the criminal justice reform was over, and criminal policymaking returned to its usual pattern of small and incremental change. Some narrowing in the numbers and diversity of scholars participating in policy discussions was inevitable, when the decisions taken were fewer in number and limited to specific topics, but this development was insignificant compared to another change in criminal law scholars' policymaking role during the 1960s. For the first time, the participation of Soviet criminal law scholars in policymaking became *institutionalized*; that is, participation became a regular part of the work of the criminal law scholar and a normal rather than an unusual feature of criminal policymaking. By the middle and later years of the decade not just major legislation but most ordinary decisions in criminal policy that resulted in legislative changes involved the participation of scholars, and scholars had come to regard activities relating to new legislation as an everyday part of their jobs.

Without some of the political developments of the 1950s that facilitated the expansion of the role of scholars, such as the restoration of the law enforcement agencies as executors and contributors to criminal policy and the more open atmosphere associated with de-Stalinization, it would be impossible to imagine the institutionalization of that role in the 1960s. The immediate responsibility for this process, however, belonged to two developments related directly to criminal law scholarship itself. One was the growing utility of criminal law scholarship, because of the revival of criminological research; the other was the strengthening of ties between the scholars and law enforcement officials through the establishment in 1963 of new agency research institutes in criminal law.

During the late fifties and early sixties the empirical study of crime and its causes, crime prevention, and the administration of justice revived, under the guidance of senior criminal law scholars who had themselves done criminological research until 1935, when it was banned in the USSR.[57] The revival of criminological study within criminal law strengthened the expertise of the criminal law scholars who had already started to participate in criminal policymaking in the late 1950s and made their opinions more attractive to officials and politicians seeking help wth policy problems. The politicians insisted on a practical orientation for

Soviet criminology as a condition for approving the field's revival. At first, they seemed to regard criminology's practical contribution as relating mainly to particular districts, "where the results of study can be used to correctly determine the means which state and social agencies will exploit in the struggle against law violations." [58] But in 1963 the leaders acknowledged the significance of crime study for current policy issues. Following its acceptance of a practically oriented sociology the year before, the leadership announced its desire that legal research, especially of an empirical variety, be used more widely in policymaking. A *Kommunist* editorial proclaimed that *"it must be arranged that the conclusions and generalizations of scholars not lie on the shelves of archives but find the shortest route to those agencies that are occupied with lawmaking and with the application of legal norms* (italics in original).[59] According to the editorial, the law scholars' participation in the preparation of the Fundamental Principles of Criminal Legislation and the RSFSR Criminal Code had been exemplary, but the infrequency of such engagements was to be deplored. Moreover, *Kommunist* continued, it was especially important that those legal scholars who performed sociological research, such as criminologists, participate fully in lawmaking: "Concrete sociological research must play an important role not only in evaluating existing legal norms but also in the process of preparing new legal acts. . . . In issuing a law, the legislator is obliged to predict its social effect, in what direction it will guide the given social process. . . . To answer these questions we are calling upon the legal research institutes and upon legal science." [60]

The acceptance of criminological research and the definition of its practical role as contributing to the development of criminal policy had obvious consequences for the participation of criminal law scholars. If criminology was being accepted and supported because of its utility, and the practitioners of criminology were being urged to direct their conclusions to the "agencies occupied with lawmaking and the application of legal norms," then the scholars who performed the research would surely be drawn into the policymaking process. They would be required at the minimum to supply written memoranda whenever their research related to policy questions and they might well be asked to give oral advice and to make suggestions for policy changes as well. The reference to the scholars' role in the making of the 1958 Fundamental Principles of Criminal Legislation suggested that it was just these kinds of activities that were being encouraged.

Soviet political leaders did not merely acknowledge their appreciation of the utility of criminological and criminal law scholarship for criminal policymaking; they also took steps to ensure that the results of research and the conclusions of researchers would actually be utilized. The same *Kommunist* article announced a fundamental reorganization of the legal research institutes in Moscow, which produced three new institutes, each attached to one or more government agencies. Of these, the most important for criminology and criminal law scholarship was the All-Union Institute for the Study and Prevention of Crime, attached to the USSR Procuracy and the USSR Supreme Court and commonly referred to as "the Procuracy Institute." [61] This institute drew together most of the scholars from other institutes who were studying criminal law and procedure, criminology, and police science; in the course of the decade that followed it nearly doubled in size, with the addition of new, young criminologists and criminal law scholars.

The performance of duties set out in the Procuracy Institute's charter attached to two law enforcement agencies enabled Soviet criminal law scholars to develop a close and structured relationship with the leading officials in those agencies. The relationship was of no small importance, for the chiefs of the Procuracy and the Supreme Court, along with those of the MVD, had become fully responsible for administrative decisionmaking in criminal policy, and they were taking an increasingly large role in the initiation of changes in criminal policy as well. Let us consider briefly the two sides of this relationship—the involvement of the agencies' leading officials in the work of the institute and the scholars' involvement in the work of the agencies.

The performance of duties set out in the Procuracy Institute's charter assured that the heads of the Procuracy and of the Supreme Court would become familiar with the institute's work. These officials appointed the institute's directors and senior staff; served on its Academic Council, which regularly discussed the institute's research work; and approved the annual plans and research reports of the institute. The officials also learned about specific research projects when they received special reports from the scholars (*spravki, dokladnye zapiski*).[62] Scholars who completed research projects usually prepared these internal reports for interested government officials before writing articles for publication in open or closed format.[63] Sometimes these reports were sent to the Praesidium of the Supreme Soviet, as well as to government agencies.

The criminal law scholars' involvement in the work of the USSR Procuracy and the USSR Supreme Court was multi-faceted. The scholars helped agency operations by developing and explaining to officials new and improved methods of work and by taking part in educational programs "to raise the qualifications" of officials. In addition, the scholars advised the heads of the agencies in administrative decisionmaking by serving on the Supreme Court's advisory council and on the Procuracy's methodological council. As members of these councils, scholars discussed many of the Court's edicts and the Procuracy's orders in their earliest stages of preparation, and they were often called upon to prepare suggestions for or drafts of future sublegislation. Individual members of the councils were sometimes invited to attend sessions of Supreme Court plenums and of the Collegium of the USSR Procuracy.

The considerable involvement of institute scholars in the work of the law enforcement agencies and of the agency chiefs in the work of the institute encouraged the institutionalization of the scholars' role in criminal policymaking. First, through their contributions to the operations of the agencies, scholars took part both in administrative decisionmaking and in the implementation of policy decisions. Secondly, the scholars' relationship with the leading law enforcement officials gave the former a regular line of communication with key actors in the formulation of criminal policy. Whether through research reports or through private conversations, the scholars could easily pass on to the officials their suggestions regarding policy or practice, and in point of fact, they often make their views known. For their part, the law enforcement officials could easily turn to the scholars for solutions to policy problems, and the evidence suggests that they did so frequently; according to the institute's reckoning, its scholars took part in the preparation of more than twenty different legislative projects in 1965 and the same number again in 1966. Apparently, the officials did not hesitate to turn to the institute at a moment's notice; for the scholars complained repeatedly in their annual reports about "supplementary assignments" that prevented them from completing all their planned projects.[64]

The regular participation of scholars in criminal policymaking gained support in the late 1960s and early 1970s from a further source. Just as the Khrushchevian emphasis upon "democratization" had helped the expansion of criminal law scholars' participation in the late 1950s, so in the middle and late 1960s a new political theme—that of "rationalization"—reinforced the institutionalization of their role. During the course of the sixties, "rational" or "scientific" approaches in administration and policymaking became fashionable among officials, scholars, and politicians alike.

The new concern with rationalization did not leave the leading law enforcement officials untouched. A number of them, such as the minister of internal affairs, N. A. Shchelokov, came to attach great importance to rationalizing the administration of justice and to rendering policy decisions "scientifically." [65] For these ends the scholars at the Procuracy Institute and elsewhere were indispensable. In the late sixties and early seventies some studied how the principles of "scientific organization of labor" could help law enforcement agencies, while others did research on methods of ensuring that the proposals of scholars were actually introduced into law enforcement practice.[66] Still others conducted the research that served as the basis for a series of policy decisions relating to parole provisions, regulations governing the stigma "specially dangerous recidivist," and the forms of conditional judgment. As a result, the political meaning attached to the participation of criminal law scholars in criminal policymaking changed during the sixties. Whereas in 1958 their participation had been touted as a "democratic feature of Soviet political process," in 1969 it was lauded for giving legislation "a scientific basis." [67]

To explain how and why the participation of Soviet criminal law scholars in the formation of Soviet criminal policy became institutionalized in the 1960s is not to document that institutionalization or to say what the participation was like; and the question still remains what impact upon the development of criminal policy resulted from the regular participation of scholars. The longer study on which this essay is based pays considerable attention to these questions. It recounts in detail three sets of decisions taken in Soviet criminal policy during the middle and late sixties (those relating to alcoholism and hooliganism, juvenile delinquency, and parole and recidivism) and analyzes on the basis of these case studies the scope, quality, and influence of the scholars.[68] Here I simply list some of the results of this analysis.

1. During the middle and late 1960s the participation of Soviet criminal law scholars (or criminologists) in policymaking was of broad scope. They took part in nearly every decision related to their expertise, and participation in policymaking represented a substantial segment of their own professional work. In the course of policymaking activity they communicated most often with the heads of the law enforcement agencies, who themselves constituted the formal initiators of each of these policy changes.

2. The scholars' participation during the middle and late sixties was of good quality. Nearly all of it took place before decisions had been rendered on the issues at hand; and whether it took place behind the scenes or in public forums, it served the functions of communicating and advocating policy proposals, not of publicizing or executing regime decisions. The more important forms of participation were those occurring behind the scenes, such as discussions with law enforcement leaders, the writing of research memoranda, and serving on drafting and editorial commissions.

3. The criminologists exerted considerable influence on at least some of the decisions in which they participated. The outcomes of all the deci-

sions except one coincided in whole or in part with their policy preferences, and the nature of their participation was probably responsible for this situation.

4. The criminologists had a moderate impact on the development of Soviet criminal policy as a whole in the middle and late 1960s. Their participation was directly related to a new trend in policy, an emphasis on crime prevention; but that trend represented only a part of criminal policy as a whole, which during the sixties was characterized by a mixed or eclectic approach. The trend toward more emphasis on crime prevention was produced both by the direct influence of scholars through participation in decisionmaking and by indirect means, such as the influence of scholars on the attitudes and thinking of officials.

In sum, the nature and influence of Soviet criminal law scholars' participation did not deteriorate during the 1960s but instead became a component part of criminal policymaking. As a regular feature of that process, it maintained the standards of scope and quality it had achieved during the late fifties, and throughout the sixties it remained at least as influential on decisionmaking as it had been during the reform. The overall impact of criminal law scholars on criminal policy probably grew during the sixties because of the cumulative effect of their ideas about crime prevention.

¶ The Meaning of Participation

This essay has traced the development of the participation of Soviet criminal law scholars in Soviet criminal policymaking through three stages—from existence (under Stalin) to expansion (in the 1950s) to institutionalization (in the 1960s). For Western scholarship, each stage of this story has implications for the role of specialists in Soviet policymaking. Briefly, the presence of some participation by criminal law scholars during the Stalin years suggests the need for revision of the conventional image of Stalinist policymaking as almost totally excluding specialists; in some fields of policy, specialists did play a part some of the time. The expansion of criminal law scholars' participation and the actual influence of that participation on decisions in the middle and late 1950s calls in question the view of some Western observers that specialist participation during the late fifties was in general of inferior quality and little impact. The institutionalization of the scholars' role during the sixties suggests that, even though the Brezhnev regime has been more conservative than the Khrushchev in its approach to the substance of policy in some areas, it has accepted the pattern of policy formation that emerged during the Khrushchev years, in which both leading officials and academic specialists resumed important roles. As far as the policymaking *process* is concerned, there is no basis for suggesting, as some Western writers have done, that the Brezhnev years have represented a backsliding toward Stalinist political practices.[69]

Just as important as their implications for Western scholarship on specialist participation in the USSR is the meaning of our findings for the evolution of Soviet policymaking itself. Two questions seem of particular interest: how the "arrival" of Soviet criminal law scholars as regular participants affected the roles of other actors in criminal policymaking, such as law enforcement officials, Party leaders, and staff from the Central Committee apparat; and what effect the regular involvement of scholars had upon the nature of Soviet criminal policy and upon the way it was made.

The increased participation and influence of criminal law scholars took nothing away from the role of leading law enforcement officials in the formation of Soviet criminal policy; if anything it enhanced the role of those officials. Since the scholars communicated their analyses and proposals mainly to them rather than to the Party leaders or to the Central Committee staff, the law enforcement chiefs entered the highest circles of criminal policy discussion particularly well-informed—about law enforcement practice from their subordinates and about the analysis of crime trends and policy problems from the scholars. Not surprisingly, the heads of the Procuracy, Supreme Court, and MVD turn out to have been the initiators of most policy changes that took place in this period.[70]

The development of the role in criminal policymaking of criminal law scholars did not itself change the role of Party leaders in that process, but it helped to make viable a change in the Party leadership's approach toward criminal policy formation. In the middle 1950s the Party leaders began looking to the leading scholars and officials for ideas and proposals about the shape of criminal justice and using the results of discussions within the legal community as the basis for decisions about the law reform. During the 1960s the Party leaders continued to rely upon responsible officials to detect problems in law enforcement and to find effective solutions. By helping to equip law enforcement officials to perform these functions, criminal law scholars facilitated the Party leaders' new reliance upon their law enforcement chiefs.

The establishment of the role in criminal policymaking of both law enforcement officials and criminal law scholars did not mean that the Party leadership had lost either its final decisionmaking authority or its large share of the resources constituting power in the Soviet system. What had changed was the way the leaders chose to use their authority and their power. Although capable of inventing their own solutions to policy problems, they preferred to consider the options that professional crime-fighters could supply. And, although capable of overruling, ignoring, or misusing the advice that came either from officials or from specialists or both, the Party leaders did not do so most of the time. The Brezhnev leadership did not replicate the arbitrary and willful behavior of the despot Stalin or of the unpredictable Khrushchev, but tended instead to listen regularly to the arguments issuing from the legal community, to respond favorably to some of them, and to arbitrate disputes when need be.[71] There was nothing incompatible about a growing influence on policy on the part of law enforcement officials and criminal law scholars and a maintenance of authority and power by the Party leadership. If anything, a responsive approach to the views of officials and scholars seemed likely to enhance that authority.

The role of the officials of the Central Committee's Department of Administrative Organs may well have been affected by the changes in the roles of the other actors in Soviet criminal policymaking (especially of the Party leadership itself), but we know too little about their role prior to the 1960s to tell. In that decade, however, department officials appear to have played a relatively small part in the reaching of most decisions in Soviet criminal policy. Although this minor role might have resulted, at least in part, from the absence of the head of the department from 1964 to 1968, my informants in the USSR stress that lack of involvement by Central Committee staff was normal; in preceding years the Central Committee staff below the level of department head rarely engaged in decisions relating to criminal policy.[72] Within the department the small sector that supervised the legal system concentrated upon monitoring cadre selection and upon collecting information for the Party leadership; junior in age and in status to the law enforcement chiefs, most of the apparatchiki were not in a position to do more.[73] As working acquaintances of the law enforcement leaders, the Party officials often learned about policy proposals and discussions, and they occasionally prepared summary analyses of issues in criminal policy for the Party leaders.[74] But Party officials did not perform the bulk of the staff work associated with the development of new criminal legislation, which was done instead by officials at the agencies responsible for initiating the changes, scholars appointed by those agencies, or both.[75] Thus, while the Central Committee staff were not excluded from criminal policymaking, their role was not the dominant one assigned to them by some Western authors but, in comparison with leading law enforcement officials, a secondary one.[76] Consistent with this picture of the role of Central Committee Department of Administrative Organs is the nature of criminal law scholars' contacts with it. Evidently, when scholars were called "to the TsK" it was more often to help with supervisory work, such as proverka, than to consult on policy matters.[77]

The other question raised here about the consequences of the institutionalization of criminal law scholars' role concerns its effects upon Soviet criminal policy. The regular inclusion in criminal policymaking of scholars, especially of those doing criminological research, was likely to lead to some improvement both in the substance of policy and in how it was made. While not capable of "solving" the crime problem, the scholars did represent the best available expertise on crime prevention and control. As of the middle 1960s, a good number of them were doing sound empirical research on the dynamics and causes of crime and on the effectiveness of the criminal law and of its enforcement.[78]

During the sixties and early seventies a number of improvements were recorded both in the content of Soviet criminal policy and in its making. Crime prevention became established as an operative as well as a rhetorical goal in Soviet criminal policy, when a series of decisions expanded the use of prophylactic and educational measures. The result was that Soviet criminal policy became more balanced, including among its central components not only repression and stigmatization but also prevention.[79] Just as important, a sizable number of decisions taken in criminal policy in this period reflected a new empirical approach to decisionmaking. Available statistical material and sociological studies were collected and brought to bear on the policy issues under scrutiny; and knowledge, however uncertain, about the effectiveness of various measures started to replace penal philosophies as the basis for decisions. These advances in the content of criminal policy and in the way it was formulated were direct consequences of the regular role played by criminal law scholars and criminologists. However, one should add that they could not have occurred without the cooperation of law enforcement officials. During the 1960s the scholars succeeded in influencing the attitudes toward criminal policymaking of some leading officials and gained their help both in the attempt to improve features of policy and to make its execution more effective.

The improvements in criminal policy and policymaking that resulted from the role of scholars constituted not innovations but smaller changes, which had more impact upon the effectiveness of criminal policy than upon its basic premises. These were the kinds of changes to be expected; for major changes have occurred infrequently in the history of criminal policies in most industrial nations, and those that have occurred have emerged gradually over an extended period of time.[80] Moreover, most of the Soviet criminal policy community, especially its most important members, have not seemed to favor major changes in criminal policy.[81] Many of them were struggling to make the system work better, especially by improving the performance of law enforcement officials on the local level, which often failed to meet the standards expected by scholars and officials in the center. There was also much concern among some scholars to expand the utilization of criminological studies to make Soviet penal institutions more effective. But few of these persons were thoroughly critical of the existing system or desired, let alone sought, major changes.[82]

In considering the role of criminal law scholars in Soviet criminal policymaking, the question naturally arises whether the changes in that role have been typical of the development of specialist participation in other policy realms, and if so, whether or not those changes have had the same broader significance.

One cannot assume that, because by the middle 1960s criminal law scholars came to participate widely and regularly in criminal policymaking, other specialists did the same in other policy realms. It has been argued convincingly that both in the USA and in the USSR the scope and structure of the policymaking process at any one time varies from one policy realm to another.[83] There are, however, a number of reasons for believing that in the USSR of the late sixties and early seventies specialists did participate widely not only in criminal policymaking but also in the formation of policies in a variety of areas. First, some of the factors that had stimulated the expansion and institutionalization of criminal law scholars' participation were bound to have affected specialists in other policy realms. For example, the demand of the Soviet leadership for expert advice, which stimulated the revival of criminology and its use in policymaking, seemed to affect the participation of the representatives of other brands of social research. Likewise, the rationalization movement of the 1960s, which reinforced the institutionalization of the scholars' role in policymaking, seemed to encourage the participation of specialists in a variety of policy realms. Secondly, recent studies of specialist participation in the USSR have shown that by the late sixties specialists had come to play a regular part in aspects of foreign policymaking[84] and in the formation of policies for science and technology;[85] it also appears that specialists played a similar role in economic and in educational policymaking.[86] This is not to say that the timing and pattern of the development of specialist participation in these various policy realms were the same as those of criminal law scholars; in fact, the evidence suggests that in some instances serious participation by scholars began not in the 1950s but in the 1960s.[87] One way or another, however, by the early 1970s, in each of these policy areas, the relevant specialists were taking part in policymaking in a regular and serious way.

One can only speculate whether the establishment of regular participation by specialists has had the same meaning in other policy realms as in criminal law. First, the roles of other actors in the policymaking process need not have conformed to the pattern obtaining in criminal policymaking. It is likely that, in any policy realm where the role of specialists was institutionalized, ministerial leaders were also major participants, but Party leaders and Central Committee apparatchiki may have played a more active part in some of them. There were a few policy realms of such importance as to occupy Party leaders on a daily basis (for example, aspects of foreign and of economic policies); in other policy areas, like the criminal, the leaders probably left the diagnosis of problems and proposal of remedies largely in the hands of officials and specialists.[88] It is also likely that Central Committee apparatchiki were important participants in the formation of some policies, especially in areas where they administered the policies (such as relations with Communist parties in other countries or the activities of political officers in the armed forces); but there were probably other realms, where, as in criminal policy, the apparatchiki took second place to the ministerial leaders.

Secondly, the effects of regular specialist participation upon the substance of policies may also have varied from one realm of policy to another. Although in most areas the presence of specialists was likely to lead to little more than small improvements in the direction of better-planned and more effective policy choices, it was possible that specialists facilitated the introduction of policy innovations in some of them. Western experience suggests that politicians tend to adopt innovations in policies when two conditions are present: a special need for major change, created either by a crisis or by the cumulative effects of social change; and consensus among most members of the policy community that an innovative response is required.[89] If in the USSR of the seventies or eighties a critical situation were to develop in some area of policy, specialists might well play a key part in mobilizing opinion within the policy community to meet the challenge. And if they succeeded, chances are that the Party leaders would respond favorably as well.

Notes

¶ Introduction

1. Roger E. Kanet, "The Behavioral Revolution and Communist Studies," in *The Behavioral Revolution in Communist Studies,* ed. Rogert E. Kanet (New York: Free Press, 1971), p. 2. My review of the book is in *Problems of Communism* 22 (January–February 1973): 81–85.
2. David Easton, *The Political System* (New York: Knopf, 1953), p. 137.
3. Roy C. Macridis, "Comparative Politics and the Study of Government: The Search for Focus," *Comparative Politics* 1 (October 1968): 88. Reprinted in Roy C. Macridis and Bernard E. Brown, *Comparative Politics: Notes and Readings,* 4th ed. (Homewood, Ill.: Dorsey Press, 1972), pp. 94–95. Macridis here is suggesting a more political focus for research in political science, in order to overcome what he sees as a tendency for the "gradual disappearance of the political" in the discipline.
4. A provocative case for political continuity in the midst of modernization is made by George Fischer in his *Soviet System and Modern Society* (New York: Atherton, 1968). See also his distinction between "industrialism" and politics in "Monism as a Model of Modern Society," in *Opinion-Making Elites in Yugoslavia,* ed. A. H. Barton et al. (New York: Praeger, 1973), pp. 282–94.
5. James Q. Wilson, *Political Organizations* (New York: Basic Books, 1973), pp. 195, 30.
6. See Amitai Etzioni, "Two Approaches to Organizational Analysis," in *The Sociology of Organization,* ed. Oscar Grusky and George A. Miller (New York: Free Press, 1970), pp. 218–21.
7. Wilson, *Political Organizations,* p. 31.
8. Leon Trotsky, *The Revolution Betrayed,* trans. Max Eastman (Garden City, N.Y.: Doubleday, Doran, 1937).
9. Alexander J. Groth, "CPSU Decision-Making, Modernization, and Evolution of the USSR" (unpublished paper, 1974).
10. Amitai Etzioni, *A Comparative Analysis of Complex Organizations* (Glencoe, Ill.: Free Press, 1961), pp. 13–15.
11. Wilson, *Political Organizations,* p. 49.
12. Leslie Lipson, *The Democratic Civilization* (New York: Oxford University Press, 1964), p. 124. It is still early to know whether the post-Franco democracy in Spain will survive.
13. For a summarization see William Taubman, "The Change to Change in Communist Systems: Modernization, Postmodernization, and Soviet Politics," in

Soviet Politics and Society in the 1970's, ed. Henry W. Morton and Rudolf T. Tökes (New York: Free Press, 1974), pp. 369–91.
14. Dankwart A. Rustow, "Communism and Change," in *Change in Communist Systems,* ed. Chalmers A. Johnson (Stanford: Stanford University Press, 1970), p. 350.
15. See Tibor Szamuely's untitled article in *Survey,* no. 72 (Summer 1969), pp. 51–69.
16. Karl W. Deutsch, "Communication Models and Decision Systems," in *Contemporary Political Analysis,* ed. James C. Charlesworth (New York: Free Press, 1967), p. 294.
17. Curt Tausky, *Work Organizations: Major Theoretical Perspectives* (Itasca, Ill.: Peacock Publishers, 1970), p. 97.
18. Peter M. Blau, *The Dynamics of Bureaucracy,* rev. ed. (Chicago: University of Chicago Press, 1963), p. 300.
19. Michel Crozier, *The Bureaucratic Phenomenon* (Chicago: University of Chicago Press, 1964), pp. 195–96.
20. Ibid., pp. 197–98.
21. Wilbert E. Moore, *Social Change* (Englewood Cliffs, N.J.: Prentice-Hall, 1963), pp. 57–58.
22. Gerald E. Caiden, *Administrative Reform* (Chicago: Aldine, 1969), p. 48. Caiden is concerned with "man-made, deliberate, planned" change or "reform," not change that is situation-based and "ceaseless, universal" (see ibid., pp. 65, 68).
23. T. H. Rigby, *Communist Party Membership in the U.S.S.R.: 1917–1967* (Princeton: Princeton University Press, 1968), p. 525.
24. Moore, *Social Change,* p. 61.
25. For an earlier use of this concept, see Ernest J. Simmons, ed., *Continuity and Change in Russian and Soviet Thought* (Cambridge, Mass.: Harvard University Press, 1955).

¶ On the Adaptability of Soviet Welfare-State Authoritarianism

1. See Chalmers Johnson, ed., *Change in Communist Systems* (Stanford: Stanford University Press, 1970); T. H. Rigby, "Politics in the Mono-Organizational Society," in *Authoritarian Politics in Communist Europe,* ed. Andrew C. Janos (Berkeley: Institute of International Studies, 1976); Jerry F. Hough, "The Soviet System: Petrifaction or Pluralism?" *Problems of Communism* (March–April 1972); Jane P. Shapiro and Peter J. Potichnyj, eds., *Change and Adaptation in Soviet and East European Politics* (New York: Praeger, 1976).
2. This term was coined in Richard Lowenthal, "The Soviet Union in the Post-Revolutionary Era: An Overview," in *Soviet Politics since Khrushchev,* ed. Alexander Dallin and Thomas B. Larson (Englewood Cliffs, N.J.: Prentice-Hall, 1968).
3. What follows immediately is based upon George Breslauer, *Five Images of the Soviet Future: A Critical Review and Synthesis* (Berkeley: Institute of International Studies, 1978), in which I identify, label, and criticize the assumptions underlying five images (and five additional sub-images) of the Soviet future that are implicit in Western and Soviet-dissident literature.

4. Samuel Huntington finds the notion of "corporate pluralism" useful for capturing the character of Soviet pluralism since Khrushchev. See his "Social and Institutional Dynamics of One-Party Systems," in *Authoritarian Politics in Modern Society,* ed. Samuel P. Huntington and Clement H. Moore (New York: Basic Books, 1970), p. 35.
5. I first identified and interpreted the differences between these two phases in "Leadership and Adaptation in the Soviet Union since Stalin" (paper presented at conference on CPSU Adaptation, New Hampshire, May 1974).
6. For a fuller discussion of my interpretation of the Khrushchev administration, see George Breslauer, "Khrushchev Reconsidered," *Problems of Communism* (September–October 1976).
7. See T. H. Rigby, "The Soviet Leadership: Towards a Self-Stabilizing Oligarchy?" *Soviet Studies* (October 1970).
8. This term was first coined by Reinhard Bendix to characterize Stalinism in East Germany. See his *Work and Authority in Industry* (New York: Harper and Row, 1956), p. 390.
9. Leonid Brezhnev, *Leninskim kursom,* 5 vols. (Moscow: Politizdat, 1970–76), 1: 347; italics added.
10. *Pravda,* 28 September 1965; italics added.
11. See, for example, D. Chesnokov, in *Pravda,* 27 February 1967; the same author's "Leninskoe uchenie o sotsialisticheskom gosudarstve," *Kommunist* 13 (1967); and V. Chkhikvadze and N. Farberov, "V. I. Lenin o sotsialisticheskom gosudarstve," *Kommunist* 5 (1967). That this redefinition reflected official policy was confirmed by the Central Committee Theses on the Fiftieth Anniversary of the Revolution (*Pravda,* 25 June 1967) and by Brezhnev's major anniversary day address (*Pravda,* 7 November 1967).
12. Chkhikvadze and Farberov, "V. I. Lenin o sotsialisticheskom gosudarstve," p. 20. For an almost identical formulation by official sociologists, see *Klassy, sotsialnye sloi i gruppy v SSSR,* ed. Ts. A. Stepanyan and V. S. Semenov (Moscow: Nauka, 1968), pp. 16–17.
13. In *Current Soviet Policies IV: The Documentary Record of the 22nd Party Congress of the Communist Party of the Soviet Union,* ed. Charlotte Saikowski and Leo Gruliow (New York: Columbia University Press, 1962), p. 24.
14. Ellen Mickiewicz, "Policy Applications of Public Opinion Research in the USSR," in *Public Opinion Quarterly* (Winter 1972–73), pp. 566–78; Linda Lubrano Greenberg, "Soviet Science Policy and the Scientific Establishment," *Survey* (Autumn 1971).
15. *Pravda* (editorial), 17 October 1964.
16. Brezhnev, *Leninskim kursom,* 1: 215.
17. Contrast the discussion of "scientific decisionmaking" in Jerry Hough, "The Brezhnev Era: The Man and the System," *Problems of Communism* (March–April 1976), pp. 15–16.
18. *Pravda,* 23 April 1965 (Lenin Anniversary speech).
19. Generalized statements in this essay about the content of "leaders' speeches" are based upon a reading of all published speeches by Brezhnev and Kosygin between October 1964 and November 1977, as well as annual Lenin Day (22 April) and Revolution anniversary (7 November) speeches by representatives of the leadership. These are statements of trends that may not be reflected in *every* speech, however.
20. Brezhnev, *Leninskim kursom,* 1: 20.

21. *Pravda,* 10 December 1964 (*Current Digest of the Soviet Press,* vol. 26, no. 49, p. 8).
22. *Pravda,* 23 April 1965.
23. *XXIII syezd Kommunisticheskoi Partii Sovetskogo Soyuza: stenografichesky otchyot,* 2 vols. (Moscow: Politizdat, 1966), 2: 46.
24. See *Pravda,* 27 March 1965, for Brezhnev's report on the new agricultural program.
25. Brezhnev, *Leninskim kursom,* 1: 74.
26. Alec Nove, "Economic Policy and Economic Trends," in Dallin and Larson, *Soviet Politics since Khrushchev,* p. 90. See also Kosygin's report on the reforms in *Pravda,* 28 September 1965.
27. Brezhnev, *Leninskim kursom,* 1: 69.
28. Mervyn Matthews, *Class and Society in Soviet Russia* (London: Allen Lane, 1972), pp. 270 ff.
29. Gregory Grossman, "The Solidary Society: A Philosophical Issue in Communist Economic Reforms," in *Essays in Socialism and Planning in Honor of Carl Landauer,* ed. Gregory Grossman (Englewood Cliffs, N.J.: Prentice-Hall, 1970), p. 186.
30. See Murray Yanowitch and Wesley A. Fisher, eds., *Social Stratification and Mobility in the USSR* (White Plains, N.Y.: International Arts and Sciences Press, 1973), pp. xviii–xxiv; Stepanyan and Semenov, *Klassy, sotsialnye sloi i gruppy v SSSR,* passim; and G. Glezerman, "Sotsialnaya struktura sotsialisticheskogo obshchestva," *Kommunist* 13 (1968): 28–39.
31. The first elaboration by an official spokesman for dominant forces within the regime came before Khrushchev's overthrow; see G. Glezerman in *Kommunist* 12 (1964): 44–54.
32. For a summary of this literature, see A. S. Aizikovich, "Vazhnaya sotsiologicheskaya problema," *Voprosy filosofii* 11 (1965).
33. The concept "system-management" was first introduced into Soviet studies in Alfred Meyer's highly original "Authority in Communist Political Systems," in *Political Leadership in Industrialized Societies,* ed. Lewis J. Edinger (New York: John Wiley and Sons, 1967), pp. 84–107.
34. Aryeh L. Unger, "Politinformator or Agitator: A Decision Blocked," in *Problems of Communism* (September–October 1970). See also the very perceptive discussion of the "relational" role of the Party in post-Stalinist Marxist-Leninist states, with specific reference to the agitator's role, in Kenneth T. Jowitt, "Inclusion and Mobilization in European Leninist Regimes," *World Politics* (October 1975). Jowitt has also initiated important ways of reconceptualizing the role of the aktiv in these systems; see his "State, National, and Civic Development in European Leninist Regimes" (paper presented at the annual meeting of the American Political Science Association, San Francisco, September 1975).
35. I outline the difference in policies between a "right-wing" and a "left-wing" version of welfare-state authoritarianism, though without gainsaying the possibility of numerous centrist versions, in *Five Images of the Soviet Future.*
36. See, for example, Lowenthal, "The Soviet Union in the Post-Revolutionary Era," p. 7.
37. On the hopes for further development of the political contract, see A. I. Lepeshkin, in *Sovetskoye gosudarstvo i pravo* (February 1965), pp. 5–15; F. Burlatsky in *Pravda,* 10 January 1965; and A. Rumyantsev in ibid., 21 February 1965 and 9 September 1965. On hopes for further development of

the social contract as well, see Alexander Yanov, *Detente after Brezhnev* (Berkeley: Institute of International Studies, 1977). It does not follow that all these individuals, and others, were in agreement on the desirability of *both* the political and social contract of elitist liberalism.

38. On residential agitation, see Aryeh Unger, *The Totalitarian Party* (London: Cambridge University Press, 1974), pp. 128 ff.
39. The useful concept "role expansion" was first suggested to characterize this phenomenon by Grey Hodnett in "Succession Contingencies in the Soviet Union," *Problems of Communism* (March–April, 1975).
40. Jowitt ("Inclusion and Mobilization") has introduced into Soviet studies the important Weberian distinction between "status" and "role."
41. See, for example, Brezhnev's speech at the Twenty-fifth Party Congress (*Pravda,* 25 February 1976).
42. For the new Soviet Constitution as amended and ratified, see *Pravda,* 8 October 1977.
43. For discussion of the changing administrative and political relationships between Party and state, see T. H. Rigby and R. F. Miller, *Political and Administrative Aspects of the Scientific and Technical Revolution in the USSR,* Occasional Paper no. 11, Department of Political Science, Research School of Social Sciences, Australian National University (Canberra, 1976).
44. L. I. Brezhnev, *Ob osnovnykh voprosakh ekonomicheskoi politiki KPSS na sovremennom etape,* 2 vols. (Moscow, 1975), 1: 417–18. The speech was not published in the Soviet Union at the time, but Brezhnev repeated the same message, verbatim, in a publicized speech of 13 April 1970 (*Pravda,* 14 April 1970).
45. Rigby and Miller, *Political and Administrative Aspects,* p. 82.
46. For the initial change in line, see Brezhnev in *Pravda,* 14 April 1970 (echoing the message of the December 1969 plenum), and Kosygin in *XXIV s"ezd.,* 2: 14.
47. Typical was the formulation of Brezhnev at the Twenty-fifth Party Congress, "Trust and respect for people must be combined with strict demandingness for the assigned task . . ." (*Pravda,* 25 February 1976).
48. See "On the Work of the Party Committee of the USSR Academy of Sciences' P. N. Lebedev Physics Institute," *Partynaya zhizn* 21 (1970): 8–10.
49. This generalization applies to Brezhnev's speeches; Kosygin has largely avoided use of the terminology of scientific decisionmaking. For an additional revealing comparison, contrast Demichev in *Pravda* (23 April 1965) with Demichev in *Kommunist* 15 (1971).
50. *Pravda,* 7 November 1970.
51. See Yanov, *Detente after Brezhnev.*
52. Matthews, *Class and Society,* p. 305.
53. For a very useful discussion of the distinction between "institutionalization" and "constitutionalization," see Grey Hodnett, "The Pattern of Leadership Politics" (mimeo, September 1977).
54. See George Breslauer, "The Twenty-fifth Party Congress: Domestic Issues," in *The Twenty-fifth Congress of the CPSU,* ed. Alexander Dallin (Stanford: Hoover Institution Press, 1977).
55. *Pravda,* 5 June 1977, 18 June 1977.
56. See Erik Hoffmann, "The 'Scientific Management' of Soviet Society," in *Problems of Communism* (May–June 1977).
57. *XXIV s"ezd,* 1: 93; *Pravda,* 25 February 1976.

58. *XXIV s"ezd,* 1: 126.
59. These figures are tentative but the best guess available; see Rigby and Miller, *Political and Administrative Aspects,* p. 31.
60. See Gregory Grossman, "The Brezhnev Era: An Economy at Middle Age," *Problems of Communism* (March–April 1976).
61. This doctrinal change was emphasized by Leonid Brezhnev in a speech in Kiev on July 26, 1973 (*Leninskim kursom,* 4: 218).
62. *Sovetskaia Belorussiya,* 1 June 1971, as noted in Werner Hahn, *The Politics of Soviet Agriculture, 1960–1970* (Baltimore: Johns Hopkins University Press, 1972), p. 250.
63. *XXIV s"ezd,* 1: 69–71, 75–77.
64. Quoted in Hedrick Smith, *The Russians* (New York: Quadrangle, 1976), p. 215.
65. See the discussion in Stanley Rothman and George Breslauer, *Soviet Politics and Society* (St. Paul: West Publishing Company, 1978), pp. 120–21.
66. *XXIV s"ezd,* 2: 216. Moreover, in 1977 Brezhnev claimed "that some 10,000 administrators are fired annually because of citizens' complaints" (*San Francisco Sunday Examiner and Chronicle,* 29 January 1978). This figure is surely inflated, and we are told nothing about the fates of those managers (are they demoted, or simply moved to a comparable job elsewhere?). But even if the claim is only partially true, the phenomenon would be consistent with the strategy just described.
67. For a Kremlinological analysis that attempts to avoid this problem, see Breslauer, "The Twenty-fifth Party Congress."
68. An additional, important finding is the high correlation between changes in articulated policy premises and changes in actual policy. Once we control for the symbolic rhetoric, a careful analysis of Soviet leaders' speeches can be an important guide to their political behavior.
69. See Yanov, *Detente after Brezhnev.*
70. Breslauer, *Five Images of the Soviet Future.* A fuller evaluation of the viability of different political coalitions would require investigation of foreign policy premises as well, and of their compatibility with clusters of domestic policy premises.
71. Thus, in "The Twenty-fifth Party Congress" I have documented Brezhnev's apparent dissatisfaction with the pace of administrative reform.

¶ Economic Reform and Adaptation of the CPSU

1. Thomas Schelling, *The Strategy of Conflict* (Cambridge, Mass.: Harvard University Press, 1970).
2. This idea finds its most thorough development in J. Zielinski's *Economic Reforms in Polish Industry* (New York: Oxford University Press, 1973).
3. For a more detailed treatment, see Robert W. Campbell, "Price, Rent and Decisionmaking: The Economic Reform in Soviet Oil and Gas Production," in *Jahrbuch der Wirtschaft Osteuropas,* ed. H. W. Göttinger, vol. 2 (München: Günter Olzog Verlag, 1971), pp. 291–314.
4. Cambridge, Mass.: Harvard University Press, 1966.
5. Another statement of the same thesis is found in Stephen White's "Contradic-

tion and Change in State Socialism," *Soviet Studies* (January 1974), which aims to shoot down some recent writing by sociologists alleging a cleavage between the Party and the managerial-technical elite.

6. Talcott Parsons, "Some Reflections on the Place of Force in Social Processes," in *Internal War,* ed. Harry Eckstein (New York: Free Press, 1964). Reprinted in Marvin E. Olsen, *Power in Societies* (New York: Macmillan, 1970).
7. These changes are described in Alice C. Gorlin, "The Soviet Economic Associations," *Soviet Studies* (January 1974); and Leon Smolinski, "Toward a Socialist Corporation: Soviet Industrial Reorganization of 1973," *Survey* (Winter 1974).
8. "The Industrial Combine and the Post-Command Economy" (paper presented at the Western Economic Association meetings in August 1973).
9. See, especially, Jerry F. Hough, *The Soviet Prefects: The Local Party Organs in Industrial Decisionmaking* (Cambridge, Mass.: Harvard University Press, 1969).

¶ Administrative Rationality, Political Change, and the Role of the Party

1. See the general discussions by Vincent Ostrom, *The Intellectual Crisis in American Public Administration,* rev. ed. (University: University of Alabama Press, 1974); and Dwight Waldo, ed., *Public Administration in a Time of Turbulence* (Scranton: Chandler Publishing Co., 1971).
2. Harold J. Leavitt, William R. Dill, and Henry B. Eyring, *The Organizational World* (New York: Harcourt Brace Jovanovich, 1973), p. 6.
3. See James D. Thompson, *Organizations in Action* (New York: McGraw-Hill Book Company, 1967); John W. Hunt, *The Restless Organization* (Sydney and New York: John Wiley and Sons, 1972); William G. Scott and Terence R. Mitchell, *Organization Theory: A Structural and Behavioral Analysis,* rev. ed. (Georgetown, Ontario: Richard D. Irwin and The Dorsey Press, 1972); and Tom Burns and G. M. Stalker, *The Management of Innovation* (London: Tavistock, 1961).
4. Joseph Litterer, "Conflict in Organization: A Reexamination," in *Modern Management: Issues and Ideas,* ed. David R. Hampton (Belmont, Calif.: Dickenson Publishing Co., 1969), p. 121. See also the discussions on this theme by Peter Blau and W. Richard Scott, *Formal Organizations* (San Francisco: Chandler Publishing Co., 1962); James G. March and Herbert A. Simon, *Organizations* (New York: John Wiley and Sons, 1959); John M. Thomas and Warren G. Bennis, eds., *Management of Change and Conflict: Selected Readings* (Baltimore, Md.: Penguin Books, 1972); Kenneth Boulding, *Conflict Management and Organization* (Ann Arbor: Foundation for Research on Human Behavior, 1961); and Chris Argyris, *Integrating the Individual and the Organization* (New York: John Wiley and Sons, 1964).
5. William G. Scott, "Organization Theory: An Overview and an Appraisal," in *Management, Organizations, and Human Resources: Selected Readings,* ed. Herbert G. Hicks (New York: McGraw-Hill Book Co., 1972); James D. Thompson, *Organizations in Action,* and S. Terreberry, "The Evolution of Organization Environments," in Thomas and Bennis, *Management of Change and Conflict.*
6. See Craig C. Lundberg, "An Open Letter on Organization Theory," in *Con-*

temporary Management: Issues and Viewpoints, ed. Joseph W. McGuire (Englewood Cliffs, N.J.: Prentice-Hall, 1974), pp. 145–46. See also the discussion by Paul R. Lawrence and Jay W. Lorsch in *Organization and Environment: Managing Differentiation and Integration* (Boston: Harvard Business School, Division of Research, 1967).

7. Philip Selznick, "Leadership in Administration," in Hampton, *Modern Management,* p. 334.
8. Ostrom, *The Intellectual Crisis in American Public Administration,* p. 47. Weber's interpreters may be the source of the stereotype, or the external constraints may have increased since Weber's time.
9. See Thompson, *Organizations in Action,* pp. 3–24, 66–82. For further discussion, see Victor A. Thompson, *Bureaucracy and Innovation* (University: University of Alabama Press, 1969); and Stanley H. Udy, Jr., "Administrative Rationality, Social Setting, and Organizational Development," in *New Perspectives in Organization Research,* ed. W. W. Cooper, H. J. Leavitt, and M. W. Shelly II (New York: John Wiley and Sons, 1964), pp. 173–92.
10. Thompson, *Organizations in Action,* p. 67.
11. Thomas and Bennis, *Management of Change and Conflict,* p. 98. See also D. Katz and R. Kahn, *The Social Psychology of Organizations* (New York: John Wiley and Sons, 1966).
12. Selznick, "Leadership in Administration," pp. 335–36. See also Fred E. Fiedler, *A Theory of Leadership Effectiveness* (New York: McGraw-Hill Book Co., 1967); and Howard M. Carlisle, *Situational Management: A Contingency Approach to Leadership* (New York: AMACOM, 1973).
13. Thomas and Bennis, *Management of Change and Conflict,* pp. 20–21; Victor H. Vroom, "The Search for a Theory of Leadership," in McGuire, *Contemporary Management,* pp. 396–99.
14. See the excellent discussion by Scott and Mitchell in *Organization Theory,* pp. 189–91, 221–22.
15. McGuire, *Contemporary Management,* p. 146. See the collection of essays on organizational design and development in James D. Thompson, ed., *Approaches to Organizational Design* (Pittsburgh: University of Pittsburgh Press, 1966).
16. For general discussion of the matrix organization, see John F. Mee, "Matrix Organization," in Hampton, *Modern Management;* Thompson, *Bureaucracy and Innovation,* pp. 25–26; and Chris Argyris, "Today's Problems with Tomorrow's Organizations," in Thomas and Bennis, *Management of Change and Conflict,* pp. 180–208.
17. For background information, see Paul Cocks, "The Rationalization of Party Control," in *Change in Communist Systems,* ed. Chalmers Johnson (Stanford: Stanford University Press, 1970), esp. pp. 154–61.
18. For a very perceptive discussion of the weaknesses of the monocratic paradigm in the Soviet setting, see Merle Fainsod, "Bureaucracy and Modernization: The Russian and Soviet Case," in *Bureaucracy and Political Development,* ed. Joseph LaPalombara (Princeton: Princeton University Press, 1963), pp. 233–67.
19. Cocks, "The Rationalization of Party Control," pp. 157–61.
20. These ideas were set down by Rozmirovich in her *Metodologiya i praktika tekhniki upravleniya* (Moscow: 1926) and her *Osnovnye direktivy po ratsionalizatsii uchrezhdenii* (Moscow: 1930). The quotations given here appeared in the following articles attacking her views: M. Gribanov, "Teoreticheskie korni metoda proizvodstvennoi traktovki v ratsionalizatsii upravleniya," *Organizatsiya upravleniya,* no. 1 (1932), pp. 27–41; T. I. Tolokonikov, "Kak byt s meto-

dom proizvodstvennoi traktovki uchrezhdenii?" ibid., no. 1 (1931), pp. 10–14; V. Isakov, "K voprosu o polozhenii na teoreticheskom fronte v oblastnoi ratsionalizatsii sotsialisticheskogo proizvodstva i upravleniya," ibid., no. 1 (1932), pp. 3–26.

21. "Uluchshenie gosapparata," *Voprosy sovetskogo khozyaistva i upravleniya,* no. 1 (January 1924), p. 84.
22. Quoted in G. Vorobeichuk and V. Zhurov, "K voprosam ratsionalizatsii gosapparata," *Organizatsiya upravleniya,* no. 3 (1932), p. 61. The system of "responsible supervisors," earlier advocated by the CCC-RKI, was by then questioned even in principle (ibid., no. 1 [1932], p. 22). Even Nefedov's article that had criticized this system a year before also came under attack for not having tied the issue properly to the principle of one-man management. See Vorobeichuk and Zhurov, "K voprosam ratsionalizatsii gosapparata," pp. 59–70.
23. Moshe Lewin, "The Disappearance of Planning in the Plan," *Slavic Review* 32, no. 2 (June 1973): 285. For a more detailed discussion, see also his excellent study *Political Undercurrents in Soviet Economic Debates: From Bukharin to the Modern Reformers* (Princeton: Princeton University Press, 1974).
24. M. Gribanov, "Teoreticheskie korni metoda proizvodstvennoi traktovki v ratsionalizatsii upravleniya"; V. Isakov, "K voprosu o polozhenii na teoreticheskom fronte v oblastnoi ratsionalizatsii sotsialisticheskogo proizvodstva i upravleniya," *Organizatsiia upravleniia,* no. 1 (1932), pp. 3–26. For an excellent discussion of Bukharin's views, see Stephen F. Cohen, *Bukharin and the Bolshevik Revolution: A Political Biography, 1888–1938* (New York: Alfred A. Knopf, 1973).
25. Lewin, *Political Undercurrents in Soviet Economic Debates,* p. 110.
26. *XVI S"ezd VKP(b)*, p. 122; Stalin, *Works* 11: 71.
27. Alec Nove, *Economic Rationality and Soviet Politics, or Was Stalin Really Necessary?* (New York: Praeger, 1964), p. 27.
28. Lewin, *Political Undercurrents in Soviet Economic Debates,* p. 101; see also ibid., pp. 105, 109–10, and Lewin's "Disappearance of Planning in the Plan."
29. "Effectiveness" refers to a system's capacity to attain certain results, without regard to the effort and resources used in attaining those results. "Efficiency," on the contrary, refers to the relationship between the magnitude of the results and the magnitude of the effort and resources invested.
30. Supervisory control is usually minimal in a system that patterns control into structure. See the discussion on this theme by William R. Rosengren in "Structure, Policy, and Style: Strategies of Organizational Control," *Administrative Science Quarterly* (June 1967), pp. 140–59.
31. See the article by Sanford Lieberman in this volume.
32. Lewin, "The Disappearance of Planning in the Plan," p. 277.
33. Jerry F. Hough, *The Soviet Prefects: The Local Party Organs in Industrial Decision-making* (Cambridge, Mass.: Harvard University Press, 1969), p. 289.
34. T. H. Rigby, "Politics in the Mono-Organizational Society" (unpublished paper, summer 1973).
35. Alfred G. Meyer, *The Soviet Political System: An Interpretation* (New York: Random House, 1965), pp. 207–8.
36. Ibid., p. 209.
37. Reinhard Bendix, "Bureaucracy and the Problem of Power," in *Reader in Bureaucracy,* ed. Robert Merton et al. (Glencoe, Ill.: Free Press, 1952), p. 129.
38. *Pravda,* 4 November 1971.
39. Gregory Grossman, "Soviet Growth: Routine, Inertia, and Pressure," *Ameri-*

can Economic Review 50, no. 2 (May 1960): 62–72; Herbert S. Levine, "Pressure and Planning in the Soviet Economy," in *Industrialization in Two Systems: Essays in Honor of Alexander Gerschenkron,* ed. Henry Rosovsky (New York: Wiley, 1966), pp. 266–86. The role of the Party in overcoming organizational exclusiveness and inertia is also stressed by Alec Nove in his "Soviet Political Organization and Development," in *Politics and Change in Developing Countries: Studies in the Theory and Practice of Development,* ed. Colin Leys (London: Cambridge University Press, 1969), pp. 65–84.

40. Meyer, *The Soviet Political System,* p. 222.
41. Joseph Stalin, *Mastering Bolshevism* (New York: 1945), p. 5.
42. Donald Ralph Kingdom, *Matrix Organization: Managing Information Technologies* (London: Tavistock, 1973), pp. xi–xii; David I. Cleland and William R. King, *Systems Analysis and Project Management* (New York: McGraw-Hill Book Co., 1968), p. 158.
43. Fremont A. Shull, Jr., *Matrix Structure and Project Authority for Optimizing Organizational Capacity* (Carbondale: Southern Illinois University, School of Business, 1965); John Stanley Baumgartner, *Project Management* (Homewood, Ill.: Richard D. Irwin, 1963), p. 8.
44. Kingdom, *Matrix Organization,* p. 18; Cleland and King, *Systems Analysis and Project Management,* pp. 154–55.
45. Quoted in ibid., p. 173.
46. Cleland and King, *Systems Analysis and Project Management,* pp. 172–76.
47. Shull, *Matrix Structure and Project Authority for Optimizing Organizational Capacity,* p. 65; Cleland and King, *Systems Analysis and Project Management,* pp. 153, 172.
48. Kingdom, *Matrix Organization,* pp. 29, 103–7; Cleland and King, *Systems Analysis and Project Management,* p. 172.
49. R. Wayne Young, *Project Management from the Project Manager's Viewpoint* (Stanford: Stanford University, Graduate School of Business, 1968), p. 6.
50. Argyris, "Today's Problems and Tomorrow's Organizations," p. 185; Cleland and King, *Systems Analysis and Project Management,* pp. 10, 174; Baumgartner, *Project Management,* p. 9. For an excellent discussion of similar problems and attitudes among party functionaries, see Jerry F. Hough, "The Party Apparatchiki," in *Interest Groups in Soviet Politics,* ed. H. Gordon Skilling and Franklyn Griffiths (Princeton: Princeton University Press, 1971), pp. 47–92.
51. See Young, *Project Management from the Project Manager's Viewpoint,* p. 25; and Baumgartner, *Project Management,* pp. 81–84. On the Soviet side, see Hough's "Party Apparatchiki" and also his "Bureaucratic Model and the Nature of the Soviet System," *Journal of Comparative Administration* 5, no. 2 (August 1973): 134–67.
52. Young, *Project Management from the Project Manager's Viewpoint,* pp. 18, 33, 43–44.
53. Kingdom, *Matrix Organization,* pp. xii, 20, 59; Baumgartner, *Project Management,* p. 75; Argyris, "Today's Problems and Tomorrow's Organizations," pp. 185, 198. For an interesting discussion about the Soviet context, see Erik Hoffmann, "Role Conflict and Ambiguity in the Communist Party of the Soviet Union," in *The Behavioral Revolution and Communist Studies,* ed. Roger E. Kanet (New York: Free Press, 1971), pp. 233–58.
54. Kingdom, *Matrix Organization,* p. 28.
55. For further discussion of the problematics and dynamics of matrix organiza-

tions, see ibid., pp. 47–50, 87–88, 103–7; Cleland and King, *Systems Analysis and Project Management,* pp. 13–15, 178; and Argyris, "Today's Problems and Tomorrow's Organizations," p. 184.

56. Instead of a resurrected Central Control Commission-RKI, the PSCC amounted essentially to a restored Rabkrin, which could serve as a strong supervisory arm of the Party and government in the economy. It had no intra-party control functions.

¶ Information Processing in the Party: Recent Theory and Experience

1. See Erik P. Hoffmann, "Soviet Metapolicy: Information Processing in the Communist Party of the Soviet Union," *Journal of Comparative Administration* 5, no. 2 (August 1973): 200–232. On "metapolicy"—policy on how to make policy—see Yehezkel Dror, *Public Policy Reexamined* (San Francisco: Chandler, 1968). I use the term in a somewhat more restricted sense than Dror, meaning by it fundamental procedures, practices, and rules concerning the formulation and determination of policies, as distinguished from policymaking on substantive issues or policy outputs in specific issue-areas. Formal and informal policymaking processes and institutional arrangements are themselves the products of past policy decisions and environmental influences. These policies on policymaking are subjected to periodical reevaluation and change (evolutionary or revolutionary) in light of new leadership goals, values, beliefs, priorities, and calculations and changing domestic, international, and technological factors and relationships.
2. E.g., V. G. Afanasyev, *Nauchno-tekhnicheskaia revoliutsiia, upravlenie, obrazovanie* (Moscow: Politizdat, 1972), pp. 226–28 ff.; N. A. Zolotaryev and P. I. Kotelnikov, eds., *Organizatsionno-partynaya rabota,* vyp. 2 (Moscow: Politizdat, 1973), pp. 321, 358, 366 ff.
3. E.g., *Politicheskaia informatsiya* (Moscow: Politizdat, 1973), pp. 10 ff.
4. G. T. Zhuravlyev, *Sotsialnaia informatsiya i upravlenie ideologicheskim protsessom* (Moscow: Mysl, 1973), pp. 50–51.
5. E.g., G. E. Glezerman, *Istoricheskii materializm i razvitie sotsialisticheskogo obshchestva* (Moscow: Politizdat, 1973).
6. E.g., Afanasyev, *Nauchno-tekhnicheskaya revoliutsiya* ,pp. 223, 231, 240; Zolotaryev and Kotelnikov, *Organizatsionno-partynaya rabota,* vyp. 2, p. 371.
7. *Materialy XXIV sezda KPSS* (Moscow: Politizdat, 1971), pp. 94, 208.
8. "Vnutripartynaya informatsiya—vazhny instrument rukovodstva," *Partynaya zhizn* 16 (August 1971): 3–8.
9. L. A. Slepov, *Vozrastanie rukovodyashchei roli partii v stroitelstve kommunizma* (Moscow: Mysl, 1972), p. 43.
10. *Ustav Kommunisticheskoi Partii Sovetskogo Soyuza* (Moscow: Politizdat, 1973), I/3/b, p. 11; III/26, pp. 26–27; IV/35, 42/f, pp. 32, 38.
11. Slepov, *Vozrastanie rukovodyashchei roli partii,* p. 73; italics added.
12. N. I. Zhukov, *Filosofskie osnovy kibernetiki,* 2nd ed. (Minsk: Izdatelstvo BGU, 1973); *Informatsiya* (*Filosofsky analiz informatsii—tsentralnogo poniatiya kibernetiki*), 2nd ed. (Minsk: Nauka i tekhnika, 1971).
13. V. I. Siforov, "Metodologicheskie voprosy nauki ob informatsii," *Voprosy filosofii* 7 (August, 1974): 105–9.
14. E.g., V. G. Afanasyev and A. D. Ursul, "Sotsialnaia informatsiya," *Voprosy*

filosofii 10 (1974): 61–74; A. D. Ursul, *Otrazhenie i informatsiya* (Moscow: Nauka, 1973); *Informatsiya* (Moscow: Nauka, 1971).

15. See V. G. Afanasyev, *Ob intensifikatsii razvitiya sotsialisticheskogo obshchestva* (Moscow: Mysl, 1969), pp. 84 ff.; Afanasyev, *Nauchno-tekhnicheskaya revoliutsiya,* pp. 225–26 ff.; and Afanasyev's best-known work, *Nauchnoe upravlenie obshchestvom,* 2nd ed. (Moscow: Politizdat, 1973).
16. V. G. Afanasyev, *Sotsialnaia informatsiya i upravlenie obshchestvom* (Moscow: Politizdat, 1975), pp. 61–77.
17. V. G. Afanasyev, "Nauchnoe rukovodstvo sotsialnymi protsessami," *Kommunist* 12 (August 1965): 65–66.
18. Afanasyev, *Ob intensifikatsii razvitya,* pp. 84–86 ff.
19. Zhuravlyev, *Sotsialnaia informatsiya,* pp. 29–30 ff.
20. Afanasyev, *Sotsialnaia informatsiya,* p. 155; V. G. Afanasyev, "Upravlenie i reshenie," *Kommunist* 17 (November 1974), pp. 43–44.
21. Zhuravlyev, *Sotsialnaia informatsiya,* pp. 115–26 ff.
22. E.g., Afanasyev, *Nauchno-tekhnicheskaya revoliutsiya,* pp. 227–28 ff.
23. Ibid., pp. 223, 228.
24. Afanasyev, *Sotsialnaia informatsiya,* pp. 146–76; Afanasyev, "Upravlenie i reshenie," pp. 38–48; Afanasyev and Ursul, "Sotsialnaia informatsiya," pp. 67–69 ff.
25. E.g., Afanasyev, "Upravlenie i reshenie," pp. 46–48; Afanasyev and Ursul, "Sotsialnaia informatsiya," pp. 67–74.
26. See V. G. Afanasyev, ed., *Nauchnoe upravlenie obshchestvom,* vols. 1–8 (Moscow: Mysl, 1967–74). For comparative analyses of the ideas of Afanasyev and other Soviet and Western writers, with emphasis on the role of feedback in decisionmaking, see Donald Schwartz, "Recent Soviet Adaptations of Systems Theory to Administrative Theory," *Journal of Comparative Administration* 5, no. 2 (August 1973): 233–64; "Decisionmaking, Administrative Decentralization, and Feedback Mechanisms: Comparisons of Soviet and Western Models," *Studies in Comparative Communism* 7, nos. 1–2 (Spring–Summer, 1974): 146–83; and "Information and Administration in the Soviet Union: Some Theoretical Considerations," *Canadian Journal of Political Science* 7, no. 2 (June 1974): 228-47.
27. E.g., L. F. Isakov, *Nauchno-tekhnicheskaya informatsiya v stroitelstve* (Moscow: Stroiizdat, 1973).
28. O. V. Kozlova and I. N. Kuznetsov, *Nauchnye osnovy upravleniya proizvodstvom* (Moscow: Ekonomika, 1970), pp. 107, 173 ff.
29. G. G. Vorobyov, *Informatsionnaya kultura upravlencheskogo truda* (Moscow: Ekonomika, 1971); *Informatsiya v rabote rukovoditelya* (Moscow: Ekonomika, 1968). For the major Western study of information in Soviet industrial decisionmaking, see Jerry F. Hough, *The Soviet Prefects: The Local Party Organs in Industrial Decision-making* (Cambridge, Mass.: Harvard University Press, 1969).
30. D. M. Gvishiani, *Organizatsiya i upravlenie,* 2nd ed. (Moscow: Nauka, 1972), pp. 526–27.
31. See especially the writings of A. A. Belyakov and I. A. Shvets, respectively, former and present head of the Party Information Sector of the Department of Organizational-Party Work of the CPSU Central Committee apparatus. Their major work is *Partynaya informatsiya* (Moscow: Politizdat, 1970). See also their "Partynaya informatsiya," in *Lektsii po partynomu stroitelstvu,* vyp. 1

(Moscow: Mysl, 1971), 1: 394–419 (attribution on p. 2); and "Informatsiya—deistvenny instrument partynogo rukovodstva," *Kommunist* 4 (March 1969): 53–64.

32. *Partynoe stroitelstvo,* 3rd ed. (Moscow: Mysl, 1972), pp. 242–44.
33. V. G. Zamaryanov, "O nauchnoi organizatsii truda v partynom rabote," in *Problemy partynogo stroitelstva* (Moscow: Politizdat, 1972), p. 286.
34. E.g., I. G. Petrov and A. S. Seregin, "O nekotorykh aspektakh issledovaniya sotsialno-politicheskoi informatsii," in *Problemy nauchnogo kommunizma,* vyp. 5 (Moscow: Mysl, 1971), p. 327.
35. *Partynoe stroitelstvo,* p. 242.
36. Leonid Brezhnev, "Otchetny doklad Tsentralnogo Komiteta KPSS XXIV sezdu Kommunisticheskoi Partii Sovetskogo Soyuza," in *Materialy XXIV sezda KPSS,* p. 94.
37. I. A. Shvets, "Vnutripartynaya informatsiya kak instrument rukovodstva, sredstvo vospitaniya i kontrolya," in *Problemy partynogo stroitelstva,* pp. 180–81.
38. A. F. Kadashev, "O nauchnom podkhode v partiinoi rabote," in *Problemy partynogo stroitelstva,* p. 79.
39. Zolotarev and Kotelnikov, *Organizatsionno-partynaya rabota,* pp. 366, 368–69.
40. P. A. Rodionov, "Leninskii stil partynoi raboty," *Pravda,* 21 January 1975, p. 3.
41. V. Zasorin, "Kollektivnost v rabote—vazhneishaya cherta leninskogo stilya," *Partynaya zhizn* 3 (February 1969): 14.
42. See the reference to a February 1969 "special decision" of the Central Committee to take necessary measures to improve "Party-political information," *Leninskie organizatsionnye printsipy i voprosy partynogo stroitelstva na sovremennom etape* (Moscow: Politizdat, 1971), p. 115. See also Zolotarev and Kotelnikov, *Organizatsionno-partynaya rabota,* p. 359; and Hoffmann, "Soviet Metapolicy," pp. 207–23.
43. *Nekotorye voprosy organizatsionno-partynoi raboty* (Moscow: Politizdat, 1973), pp. 209–10; Zolotarev and Kotelnikov, *Organizatsionna-partynaya rabota,* pp. 357, 359; Shvets, "Vnutripartynaya informatsiya kak instrument rukovodstva, pp. 170–71.
44. *Nekotorye voprosy organizatsionno-partynoi raboty,* pp. 222–23.
45. M. Rusakov, "Informatsiya—vazhny instrument rukovodstva," *Partynaya zhizn* 14 (July 1969): 35–38; Hoffmann, "Soviet Metapolicy," pp. 214–17.
46. A. Pravdin (interviewed by Mervyn Matthews), "Inside the CPSU Central Committee," *Survey* 20, no. 4 (Autumn 1974): 97.
47. Ibid., pp. 97–98.
48. See, e.g., *Nekotorye voprosy organizatsionno-partynoi raboty,* pp. 276–311; and A. N. Kushnikov and V. I. Sopelko, "Sotsialnye issledovaniya v partynoi rabote," in *Problemy nauchnogo kommuniza,* vyp. 8, pp. 123–46.
49. E.g., "O praktike provedeniya partynykh sobranii v Yaroslavskoi gorodskoi partynoi organizatsii" (Postanovlenie Ts. K. KPSS, 11/3/69), in *Spravochnik partynogo rabotnika,* vyp. 10 (Moscow: Politizdat, 1970), pp. 278–83; Hoffmann, "Soviet Metapolicy," pp. 221–23. For comparison with the Khrushchev years, see Erik P. Hoffmann, "Ideological Administration under Khrushchev: A Study of Intra-Party Communication," *Canadian Slavic Studies* 4, no. 4 (Winter, 1970): 736–66.
50. Zasorin, "Kollektivnost v rabote," p. 16.

51. See, e.g., S. Roomets, *Perfokarty i ikh primenenie* (Tallin: Sovet narod. khoz. Estonskoi SSR, 1965); G. G. Vorobyev, *Perfokartnyi metod dokumentalnogo ucheta v narodnom khozyaistve* (Moscow: Ekonomika, 1967); Kh. A. Randalu, *Perfokarty v pravovoi nauke i praktike* (Moscow: Yuridicheskaya literatura, 1969); and I. I. Guselnikov and A. F. Turpitko, *Perfokarty s kraevoi perforatsiei* (Moscow: Vysshaya shkola, 1967).
52. I. A. Shvets, "Vnutripartynaya informatsiya—instrument rukovodstva, sredstvo vospitaniya i kontrolya," *Partynaya zhizn* 12 (June 1975): 26.
53. E.g., Belyakov and Shvets, "Partynaya informatsiya," p. 411; *Nekotorye voprosy organizatsionno-partynoi raboty*, pp. 224–25.
54. These viewpoints are expressed in the following: Belyakov and Shvets, *Partynaya informatsiya*, pp. 82–95; N. M. Tarasenko, *Informatsiya v partynykh organakh* (Tula: Priokskoe knizhnoe izdatelstvo, 1971); *Nekotorye voprosy organizatsionno-partynoi raboty*, pp. 45–56, 224–26; V. G. Zamaryanov, "Problemy nauchnoi organizatsii truda v rabote partynogo apparata," in *Kommunisty i ekonomicheskaya reforma* (Moscow: Mysl', 1972), pp. 312–22; V. A. Kadeikin, *Problemy nauchnogo pokhoda v partynoi rabote* (Moscow: Mysl, 1974), pp. 5–6, 111–12 ff. Skepticism about modern information-processing technology is often conveyed by cursory treatment of the subject, or by outright silence, in the Party press. On related disagreements among Party apparatchiki, see Darrell Hammer, "Brezhnev and the Communist Party," *Soviet Union* 2, no. 1 (1975), esp. pp. 8–12.
55. In addition to discussions of the kind cited in note 54, above, see the recent Soviet literature on "democratic centralism," "collective leadership," and "the scientific management of society." Some noteworthy new Soviet works are reviewed in Erik P. Hoffmann, "The 'Scientific Management' of Soviet Society," *Problems of Communism* 27, no. 3 (May–June 1977): 59–67.
56. I. M. Reutskii and D. V. Evdokimov, *Informatsiya—instrument partynogo rukovodstva* (Moscow: Moskovsky rabochy, 1974), pp. 37–38.
57. Belyakov and Shvets, *Partynaya informatsiya*, pp. 88–89.
58. E.g., Tarasenko, *Informatsiya v partynykh organakh*, pp. 42 ff.
59. Reutskii and Evdokimov, *Informatsiya*, p. 39.
60. E.g., Zasorin, "Kollektivnost v rabote," p. 16; *Spravochnik partynogo rabotnika*, vyp. 10.
61. Belyakov and Shvets, *Partynaya informatsiya*, p. 72.
62. Ibid., pp. 72–73.
63. Zhuravlyev, *Sotsialnaia informatsiya*, pp. 79–94 ff., esp. pp. 87–92.
64. S. Arbuzov, "Sbor i analiz vnutripartynoi informatsii," *Partynaya zhizn* 4 (February 1972): 42–43.
65. See Belyakov and Shvets, *Partynaya informatsiya*, pp. 68–69.
66. For historical perspective, see V. G. Zamaryanov, "Nauchnaia organizatsiya truda v partynom apparate v 20-e gody," *Voprosy istorii KPSS* 4 (1973): 66–77; Paul Cocks, "The Rationalization of Party Control," in *Change in Communist Systems*, ed. Chalmers Johnson (Stanford: Stanford University Press, 1970) pp. 153–90. For comparative perspective, see Michel Oksenberg, "Methods of Communication within the Chinese Bureaucracy," *China Quarterly* 57 (January–March 1974): 1–39; Congressional Research Service, *The Congress and Information Technology* (Washington: Government Printing Office, 1974); *Information Systems Technology in State Government* (Lexington, Ky.: Council of State Governments, 1975).

67. E.g., Leonid Brezhnev, "Otchetny doklad Tsentralnogo Komiteta KPSS XXIV sezdu," p. 57; italics in original.
68. Cf. Jerry Hough, "The Soviet System: Petrification or Pluralism?" *Problems of Communism* 21, no. 2 (March–April 1972): 25–45; Sidney Ploss, "New Politics in Russia?" *Survey* 19, no. 4 (Autumn 1973): 23–35.
69. V. V. Shcherbitsky, "Postoinno sovershenstvovat rabotu po organizatsii i proverka vypolneniya partynykh reshenii," *Partynaya zhizn* 2 (January 1975): 11; italics added.
70. See Erik P. Hoffmann, "Technology, Values, and Political Power in the Soviet Union: Do Computers Matter?" in *Technology and Communist Culture,* ed. Frederic Fleron (New York: Praeger, 1977), pp. 397–436.

¶ Environmental Problems as a New Policy Issue

1. David Easton, *A Framework for Political Analysis* (Englewood Cliffs, N.J.: Prentice-Hall, 1965), pp. 103–35.
2. See, for example, Frederic J. Fleron, "Toward a Reconceptualization of Political Change in the Soviet Union," *Comparative Politics* 1 (January 1968): 228–44, and "Cooptation as a Mechanism of Adaptation to Change: The Soviet Political Leadership System," *Polity* 2 (Winter 1969): 176–201; Robert H. Donaldson, "The 1971 Soviet Central Committee: An Assessment of the New Elite," *World Politics* 25 (September 1972): 382–409; and George Fischer, *The Soviet System and Modern Society* (New York: Atherton, 1968).
3. Paul Cocks, "The Rationalization of Party Control," in *Change in Communist Systems, ed. Chalmers Johnson* (Stanford: Stanford University Press, 1970), pp. 153–90; Donald V. Schwartz, "Recent Soviet Adaptations of Systems Theory to Administrative Theory," *Journal of Comparative Administration* 5 (August 1973): 233–64, and "Decisionmaking, Administrative Decentralization, and Feedback Mechanisms: Comparisons of Soviet and Western Models," *Studies in Comparative Communism* 7 (Spring–Summer 1974): 146–83; Jerry Hough, "The Bureaucratic Model and the Nature of the Soviet System," *Journal of Comparative Administration* 5 (August 1973): 134–67.
4. See, for example, Richard M. Mills, "The Formation of the Virgin Lands Policy," *Slavic Review* 29 (March 1970): 58–69; D. D. Barry, "The Specialist in Soviet Policy-Making: The Adoption of a Law," *Soviet Studies* 16 (October 1964): 152–65; Philip D. Stewart, "Soviet Interest Groups and the Policy Process: The Repeal of Production Education," *World Politics* 22 (October 1969): 29–50; J. J. Schwartz and William Keech, "Group Influence and the Policy Process in the Soviet Union," *American Political Science Review* 62 (September 1969): 840–51; and Donald R. Kelley, "Interest Groups in the USSR: The Impact of Political Sensitivity on Group Influence," *Journal of Politics* 34 (August 1972): 860–88, and "Toward a Model of Soviet Decision Making: A Research Note," *American Political Science Review* 66 (June 1974): 701–7.
5. Jerry Hough, "The Soviet System: Petrification or Pluralism?" *Problems of Communism* 21 (March–April 1972): 35.
6. See Marshall I. Goldman, *The Spoils of Progress: Environmental Pollution in the Soviet Union* (Cambridge, Mass.: MIT Press, 1972), pp. 211–38; Friedrich Engels, *Dialectics of Nature* (Moscow: Progress Publishers, 1964); Karl Marx, *The Economic and Philosophical Manuscripts of 1844* (New York: Interna-

tional Publishers, 1964); V. L. Mote, "The Geography of Air Pollution in the USSR" (Ph.D. diss., University of Washington, 1971), chap. 2.

7. Donald R. Kelley, "Economic Growth and Environmental Quality in the USSR: Soviet Reaction to *The Limits to Growth*," *Canadian Slavonic Papers* 18 (September 1976): 266–83; see also an extensive discussion in the pages of *Voprosy Filosofii*, which appeared as a regular feature between December 1972 and April 1973.
8. *Pravda*, 12 January 1973; John M. Kramer, "Prices and the Conservation of Natural Resources in the Soviet Union," *Soviet Studies* 24 (January 1973): 364–73; Marshall I. Goldman, 'Externalities and the Race for Economic Growth in the USSR: Will the Environment Ever Win?" *Journal of Political Economy* (March–April 1972), pp. 314–27, and *Spoils*, pp. 9–76.
9. A sanitary inspector may fine an individual fifty rubles and an enterprise up to five hundred rubles, and the Russian Republic criminal code specifies up to a year's imprisonment or a three-hundred-ruble fine for pollution offenses, with up to a five-year term if the offense results in "substantial harm" to human health, agriculture, or wildlife. Prison sentences are rare (Philip R. Pryde, *Conservation in the Soviet Union* [New York: Cambridge University Press, 1972], pp. 153–54; John D. LaMothe, *Water Quality in the Soviet Union—A Review* [Washington, D.C.: Department of the Army, 1971], p. 25; David E. Powell, "The Social Costs of Modernization: Ecological Problems in the USSR," *World Politics* 23 [July 1971]: 629).
10. Kramer, "Prices and the Conservation of Natural Resources," p. 372; John W. Kramer, "The Politics of Conservation and Pollution in the USSR" (Ph.D. diss., University of Virginia, 1973), pp. 150–53; Powell, "Social Costs of Modernization," p. 630; Goldman, *Spoils*, pp. 48, 111–14.
11. Pryde, *Conservation*, p. 11.
12. *Pravda*, 10 January 1973.
13. I. P. Gerasimov, "Scientific-Technical Progress and Geography," *Materialy V syezda geograficheskogo obshchestva SSSR* (Leningrad, 1970), trans. in *Soviet Geography: Review and Translation* 12 (April 1971): 205–18; E. B. Lopatina et al., "The Present State and Future Tasks in the Theory and Methods of an Evaluation of the Natural Environment and Resources," *Izvestiya akademiya nauk SSSR: seriya geograficheskaya*, no. 4 (1970), pp. 45–54, trans. in *Soviet Geography: Review and Translation* 12 (March 1971): 142–43; V. B. Sochava, "Geography and Ecology," *Materialy V syezda geograficheskogo obshchestva SSSR* (Leningrad, 1970), trans. in *Soviet Geography: Review and Translation* 12 (May 1971): 277–91.
14. See articles by the economist P. Oldak in *Literaturnaya Gazeta*, 3 June 1970, and *Voprosy Filosofii* (February 1973); pp. 50–52; Pryde, *Conservation*, p. 165; Keith Bush, "Environmental Problems in the USSR," *Problems of Communism* 11 (July–August 1972): 27; N. Fedorenko and K. Gofman, "Problems of the Optimization of Environmental Planning and Management," *Voprosy Ekonomiki* (October 1972), pp. 38–46, trans. in *Current Digest of the Soviet Press* 25, no. 5 (Feb. 28, 1973): 1.
15. Mikhail Sholokhov, comments to the Twenty-third CPSU Congress, XXIII *syèzda kommunisticheskoi partii sovetskogo soiuza, stenograficheskii otchet* (Moscow: Politizdat, 1966), pp. 354–62; Alexander Solzhenitsyn, *Letter to the Soviet Leaders* (New York: Harper and Row, 1974). The latter's interest in the question of the environment predates the publication of this essay in the West.

16. B. Gwertzman, "New Russian Movie Discusses Industry Environmental Role," *New York Times,* 6 March 1970.
17. Robert W. Clawson and William Kolarik, "Soviet Resource Management: Political Aspects of Water Pollution Control" (paper presented at the Conference on Soviet Resource Management and the Environment, University of Washington, 7 June 1974).
18. Ibid., p. 40.
19. Ibid., pp. 25–28.
20. Kramer, *Politics,* pp. 6–10.
21. These groups might be more properly described as "opinion groups," for what unites them is a commonly held attitude toward certain environmental questions and not a single organizational base of operations. See H. Gordon Skilling, "Groups in Soviet Politics: Some Hypotheses," in *Interest Groups in Soviet Politics,* ed. H. Gordon Skilling and Franklyn Griffiths (Princeton: Princeton University Press, 1971), pp. 25–27.
22. If the American and Japanese experiences are typical, however, the creation of centralized environmental agencies in itself is not a guarantee that effective measures will be taken; see Donald R. Kelley, Kenneth R. Stunkel, and Richard R. Wescott, "The Politics of the Environment: The United States, the USSR, and Japan," *American Behavioral Scientist* 17 (May–June 1974): 751–70.
23. Goldman, *Spoils,* p. 192; Pryde, *Conservation,* pp. 9–24.
24. O. S. Kolbasov, "Legislation on Water Use in the USSR," in *Water Resources Law and Policy in the Soviet Union,* ed. Irving K. Fox (Madison: University of Wisconsin Press, 1971), pp. 208–10; Bush, "Environmental Problems," p. 28; Pryde, *Conservation,* pp. 107–12.
25. Thane Gustafson, "The New Soviet Environmental Program: Do the Soviets Really Mean Business?" Paper, Northeastern Slavic Conf., Harvard, April 1977.
26. LaMothe, *Water Quality,* p. 25.
27. *Pravda,* 10 January 1973.
28. The best discussion of this apparatus mechanism is found in Abdurakhman Avtorkhanov, *The Communist Party Apparatus* (Chicago: Henry Regnery, 1966), pp. 192–227, 263–89.
29. Pryde, *Conservation,* pp. 161–66; Kramer, *Politics,* pp. 38–75.
30. Kramer, *Politics,* pp. 24–28; the survey of environment-related articles in the media from which this profile was generated covered the national, republic, and local press and some unspecified journals; unfortunately, no list of the specific sources or information about the size of the sample was given.
31. The most comprehensive, although now dated, discussions of the political aspects of the Baikal question are to be found in Kramer, *Politics,* pp. 162–80; and Goldman, *Spoils,* pp. 177–210.
32. B. R. Buyantuev, *K narodnokhozyaistvennym problemam Baikala* (Ulan Ude: Buryatskoe knizhnoe izdatelstvo, 1960); O. Serova and S. Sarkisian, *Zhemchuzhina vostochnoi Sibiri* (Ulan Ude: Buryatskoe knizhnoe izdatelstvo, 1961).
33. *Komsomolskaya Pravda,* 26 December 1961.
34. For the early discussion, see *Literaturnaya Gazeta* of 6 February 1965, 18 March 1965, 10, 13, and 15 April 1965, 29 January 1966, and 10 and 15 February 1966.
35. *Komsomolskaya Pravda,* 11 May 1966.
36. Ibid., 11 August 1970.
37. *Literaturnaya Gazeta,* 29 January 1966.
38. *Komsomolskaya Pravda,* 11 August 1970; *Literaturnaya Gazeta,* 5 April 1972.

39. *Izvestia,* 8 February 1969.
40. *Komsomolskaya Pravda,* 11 August 1970.
41. *Pravda,* 24 September 1971.
42. *New York Times,* 5 October 1972; C. R. Goldman, "Will Baikal and Tahoe Be Saved?" *California Tomorrow* (Winter 1973–74), p. 3.
43. *New York Times,* 9 July 1973.
44. *Literaturnaya Gazeta,* 5 April 1972.
45. C. R. Goldman, "Will Baikal and Tahoe Be Saved?" p. 7.
46. *Literaturnaya Gazeta,* 5 April 1972; *Pravda,* 14 March 1974.
47. *Literaturnaya Gazeta,* 4 December 1974; *Pravda,* 20 November 1974; C. R. Goldman, "Will Baikal and Tahoe Be Saved?" pp. 9–10.
48. *Pravda,* 6 May 1975, p. 2, 13 July 1977, p. 2, 14 July 1977, p. 2, 16 July 1977, p. 2; *Izvestia,* 19 September 1976, p. 2, 3 December 1976, p. 2, 18 May 1977, p. 2.
49. *Sovetskaya Kultura,* 23 November 1977, p. 6.
50. *Literaturnaya Gazeta,* 13 February 1973.

¶ The Party under Stress: The Experience of World War II

1. Merle Fainsod, *How Russia is Ruled,* rev. ed. (Cambridge, Mass.: Harvard University Press, 1963), p. 109.
2. For an interesting discussion of Stalin and psychopolitics, see Robert C. Tucker, *The Soviet Political Mind,* rev. ed. (New York: Norton, 1971), pp. 49–118.
3. *Istoriya Velikoi Otechestvennoi voiny Sovetskogo Soiuza 1941–1945* (Moscow: Voinizdat, 1961), 2: 627 (hereafter cited as *IVOvSS*).
4. Ibid. (Moscow: Voinizdat, 1965), 6: 103.
5. Ibid., 2: 57.
6. See, for example, "O zadachakh partiinykh organizatsii v oblasti promyshlennosti i transporta, Rezolyutsiya po dokladu tov. Malenkova, prinyataya *XVIII* Vsesoyuznoi konferentsiei, VKP(b)," *Partiinoe Stroitel'stvo,* nos. 4–5 (February–March 1941), p. 151 (hereafter cited as *PS*).
7. Fainsod, *How Russia is Ruled, pp.* 196–98.
8. A. V. Mitrofanova, *Rabochii klass Sovetskogo Soiuza v pervyi period Velikoi Otechestvennoi voiny* (Moscow: Akademiia Nauk SSSR, 1960), pp. 77–78.
9. See, for example, Fainsod, *How Russia is Ruled,* pp. 193–200.
10. V. Zimin, "Nekotorye osobennosti partiinoi raboty na transporte," *PS,* nos. 23–24 (December 1944), p. 24.
11. See Fainsod, *How Russia is Ruled,* pp. 198–200. That such wide-sweeping administrative reform was not initiated before 1948 may be been because of Zhdanov's continuing support of the functional system of Party administration. See also John Armstrong, *The Politics of Soviet Totalitarianism* (New York: Random House, 1961), pp. 113–14.
12. I. V. Stalin, "Address to the Graduates of the Red Army Academies," quoted in Barrington Moore, Jr., *Soviet Politics—The Dilemma of Power* (New York: Harper and Row, Harper Torch books, 1965), p. 239.
13. Iu. P. Petrov, *Partiinoe stroitel'stvo v Sovetskoi Armii i Flote (1918–1961)* (Moscow: Voinizdat, 1964), p. 352.
14. IVOvSS, 6: 342.

15. Petrov, *Partiinoe stroitel'stvo v Armii i Flote,* p. 350.
16. *IVOvSS,* 2: 54.
17. Fainsod, *How Russia is Ruled,* p. 470.
18. M. Mackintosh, *Juggernaut* (New York: Macmillan, 1967), p. 23.
19. E. A. Rafikov, "Ukreplenie partiinykh organizatsii Krasnoi Armii v pervyi period Velikoi Otechestvennoi voiny," *Voprosy Istorii KPSS,* no. 3 (March 1964), p. 73.
20. See *Kommunisticheskaya partiya v period Velikoi Otechestvennoi voiny. Dokumenty i materialy* (Moscow: Gospolizdat, 1961), pp. 95–96; and Petrov, *Partiinoe stroitel'stvo v Armii i Flote,* pp. 360–61.
21. Petrov, *Partiinoe stroitel'stvo v Armii i Flote,* p. 352.
22. IVOvSS, 6: 365.
23. Ibid., p. 342.
24. Rafikov, "Ukreplenie partiinykh organizatsii," p. 75; Petrov, *Partiinoe Stroitel'stvo v Armii i Flote,* p. 396.
25. See "Dokumenty geroicheskikh let (1941–1945 gg.)," *Voprosy Istorii KPSS,* no. 5 (May 1965), p. 67; and Petrov, *Partiinoe stroitel'stvo v Armii i Flote,* p. 396.
26. I. M. Spirin, "Partiinie i komsomol'skie mobilizatsii v Sovetskuiu Armiiu v gody Velikoi Otechestvennoi voiny," *Voprosy Istorii KPSS,* no. 3 (March 1963), p. 35.
27. N. M. Kiryaev and I. V. Stavitskii, "Rost i ukreplenie ryadov KPSS v period Velikoi Otechestvennoi voiny," *Voprosy Istorii,* no. 9 (September 1959), p. 4.
28. T. H. Rigby, *Communist Party Membership in the USSR* (Princeton: Princeton University Press, 1968), p. 259.
29. Ibid., pp. 262–63.
30. See P. Andreev, "Moskovskaya partiinaya organizatsiya v gody Velikoi Otchestvennoi voiny," in *Kommunisticheskaya partiya v period Velikoi Otechestvennoi voiny (iiun' 1941 goda–1945 god),* ed. S. Levitin (Moscow: Moskovskii rabochii, 1960), pp. 183, 186; *Na zashchite Nevskoi tverdnyi* (Leningrad, 1965), p. 497; and N. Ia. Ivanov et al., eds., *Leningrad: Kratkii istoricheskii ocherk* (Leningrad: Lenizdat, 1964), p. 524, as quoted in Rigby, *Communist Party Membership,* p. 266.
31. M. Shamberg, "Nekotorye voprosy vnutripartiionoi raboty," *PS,* no. 4 (February 1946), p. 28.
32. *IVOvSS,* 6: 367.
33. Ibid., pp. 332, 267.
34. Rigby, *Communist Party Membership,* pp. 224–25.
35. Ibid., p. 239.
36. See, for example, M. Kozybaev, *Kompartiya Kazakhstana v period Velikoi Otechestvennoi voiny 1941–1945 gg* (Alma-Alta, 1964), pp. 246–47; and G. Sh. Kaimarazov et al., *Dagestan v gody Velikoi Otechestvennoi voiny 1941–1945 gg.* (Makhachkala: Dagestanskoe gosudarsvennor khizhizdvo, 1963), p. 313.
37. *IVOvSS,* 6: 367.
38. See Rigby, *Communist Party Membership,* p. 376.
39. V. K. Molochko, "Kommunisticheskaya partiya i massy v period stroitel'stva sotsialisma," in *Partiya i massy,* ed. K. I. Suvorov (Moscow: Mysl', 1966), p. 82. It should be noted, however, that Molochko's figures do not agree with

generally accepted statistical information on the Party's wartime enrollment.

40. *Bol'shaya Sovetskaya Entsiklopediya* (Moscow: Gosnauchizdat, 1954), 26: 146 (hereafter cited as *BSE*).
41. Ibid. (1950), 2: 429; Leonard Schapiro, *The Communist Party of the Soviet Union* (New York: Random House, 1960), p. 442.
42. *BSE* (1952), 15: 605. Zhdanov, while retaining overall control of such work, was replaced as formal head of the Propaganda and Agitation Administration in September 1940 by G. F. Aleksandrov (see *Pravda,* 7 September 1940, p. 3).
43. See *BSE* (1957), 48:263. At the same time, Shcherbakov served as first secretary of the Moscow gorkom and obkom, assistant People's Commissar for Defense, and head of the Soviet Information Bureau (ibid.).
44. See Mediator, "Die Parteigeneralität der KPdSU," *Ost-Probleme* 2, no. 29 (20 July 1950): 920; N. N. Shatalin, "O rabote s kadrami," *PS,* no. 20 (October 1943), pp. 11–19.
45. *5000 Sowjetköpfe* (Köln, 1959), p. 160.
46. *Pravda,* 22 December 1942, p. 3; *Propagandist,* no. 12 (June 1945), p. 53.
47. See M. A. Vogolagin, "V dni trevog," in A. Samsonov, *Stalingradskaya epopeya* (Moscow: Nauka, 1968), p. 393; and L. Nemzer, "The 'Apparatus' of the Central Committee, Communist Party of the Soviet Union," *American Political Science Review* 44, no. 1 (March 1950): 82.
48. Malenkov, for example, appears to have been Shatalin's patron. Their careers were to be closely connected down to 1955. See, for example, Armstrong, *The Politics of Soviet Totalitarianism,* p. 262.
49. Iu. P. Petrov. *Stroitel'stvo politorganov partiinykh i komsomol'skikh organizatsii armii i flota* (Moscow, 1968), p. 276.
50. Spirin, "Partiinye i komsomol'skie mobilizatsii," p. 35.
51. Kiryaev and Stavitskii, "Rost i ukreplenie ryadov KPSS," p. 11.
52. *Ocherki istorii Moskovskoi organizatsii KPSS* (Moscow: Moskovskii rabochii, 1966), p. 563.
53. Kiryaev and Stavitskii, "Rost i ukreplenie ryadov KPSS," p. 11.
54. Ibid.
55. *Ocherki istorii Moskovskoi organizatsii KPSS,* p. 601.
56. Iu. A. Vasil'ev, *Sibirskii arsenal' 1941–1945* (Sverdlovsk: Sredne-Uralskoe khizhizdvo, 1965), p. 233.
57. Kiryaev and Stavitskii, "Rost i ukreplenie ryadov KPSS," p. 11.
58. *Ocherki istorii Moskovskii organizatsii KPSS,* p. 601.
59. Ibid.
60. Vasil'ev, *Sibirskii arsenal',* p. 235.
61. L. Slepov, *Mestnye partiinye organy. Lektsii* (Moscow, 1954), p. 8.
62. The Party's role in agriculture will be discussed in a later section.
63. Party organizations and officials were criticized frequently in the Soviet press for their campaign-style approach to problem-solving. Such an approach, it was asserted, was incorrect because, among other things, it led to a neglect of the larger and longer-range questions of economic plan fulfillment. (See, for example, "Partiinyi rabotnik—politicheskii rukovoditel'," *PS,* nos. 17–18 [September 1943], p. 6). Nonetheless, as has been indicated, such an approach to problem-solving fitted in well with the regime's wartime needs and thus was tolerated and in some ways—the regime's own criticism notwithstanding —even encouraged.

    Similarly, Party cadres were criticized for serving as expediters (*tolkachi*) for economic administrators. (See, for example, *PS*, no. 4 [February 1943], p. 42). Clearly, such practices not only went against the precepts of Soviet administrative theory but also were illegal. The regime was in no position during the war, however, to do away with such violations of administrative theory and law. Indeed, as many Party and economic officials had discovered in the prewar period, such illegal practices introduced an element of flexibility into a basically rigid, centrally controlled economic plan and thus were important for the proper functioning of the economic system. (See Joseph S. Berliner, *Factory and Manager in the U.S.S.R.* [Cambridge, Mass.: Harvard University Press, 1957], pp. 207–30).

64. See Jerry F. Hough, *The Soviet Prefects: The Local Party Organs in Industrial Decision-making* (Cambridge, Mass.: Harvard University Press, 1969), pp. 214–34.
65. See, for example, "Zadachi partiino-politicheskoi raboty," *PS*, no. 12 (June 1942), p. 18.
66. M. Kulagin, "Rezervy nashikh predpriyati," *PS*, no. 6 (August 1942), p. 26.
67. See, for example, "Zadachi bol'shevikov Urala," *PS*, nos. 23–24 (December 1942), p. 4.
68. "Nedostatki v rabote Tadzhikskoi partorganizatsii," *PS*, no. 19 (October 1942), p. 33.
69. Ya. Storozhev, "Voprosy raboty organizatsionno-instruktorskikh otdelov partiinykh komitetov," *PS*, no. 8 (April 1943), p. 23.
70. Armstrong, *The Politics of Soviet Totalitarianism*, pp. 115–16.
71. See, for example, Ya. Storozhev, "Voprosy raboty organizatsionno-instructorskikh otdelov partiinykh komitetov," pp. 23–24.
72. See "Partiinye rabotnik—politcheskii rukovoditel'," p. 6.
73. See, for example, Storozhev, "Voprosy raboty organizatsionno—instruktorskykh otdelov," p. 23.
74. Ibid., p. 25.
75. "Partiinye rabotnik—politicheskii rukovoditel'," p. 6.
76. See ibid.; "Zadachi partiino-organizatsionnoi raboty"; and Kozybaev, *Kompartiya Kazakhstana*, pp. 239–40.
77. *PS*, no. 17–18 (September 1943), p. 36.
78. Ibid.
79. See Fainsod, *How Russia is Ruled*, p. 199.
80. *PS*, no. 20 (October 1943), pp. 14–15.
81. Ibid.
82. Ibid., p. 6.
83. Ibid., pp. 14–15.
84. Armstrong, *The Politics of Soviet Totalitarianism*, p. 116.
85. The impact of the war on the countryside was particularly severe because rural Party membership in the prewar period was already at a very low level. Moreover, the regime continued to accord agriculture a position second in importance to industrial production, and, therefore, rural organizations were forced to give up additional cadres to the industrial sector of the economy. An indication of the actual decline in membership is provided by the following examples: from 1 July 1941 to 1 January 1942, the number of Communists in the villages of the Altai krai decreased by 35.2 percent; in Yaroslav oblast, the number decreased by 33.2 percent (Iu. V. Arutunyan, *Sovetskoe krestyanstvo v gody Velikoi Otechestvennoi voiny* [Moscow, 1963], p. 51).

Viewed from a somewhat different angle, the network of kolkhoz Party organizations, on the average for the country, declined by 20 percent during the first year of the war (M. I. Likhomanov, "Organizatorskaya rabota partii v derevne v pervy perioda Velikoi Otechestvennoi voiny 1941–1942," *Voprosy Istorii KPSS,* no. 2 [February 1965], p. 63).

Of even greater importance, rural Party organizations lost a substantial number of their experienced apparatus personnel to the war effort. In Omsk oblast, for example, in the course of the first three months of the war alone, 700 members of the Party apparatus departed for the front (N. M. Kiryaev and I. V. Stavitskii, "Rost i ukreplenie ryadov KPSS," p. 11). It is claimed that analogous situations were to be found in almost all Party organizations (ibid.). The vacancies were filled, for the most part, by young cadres who often lacked not only the expertise to perform their assigned functions but also the most rudimentary habits and skills of Party work. The problem of restaffing the rural organizations continued throughout the war.

86. V. Ya. Ashanin, "Politotdel MTS v gody Velikoi Otechestvennoi voiny," *Voprosy Istorii KPSS,* no. 4 (April 1960), p. 52.
87. A. Grigoriev, "Neskol'ko vyvodov iz opyta raboty politotdelov MTS," *PS,* nos. 17–18 (September 1942), p. 20.
88. Arutunyan, *Sovetskoe krest'yanstvo,* p. 56. Their importance is also borne out by the inclusion of these posts in the nomenklatura lists of Party organizations from the obkom right up to the Central Committee of the CPSU, depending on the particular assignment (ibid.).
89. Ibid.
90. Ibid.
91. See Robert F. Miller, *One Hundred Thousand Tractors* (Cambridge, Mass.: Harvard University Press, 1970), pp. 220–48.
92. The politotdel was the primary unit in the system of political control organized under the USSR Commissariat of Agriculture.
93. *PS,* no. 12 (June 1942), p. 45.
94. Grigoriev, "Opyta raboty politotdelov MTS," p. 21.
95. Ashanin, Politotdel MTS," p. 61.
96. Robert F. Miller, *The Machine-tractor Station as an Institution for the Organization and Control of Agriculture* (Ph.D. diss., Harvard University, 1964), p. 340.
97. Ibid., p. 348.
98. V. Zhavoronkov, "Nekotorye voprosy raboty sel'skikh raikomov," *PS,* no. 15 (August 1943), p. 16.
99. Arutunyan, *Sovetskoe krest'yanstvo,* p. 55. The derisive term Arutunyan quotes is *upalnomochennye,* a rather untranslatable play on the word for plenipotentiary, *upolnomochennye.*
100. Ibid.
101. "Selskii raikom partii," *PS,* nos. 5–6 (March 1943), p. 6.
102. See, for example, I. V. Stavitskii, "Rol' voennykh sovetov v organitsii partiino-politicheskoi raboty na frontakh Velikoi Otechestvennoi voiny (1941–1945 gg.)," *Voprosy Istorii KPSS,* no. 2 (February 1968), pp. 28–29.
103. See, for example, Petrov, *Partiinoe stroitel'stvo v Armii i Flote,* pp. 355–56; and I. V. Stavitskii, "O voennykh kommissarakh perioda Velikoi Otechestvennoi voiny," *Voprosy Istorii KPSS,* no. 3 (March 1965), pp. 23–24.
104. See, for example, *Krasnaya Zvezda,* 23 August 1942; and Roman Kolkowicz,

The Soviet Army and the Communist Party: Institutions in Conflict (Santa Monica, Calif.: Rand Corporation, 1966), p. 105.

105. See Kolkowicz, *The Soviet Army,* pp. 108–9.
106. *KPSS o Vooruzhennykh Silakh Sovetskogo Souiza: sbornik dokumentov, 1917–1958* (Moscow: Gospolizdat, 1958), p. 371.
107. Petrov, *Partiinoe stroitel'stvo v Armii i Flote,* p. 376.
108. See, for example, ibid., p. 401.
109. Armstrong, *The Politics of Soviet Totalitarianism,* p. 160.
110. See, for example, D. Skiliagin et al., *Dela i liudi Leningradskoi militsii; ocherk istorii* (Leningrad: Lenizdat, 1967), p. 295; and P. I. Zyrianov, ed., *Pogranichnye voiska v gody Velikoi Otechestvennoi voiny* (Moscow: Nauka, 1968), pp. 502–3, 551–98.
111. See, for example, Arutunyan, *Sovetskoe krest'yanstvo,* p. 194.
112. For details, see A. S. Fedoseev, *Demokraticheskii tsentralism Leninskii printsip organizatsii Sovetkogo gosudarstvennogo apparata* (Moscow, 1962), pp. 188–90.

¶ Alcohol Abuse: The Pattern of Official Response

1. Cited in Walter D. Connor, *Deviance in Soviet Society* (New York: Columbia University Press, 1972), pp. 39–40.
2. See N. Ya. Kopyt's article in *Sotsialnye problemy zdavookhraneniya,* 36, no. 1 (1975): 38.
3. See the Second Report to the U.S. Congress, *Alcohol and Health,* compiled by the Secretary of Health, Education, and Welfare (Washington, D.C.: U.S. Government Printing Office, 1974), p. 6.
4. Kopyt, pp. 41–42.
5. Studies of American drinking practices offer an interesting contrast with Soviet behavior. In general, American surveys point to a strong correlation between social class and alcohol consumption. That is, "proportionately more people on the lower socioeconomic levels are abstainers than are those on the upper levels." In addition, "both moderate and heavy drinking increases as social class rises." See *Alcohol and Health,* p. 13. The Soviet pattern is the diametric opposite of the American.
6. Kopyt, p. 39; Boris M. Segal, *Alkogolizm* (Moscow: Meditsina, 1967), p. 4.
7. *Literaturnaya gazeta,* 10 July 1974, p. 11.
8. *Ekonomika i organizatsiya promyshlennogo proizvodstva,* no. 4 (1974), p. 37 (cited hereafter as *EKO*).
9. *EKO.*
10. Vladimir G. Treml, "Production and Consumption of Alcoholic Beverages in the USSR," *Journal of Studies on Alcohol* 36, no. 3 (March 1975): 286–87. Distilled spirits now account for about one-half of total consumption in the USSR, a sharp drop from the 1957 level of 78% (ibid.).
11. Yu. M. Tkachevskii, *Provovye mery borby s pianstvom* (Moscow: Izd-vo Moskovskogo Universiteta, 1974), p. 174.
12. See *Agitator,* no. 15 (1973), pp. 33–35; and *Doshkolnoye vospitaniye,* no. 12 (1973), pp. 63–66. See also I. G. Urakov and V. V. Kulikov, *Vo vred sebye i obshchestvu* (Moscow: Znanie, 1975); and Segal, *Alkogolizm,* passim.

13. *Sotsialisticheskaya industriya,* 8 June 1972, p. 3.
14. *Literaturnaya Rossiya,* 8 February 1974, p. 15; Urakov and Kulikov, *Vo vred sebye,* p. 44.
15. Urakov and Kulikov, *Vo vred sebye,* p. 49.
16. *Literaturnaya gazeta,* 10 July 1974, p. 11.
17. See, e.g., *Literaturnaya Rossiya,* 8 February 1974, p. 15; and *Literaturnaya gazeta,* 11 June 1975, p. 13.
18. See Kopyt, pp. 46–47; and Urakov and Kulikov, *Vo vred sebye,* pp. 72–73.
19. See, e.g., N. Solovieva, "Razvod, ego faktory, prichiny, povody," in *Problemy byta, braka i semi* (Vilnius, 1970), p. 62; *EKO,* p. 53; and Kopyt, p. 49.
20. Urakov and Kulikov, *Vo vred sebye,* pp. 60–61.
21. *Chelovek i zakon,* no. 6 (1973), p. 21. According to Treml's estimates, the production of alcoholic beverages by the state preempts about 3% of the net output of grains, 5% of potatoes, and 4–8% of sugar beets. The manufacture of home brew consumes at least as much again of these agricultural products (Treml, "Production and Consumption of Alcoholic Beverages," p. 287).
22. *EKO,* p. 37; Urakov and Kulikov, *Vo vred sebye,* pp. 50–52.
23. *Sotsialisticheskaya industriya,* 8 June 1972, p. 3.
24. Tkachevskii, *Provovyye mery borby,* pp. 24–25.
25. *Sovetskoye gosudarstvo i pravo,* no. 2 (1973), p. 42. See also Tkachevskii, *Pravovyye mery borby,* p. 66; and Kopyt, p. 48.
26. *Pravda,* 28 October 1974, p. 1. See also *Rabochaya gazeta,* 22 November 1974, p. 3.
27. *EKO,* p. 50 (statement by Boris Urlanis); Tkachevskii, *Pravovyye mery borby,* p. 29. Treml has estimated total tax collections from alcoholic beverages in recent years at more than twenty billion rubles annually ("Production and Consumption of Alcoholic Beverages," p. 302).
28. *Sotsialisticheskaya industriya,* 8 June 1972, p. 3; *Agitator,* no. 16 (1972), p. 48; *Trud,* 6 September 1972, p. 3; Urakov and Kulikov, *Vo vred sebye,* p. 15; Tkachevskii, *Provovye mery borby,* p. 44; *Zdravookhraneniye Rossisskoi Federatsii,* no. 2 (1971), p. 29.
29. *EKO,* p. 49.
30. *Gigiyena i sanitariya,* vol. 35 (1970).
31. *Moskovskaya pravda,* 27 February 1975, p. 2; *Voprosy filosofii,* no. 1 (1974), p. 103.
32. *Meditsinskaya gazeta,* 20 November 1970, p. 2.
33. Urakov and Kulikov, *Vo vred sebye,* p. 53.
34. *Sovetskoye zdravookhaneniye,* no. 2 (1961), p. 28.
35. *Izvestia,* 1 October 1968, p. 5. See also, e.g., *Sotsialisticheskaya industriya,* 15 September 1973, p. 1.
36. See J. Wortis, *Soviet Psychiatry* (Baltimore: Williams and Wilkins, 1950), p. 173.
37. Connor, *Deviance in Soviet Society,* p. 53.
38. *Literaturnaya Rossiya,* 8 February 1974, p. 15; *Zhurnalist,* no. 12 (1973), p. 42.
39. Urakov and Kulikov, *Vo vred sebye,* pp. 41–42. They quote the American psychologists Dollard and Miller: "Anyone can become an alcoholic if he works hard enough at it" (ibid, p. 42). See also Kopyt, p. 50.
40. See *Meditsinskaya gazeta,* 20 November 1970, p. 2.
41. *Sovetskaya Rossiya,* 26 March 1964, p. 4.

42. *Vedomosti verkhovnogo soveta RSFSR,* no. 15 (13 April 1967), in *Current Digest of the Soviet Press* 19, no. 15 (1967): 11.
43. For insights into the medical community's increasing interest in outpatient care, especially when it allows the alcoholic to work in a special plant or special section of a factory, see *Meditsinskaya gazeta,* 23 June 1972, p. 2, 8 September 1972, p. 4, 18 October 1972, p. 2, 11 May 1973, p. 2, and 16 November 1973, p. 2.
44. See Tkachevskii, *Provovye mery borby,* p. 38.
45. *Izvestia,* 13 July 1975, p. 3.
46. *Sovetskaya Rossiya,* 11 July 1972; *Agitator,* no. 4 (1975), p. 58.
47. *Kommunist Tadzhikistana,* 13 April 1975, p. 3.
48. *Sotsialisticheskaya zakonnost,* no. 8 (1973), p. 60.
49. *Meditsinskaya gazeta,* 20 November 1970, p. 2.
50. *Pravda,* 9 January 1973, p. 6. See also *Agitator,* no. 4 (1975), pp. 58–59. Tkachevskii claims that cure rates are 6–7 times higher in labor-treatment institutions than in conventional medical facilities (*Pravovyye mery borby,* pp. 38, 40). For an earlier but equally enthusiastic appraisal, see *Sotsialisticheskaya zakonnost,* no. 4 (1968), pp. 28–29.
51. *Sovetskoye gosudarstvo i pravo,* no. 2 (1973), p. 46.
52. See, e.g., *Sovetskaya yustitsiya,* no. 8 (1975), p. 24; and *Pravda,* 19 May 1975, p. 1.
53. Urakov and Kulikov, *Vo vred sebye,* p. 27.
54. *Pravda,* 17 October 1974, p. 3.
55. *Zdravookhraneniye Rossiskoi Federatsii,* no. 5 (1970), p. 19.
56. *Selskaya zhizn,* 29 January 1975, p. 4; *Literaturnaya gazeta,* 11 June 1975, p. 13.
57. See *Sovetskaya yustitsiya,* no. 21 (1973), p. 25; *Agitator,* no. 8 (1974), pp. 52–53; and *Sovetskaya Latvia,* 16 February 1975, p. 2.
58. *Sovetskoye zdravookhraneniye,* no. 2 (1961), p. 29.
59. *Sovetskaya yustitsiya,* no. 21 (1973), pp. 23–25.
60. See David E. Powell, *Antireligious Propaganda in the Soviet Union* (Cambridge, Mass.: MIT Press, pp. 104–11.
61. Approximately one-fifth of all motor vehicle accidents are said to be the result of road surface defects. Of those blamed on the negligence of drivers and/or pedestrians, 70% are attributed to the former and 30% to the latter. One out of every three accidents is said to be caused by the operator of a privately owned car or motorcycle (*Izvestia,* 15 November 1975, p. 1). See also Tkachevskii, *Pravovyye mery borby,* pp. 46, 121.
62. Tkachevskii, *Pravovyye mery borby,* p. 116.
63. Ibid, p. 115; Urakov and Kulikov, *Vo vred sebye,* pp. 54–56.
64. Tkachevskii, *Pravovyye mery borby,* pp. 44–45, 118.
65. Ibid, pp. 45, 46, 121.
66. *Izvestia,* 15 November 1975, p. 1.
67. See *Za rulem,* no. 9 (1975), pp. 26–27.
68. *Chelovek i zakon,* no. 6 (1973), p. 22; see David E. Powell, "Alcoholism in the USSR," *Survey* 78, no. 1 (Winter 1971): 131, fn. 40.
69. *Sovetskaya yustitsiya,* no. 7 (1972), p. 4.
70. *Sovetskoye gosudarstvo i pravo,* no. 2 (1973), p. 41; *Sovetskaya Rossiya,* 20 June 1970; *Sovetskoye zdravookhraneniye,* no. 2 (1972), p. 68.

71. *Sovetskoye zdravookhraneniye,* no. 2 (1972), pp. 65–69; *Sovetskoye gosudarstvo i pravo,* no. 2 (1973), p. 41.
72. *Sovetskaya yustitsiya,* no. 19 (1972), pp. 25–27. See also *Sovety deputatov trudyashchikhsya,* no. 11 (1972), pp. 62–64; *Sovety deputatov trudyashchihsya,* no. 9 (1973), pp. 94–99.
73. Treml, "Production and Consumption of Alcoholic Beverages," p. 287.
74. See, e.g., *Sovetskaya Rossiya,* 7 January 1970.
75. *Kierunki* (a Polish newspaper), 12 November 1967; *Staat und Recht* (an East German journal) 16, no. 11 (1967).
76. See *Meditsinskaya gazeta,* 20 November 1970, p. 2; and *Zdravookhraneniye Rossiskoi Federatsii,* no. 5 (1972), pp. 17, 19. See also *Literaturnaya Rossiya,* 8 February 1974, p. 15; and *Meditsinskaya gazeta,* 20 November 1970, p. 2.

¶ Specialists in Policymaking: Criminal Policy, 1938–70

1. Examples of a low assessment of specialists' role in Soviet policymaking include Zbigniew Brzezinski and Samuel Huntington, *Political Power USA/USSR* (New York: Viking, 1964), pp. 191–234; and Sidney Ploss, "New Politics in Russia?" *Survey* 19, no. 4 (Autumn 1973): 23–35. A different appraisal is found in Franklyn Griffiths, "A Tendency Analysis of Soviet Policymaking," *Interest Groups in Soviet Politics,* ed. H. Gordon Skilling and Franklyn Griffiths (Princeton: Princeton University Press, 1971), pp. 335–78; and Jerry F. Hough, "The Soviet System: Petrification or Pluralism?" *Problems of Communism* 21 (March–April 1972): 25–45.
2. By a government's criminal policy I mean its policy toward all activities associated with the control and prevention of ordinary criminal behavior. These activities include the determination of the criminal law, the administration of criminal justice by police and courts, the maintenance of a penal system, and the establishment of measures of crime prevention. However, I do not regard as a part of criminal policy government activities relating to the control of political dissidence or deviance.
3. See H. Gordon Skilling, "Group Conflict in Soviet Politics," *Interest Groups in Soviet Politics,* p. 391; and Merle Fainsod, *How Russia Is Ruled,* 1st ed. (Cambridge, Mass.: Harvard University Press, 1953), pp. 350–53.
4. See V. I. Ivanov, "Razvitie kodifikatsii ugolovnogo zakonodatelstva," in *Razvitie kodifikatsii sovetskogo zakonodatelstva* (Moscow: Yur. lit., 1968), pp. 205–6.
5. B. S. Utevskii and B. S. Osherovich, *Dvadtsat let vsesoyuznogo instituta yuridicheskikh nauk* (Moscow: Gosyurizdat, 1945) .
6. Interviews. During the course of an academic year in Moscow and a later three-week visit to the USSR, I held a substantial number of interviews with Soviet criminal law scholars and a smaller number with Soviet law enforcement officials of the middle and lower levels. I have provided a full list of the persons with whom I had formal interviews or useful discussions in the book upon which this essay is based. See Peter H. Solomon, Jr., *Soviet Criminologists and Criminal Policy* (New York: Columbia University Press, 1978), pp. 220–22.
7. "Vo Vsesoyuznom institut yuridicheskikh nauk: Rabota sektsii ugolovnogo

prava," *Sovetskaya yustitsiya* (hereafter *SIu*), nos. 23–24 (1938), p .61; "Pervaya nauchnaya sessiya vsesoyuznogo instituta yuridicheskikh nauk," in *Trudy pervoi nauchnoi sessii Vsesoyuznogo instituta yuridicheskikh nauk, 27 yanvariya-3 fevralya 1939,* ed. I. T. Golyakov (Moscow: VIIuN, 1940), p. 2. For a summary report of the conference proceedings, see "Vo vsesoyuznom institute yuridicheskikh nauk, nauchnaya sessiya," *SIu, no.* 8 (1939), pp. 21–22, no. 9 (1939), pp. 26–30, no. 10 (1939), pp. 22–29.

8. *Informatsionny byulleten VIIuN,* no. 5 (1939), p. 6; B. Khlebnikov, "Nauchno-issledovatelskaya rabota v oblasti ugolovnogo prava v 1939 g. (Svodnyi plan institutov NKIU SSSR," ibid., no. 6 (1939), pp. 12–16; *Ugolovnyi kodeks SSSR. Proekt* (Moscow: Vsesoyuzny institut yuridicheskikh nauk, 1939). For discussions, see *SIu* and *Sotsialisticheskaya zakonnost* (cited hereafter as *SZ*) for 1939 and 1940.
9. A. A. Gertsenzon, "Puti razvitiya sovetskoi nauki ugolovnogo prava," *Sovetskoe gosudarstvo i prava* (cited hereafter as *SGiP*), no. 11 (1947), p. 81.
10. See Harold Berman, *Justice in the USSR,* rev. ed. (New York: Vintage, 1963), pp. 37–58.
11. M. D. Shargorodsky, "Analogiya v istorii ugolovnogo prava i v sovetskom prave," *SZ,* no. 7 (1938), p. 59.
12. A. Ia. Vyshinsky, *K polozheniyu na fronte pravovoi teorii* (Moscow: Gosyurizdat, 1937), p. 32.
13. "Vo vsesoiuznom institute"; and interview with A. A. Gertsenzon. Professor Gertsenzon indicated to me that of all his activities in criminal policymaking during the course of forty-five years as a criminal law scholar, it was his initiative of the struggle against the principle of analogy of which he was most proud.
14. While Vyshinsky was simultaneously Procurator-General Director of the Institute of Law, and editor of *Sovetskoe gosudarstvo i pravo,* Golyakov was Chairman of the USSR Supreme Court, Director of the All-Union Institute of Juridical Sciences, and editor of *Sovetskaya yustitsiya.*
15. I. T. Golyakov, "Osnovnye problemy nauki sovetskogo sotsialisticheskogo prava," in *Trudy pervoi nauchnoi sessii,* pp. 29–30. Golyakov gave as an example of the faulty use of analogy the case of a man who "for performing a few cuttings according to the Muslim tradition" was convicted by analogy of abortion.
16. A. A. Gertsenzon, "Osnovnye printsipy i polozheniya proekta ugolovnogo kodeksa SSSR," loc. cit., pp. 146–49; "Preniya po dokladu A. A. Gertsenzona i sodokladi B. S. Utevskogo i V. S. Trakhtereva," loc. cit., pp. 170–94.
17. Gertsenzon, "Osnovnye printsipy," pp. 148–49.
18. "Preniya po dokladu A. A. Gertsenzona," pp. 171, 180–81.
19. *Informatsionny biulleten VIIuN,* no. 5 (1939), p. 6.
20. P. V. "Ponyatie analogii v sovetskom ugolovnom prave i praktika ee primenenia," *SIu,* no. 3 (1939), pp. 8–13; G. Nadzharov [aspirant, All-Union Legal Academy], "O primenenii analogii v sovetskom ugolovnom prave," *SZ,* no. 6 (1939), pp. 64–66; R. Stepanova, "Za sokhranenie instituta analogii v sovetskom ugolovnom prave," *SZ,* no. 12 (1939), pp. 59–63; M. D. Shargorodsky, "Problemy proekta Ugolovnogo Kodeksa SSSR," pt. 1, *SIu,* no. 5 (1940), pp. 10–15; interviews.
21. Gertsenzon, "Puti razvitiia." I have found no evidence to support Barry and Berman's suggestion that the draft code failed to meet Stalin's approval. See

Donald Barry and Harold Berman, "The Jurists," *Interest Groups in Soviet Politics,* p. 318.

22. A. A. Piontkovsky, *Staliniskaya konstitutsiya i proekt ugolovnogo kodeksa SSSR* (Moscow: Gosyurizdat, 1947), pp. 10–12; interviews.
23. Interviews.
24. One mark of the criminal law scholars' status was the appointment of three of them—I. T. Golyakov, M. M. Isaev, and A. A. Piontkovsky—to the USSR Supreme Court. Scholars had not been seated on the high court during the Khrushchev or Brezhnev years. See V. V. Kulikov and Kh.B. Sheinin, "Verkhovny sud SSSR i yuridicheskaya nauka," *SGiP,* no. 3 (1974), p. 7. The All-Union Institute of Juridical Sciences had close ties both with the Commissariat (later Ministry) of Justice to which it was attached and with the USSR Supreme Court, with which it shared its director in the person of I. T. Golyakov.
25. See Solomon, *Soviet Criminologists and Criminal Policy,* pp. 27–32. When the NKVD SSSR was formed in 1934, it drew together the penal institutions that had been administered by the OGPU and by Narkomyust.
26. See John N. Hazard, *Law and Social Change in the USSR* (London: Stevens and Sons, 1953), p. 88; and N. V. Zhogin, "Ob izvrashchenyakh Vyshinskogo v teorii sovetskogo prava i praktike," *SGiP,* no. 3 (1964), pp. 26–27.
27. The judicial chiefs retained control over the administration of the court system and the application through the courts of the criminal law. See Berman, *Justice in the USSR,* pp. 7–9. However, the 1938 Law on Court Organization removed legislative initiative from the list of the Supreme Court's official functions; this formal right was returned to the court only in 1957. See S. G. Bannikov, "Zakonodatelnaya initsiativa Verkhovnogo suda SSSR," *SGiP,* no. 3 (1974), p. 14.
28. Brzezinski and Huntington claimed that specialist participation in the late 1950s served to mobilize support for decisions already taken more than to initiate or to advocate policy proposals (Brzezinski and Huntington, *Political Power USA/USSR*).
29. Donald Barry was unsure whether legal scholars in the late 1950s were concerned with the substance of the law as opposed to its legal form. See his "Specialists in Soviet Policy-making; The Adoption of a Law," *Soviet Studies* 14 (1964).
30. During the next few years the USSR Supreme Court regained jurisdiction for most categories of cases previously handled administratively by the NKVD or MGB; the MVD took over from the security police the administration of the prison system; and the USSR Procuracy revived its role in supervising the administration of justice. For legislation helping to restore the Procuracy's supervisory function, see "Polozhenie o prokurorskom nadzore, utverzhdeno 24 maya, 1955," in *Sbornik zakonov SSSR i Ukazov Prezidiuma Verkhovnogo Soveta SSSR, 1938–1967,* 3 vols. (Moscow: Yur. lit., 1968–70), 2:573–85; see also "Ob amnestii, Ukaz Prezidiuma Verkhovnogo Soveta ot 27 marta 1953 G.," in ibid., pp. 627–28.
31. Interviews; see also A. A. Piontkovsky, "Osnovnye voprosy proekta ugolovnogo kodeksa SSSR," *SZ,* no. 1, (1954): 25–38.
32. Ivanov, "Razvitie kodifikatsii ugolovnogo zakonodatelstva," p. 206; interviews; *SGiP* and *SZ* for summer and fall of 1954. And see *Teoreticheskaia konferentsiia po voprosam proekta UK SSSR: tezisy dokladov* (Leningrad: LGU, 1955). My thanks to Morris McCain of Yale University for showing me his notes on this source.

33. "Za povyshenie roli pravovoi nauki v kodifikatsii sovetskogo zakonodatelstva," *SGiP,* no. 1 (1956), p. 4. See also D. S. Karev, "O kodifikatsii i sistematizatsii zakonodatelstva SSSR i soyuznykh respublik," *SZ,* no. 2 (1956), p. 7; and A. N. Vasilev, "K proektu UK SSSR," *SGiP,* no. 7 (1954), p. 120.
34. Ibid., p. 12.
35. N. S. Khrushchev, "Secret Speech Concerning the Cult of the Individual" (delivered at the Twentieth Congress of the CPSU, 25 February 1956, in *The Anti-Stalin Campaign and International Communism,* ed. The Russian Institute of Columbia University (New York: Columbia University Press, 1956), pp. 1–90.
36. Traditionally, *obshchestvennost'* referred not to the public as a whole, but to its more informed and active segments.
37. A. A. Ushakov, "V. I. Lenin i kodifikatsiia sovetskogo prava," *SGiP,* no. 5 (1956), pp. 1–10; O. I. Chistyakov, "Organizatsiia kodifikatsionnykh rabot v pervye gody sovetskoi vlasti (1917–23)," ibid., pp. 10–22.
38. Chistyakov, p. 22.
39. For the legal basis of the change, see "Ob otnesnenii k vedeniyu soyuznykh respublik zakonodatelstva ob ustroistve sudov soiuznykh respublik, prinyatiya grazhdanskogo, ugolovnogo i protsessualnykh kodeksov," Zakon priniatii Verkhovnym Sovetom SSSR 11 fevralia 1957 g., *Vedomosti Verkhovnogo Soveta SSSR,* no. 4 (1957), p. 63.
40. Interviews.
41. Thus, B. S. Utevsky, a leading penologist and head of the kafedra of corrective-labor law at the MVD Higher School, was recruited to the commission to prepare the section related to punishment. He reportedly discussed it with his colleagues in the kafedra before submitting it to the drafting commission (interviews).
42. See "V Institute Prava AN SSSR," *SGiP,* no. 3 (1957), pp. 123–30; "Vo Vsesoyuznom Institute Yuridicheskikh Nauk," *SGiP,* no. 6 (1957), pp. 125–30; "Rabotu po kodifikatsii sovetskogo zakonodatelstva—na uroven novykh zadach," *SZ,* no. 5 (1957), pp. 1–5.
43. "Rabotu po kodifikatsii," p. 5.
44. See John Gorgone, "Soviet Jurists in the Legislative Arena," *Soviet Union,* II, no. 1 (1976), pp. 1–36.
45. "Rabotu po kodifikatsii."
46. "Vazhnyi shag v dalneishem razvitii sovetskoi demokratii," *SGiP,* no. 7 (1957), p. 9; interviews.
47. Interviews; see also M. A. Gedvilas and S. G. Novikov, "O deyatelnosti komissii zakonodatelnykh predpolozhenii Verkhovnogo Soveta SSSR," *SGiP,* no. 9 (1957), pp. 18–24.
48. "Osnovnye nachala ugolovnogo zakonodatelstva Soyuza SSSR i soyuznykh respublik (proekt)," *SGiP,* no. 6 (1958), pp. 3–12; *SZ,* no. 6 (1958), pp. 7–16; *Sovety deputatov trudyashchikhsya,* no. 6 (1958), pp. 19–27.
49. See *SGiP* and *SZ,* nos. 7–12 (1958).
50. "Vazhnyi shag," pp. 1–9.
51. "V Komissiakh Zakonodatelnykh Predpolozhenii Soveta Soyuza i Soveta Natsionalnostei Verkhovnogo Soveta SSSR," *SGiP,* no. 6 (1958), p. 1, and *SZ,* no. 6 (1958), p. 7; interviews.
52. Solomon, *Soviet Criminologists and Criminal Policy.*
53. The abuses included cheating, faking of documents, and concealment of defective goods. Often, some prisoners, especially recidivists, would force other in-

mates to fulfill their work norms for them. In some colonies, as a result, recidivists were released earlier than first offenders (A. Lyubavin and A. L. Remenson, "Dosrochnoe osvobozhdenie v poryadke zacheta rabochikh dnei," *SZ*, no. 6 [1957], pp. 14–19).

54. For documentation and a full account of the parole decisions in 1957–58, see Solomon, *Soviet Criminologists and Criminal Policy*, pp. 42–45 and p. 179.
55. For documentation and a full account of the recidivism decisions of 1957–59, see ibid., pp. 45–48 and p. 180.
56. Interviews. Gorgone, "Soviet Jurists in the Legislative Arena." Obviously, it is possible that the leadership injected its views into the debates among the scholars and officials, but neither my research nor Gorgone's discovered any signs of Party manipulation of participants in the discussions.
57. For an account of Soviet criminology's demise in the 1930s and revival in the 1950s and 1960s, see Peter H. Solomon, Jr., "Soviet Criminology: Its Demise and Rebirth, 1928–1963," *Soviet Union* 1, no. 2 (1974): 122–40.
58. N. R. Mironov, "O nekotorykh voprosakh preduprezhdeniya prestupnosti i drugikh antiobshchestvennykh yavlenii i borby s nimi v sovremennykh usloviyakh," *SGiP*, no. 5 (1961), p. 9.
59. "Yuridicheskaya nauka v usloviyakh kommunisticheskogo stroitelstva," *Kommunist*, no. 16 (1963), p. 33.
60. Ibid., p. 27.
61. The other two agency institutes were the All-Union Institute of Soviet Legislation (VNIISZ), attached to the Juridical Commission of the USSR Council of Ministers, and the All-Union Research Institute for the Defense of the Social Order, attached to the ministry of that name.
62. "Polozhenie o Vsesoiuznom institute po izucheniiu prichin i razrabotke mer preduprezhdenii prestupnosti," utverzhdeno Gen. Prok. SSSR i Pred. Verkhovnogo suda SSSR, 15 iunia 1963, in *Sbornik deistvuyushchikh prikazov i instruktsii generalnogo prokurora SSSR* (Moscow: Yur. lit., 1966). For a list of the many such reports prepared during 1965 and 1966, see "Otchet Vseoyuznogo instituta po izucheniyu prichin i razrabotke mer preduprezhdenii prestupnosti o vypolnenii nauchnykh issledovanii za 1965 god," *Informatsionnoe pismo* [instituta], no. 4 (Moscow, 1966); and "Otchet Vsesoyuznogo instituta po izucheniyu prichin i razrabotke mer preduprezhdenii prestupnosti o vypolenii nauchnykh issledovanii za 1966 god," *Informatsionnoe pismo* [instituta], no. 9 (1967).
63. Some research projects were reported only to their sponsors, without any dissemination of the results even in internal publications. Examples include a major statistical study of crime in the USSR during the period 1917 to 1967 and a study of the application and effectiveness of the death penalty. In the latter case, the scholars prepared *spravki* on the application of the death penalty in prerevolutionary Russia, on the death penalty in Western legislation and its application in the West, on the history of Soviet legislation on the death penalty, and on the use of the death penalty in the USSR between 1920 and 1927 ("Otchet . . . za 1965").
64. "Otchet . . . za 1965"; "Otchet . . . za 1966"; interviews.
65. N. A. Shchelokov, "Pomogat cheloveku stat luchshe," *Pravda*, 31 July 1967, p. 3; "Problemy borby s presupnostyu nesovershennoletnikh i zadachi organov okhrany obshchestvennogo poryadka SSSR," in *Problemy borby s prestupnostyu nesovershennoletnikh i zadachi organov okhrany obshchestvennogo poryadka*

SSSR (*Materialy nauchno-prakticheskoi konferentsii*) (Moscow, 1967), pp. 1–21. See also N. Shchelokov, "Glavnoe—preduprezhdenie pravonarushenii," *SZ,* no. 8 (1967).

66. V. K. Zvirbul, *Deiatelnost prokuratury po preduprezhdeniyu prestupnosti* (*Nauchnye osnovy*) (Moscow: Yur. lit., 1971); *Sovershenstvovanie prokurorskogo nadzora v SSSR* (*Sbornik statei*) (Moscow: Vsesoyuzny Institut po izucheniyu prichin prestupnosti, 1973); A. Safonov, "Opyt vnedreniya nauchnykh rekomendatsii v praktiku," *SZ,* no. 5 (1973); N. Kosoplechev et al., "Nauchnye rekomendatsii po kriminologii raionnym i gorodskim prokuroram," *SZ,* no. 11 (1973).
67. R. Nishanov, "O proektakh zakonov," *Izvestiia,* 12 July 1969, p. 1.
68. See Solomon, *Soviet Criminologists and Criminal Policy,* chaps. 5–9. I focused there upon decisions relating to the criminal justice system and the criminal law. I did not consider decisions in criminal procedure, but it was already clear from Western literature that the scholars expert in this area played a large part in decisions there. See John N. Hazard, "Social Control through Law," *Politics in the USSR,* ed. Alexander Dallin and Alan F. Westin (New York: Harcourt, Brace and World, 1966); *Soviet Law and Government* 9, no. 4 (Spring 1971); and Gorgone, "Soviet Jurists in the Legislative Arena."
69. The fullest presentation of this interpretation of Soviet political developments under Brezhnev is Sidney Ploss's "New Politics in Russia?" pp. 28–31. Ploss argued that from 1968, the Brezhnev regime had managed to curtail the public dimension of specialist participation. Although Ploss's contention may have held true for agricultural policy (the area he cites), there is no evidence that it applied to criminal policy. Moreover, there was no sign of curtailment of specialists' roles *behind the scenes* in any policy realm; and in some fields, such as science policy, the scope of specialist participation increased during the 1970s.
70. The initiators of the decisions studied were as follows: for juvenile delinquency, the USSR Procuracy; for alcoholism and hooliganism, the USSR Supreme Court *and* the MVD (each pushing different lines of attack); for parole and recidivism, the USSR Supreme Court. It is interesting to note the pride of members of the Supreme Court in their roles in these decisions: see Bannikov, "Zakonodatelnaya initsiativa Verkhovnogo suda SSSR," pp. 16–17.
71. The behavior pattern of the Brezhnev leadership in criminal policymaking corresponded to the model outlined by Jerry F. Hough and termed by him "institutional pluralism." This description was not meant to suggest all the characteristics of democratic pluralism. Hough used the word "pluralism" in order to stress that such central features of democratic pluralism as broad-ranging policy debates, with the leaders serving as mediators or brokers, have been present in Soviet policymaking. But, as Hough was aware, there are other features of democratic pluralism that the institutional variety does not share. First, a cardinal institution of democratic pluralism, the organized interest group, has no place in institutional pluralism; political actors have kept their debates within the framework of Party and state institutions and have not formed separate organizations for lobbying. Secondly, the model of institutional pluralism does not assume that the press and publishing houses are largely free from political influence, as does democratic pluralism. Thirdly, institutional pluralism does not require such wide boundaries of political discourse as does democratic pluralism; it does not include, for example, the right

to criticize political leaders by name. Fourthly, institutional pluralism can exist in a setting where political power is concentrated, whereas democratic pluralism assumes dispersal of power and authority. For an outline of the model "institutional pluralism," see Hough, "The Soviet System: Petrification or Pluralism?"

72. Interviews; see also Frederick Barghoorn, *Politics in the USSR*, 1st ed. (Boston: Little, Brown, 1966), p. 349. For elaboration see Jerry F. Hough, *The Soviet Union and Social Science Theory* (Cambridge, Mass.: Harvard University Press, 1977) and Merle Fainsod and Jerry F. Hough, *How Russia is Ruled* (Third edition; Cambridge, Mass.: Harvard University Press, 1978).

73. The head of the Department of Administrative Organs, which was responsible for supervising army activities, the security police, and the law enforcement agencies, was a politician of high stature reporting directly to a secretary of the Central Committee. Although he supervised the work of the leading law enforcement officials, even he was not necessarily superior to them, especially when, as in the case of Procurator General R. A. Rudenko, they were members of the Central Committee. The department head was assisted by one or two deputy chiefs in managing the work of the department's sections, including a legal affairs section responsible for the courts, Procuracy, and MVD. It appears that the head of this section has had lower stature than a deputy minister in one of those agencies, for two recent heads of the section were later transferred to positions as deputy ministers. Nikitin became a deputy minister of internal affairs in 1966 and Sukharev, his successor as section head, became a deputy minister of Justice in 1970.

74. For example, in connection with the 1966 Party-state edict on crime control, Party officials prepared a comprehensive summary of Soviet criminal policy, which stated goals and general principles and noted recent and anticipated decisions on concrete questions. See "O borbe s prestupnostyu," Postanovlenie TSK KPSS i Soveta Ministrov ot 23 iyulya 1966 (no open source) or, for a description of its content, "v TSK KPSS, Prezidiume Verkhovnogo Soveta SSSR i Soveta Ministrov SSSR," *Byulleten Verkhovnogo Suda SSSR,* no. 4 (1966).

75. One reason suggested was that the department's staff was too small. The legal affairs section had six or seven members, including just one instructor to supervise the court system. The USSR Supreme Court, the Procuracy, and the Ministry of Internal Affairs were far better equipped to perform the paperwork of compiling memoranda to support their policy proposals (interviews).

76. Brzezinski and Huntington wrote, "The initiative in formulating most important policy measures probably rests with the Central Committee Secretaries and the departments of the central apparat" (*Political Power USA/USSR,* p. 204). Abdurakhman Avtorkhanov claimed that "the Central Committee departments are the main channel for the preparation of decisions." See his *Communist Party Apparatus* (Chicago: H. Regnery Co., 1966), p. 217. See also Ploss, "New Politics in Russia?" p. 35.

77. Interviews.

78. In the USSR, just as in the West, there were limitations to the expertise of criminologists; on a spectrum of knowledge ranging from "hard" to "soft," theirs was relatively soft. See James Q. Wilson, "Crime and the Criminologists," *Commentary* 58, no. 1 (July 1974): 47–53. The first Soviet criminological research after the post-Stalin revival of criminology was even weaker than its Western counterpart, but by the middle 1960s the work of the better Soviet

researchers met Western standards. For examples of Soviet criminology in both periods, see Peter H. Solomon, Jr., "A Selected Bibliography of Soviet Criminology," *Journal of Criminal Law, Criminology and Police Science* 61, no. 3 (1970): 393–432.

79. The 1966 Party-state edict on crime control reflected this balance. According to Professor Gertsenzon, the edict "determined the basic lines of Soviet criminal policy for contemporary conditions." Gertsenzon also regarded the edict as representing a mixture of prophylactic and repressive approaches (A. A. Gertsenzon, *Ugolovnoe pravo i sotsiologia* [Moscow: Yur. lit., 1971], p. 191).
80. See Edwin Lemert, *Social Action and Legal Change: Revolution within the Juvenile Court* (Chicago: Aldine, 1970), pp. 1–30.
81. Interviews.
82. When one scholar did suggest an innovation in criminal policy, he was severely rebuffed by his peers. During 1959–61, Professor I. S. Noi of Saratov repeatedly urged that a large number of Soviet offenders be declared nonimputable and placed in mental hospitals rather than in prisons. In proposing this innovation for which there was no real support, Noi seemed to have challenged two basic assumptions of Soviet criminal policy, both the prevailing concept of criminal responsibility and the premise that crime was socially caused. For details, see Peter H. Solomon, Jr., "Specialists in Soviet Policy-making: Criminologists and Criminal Policy in the 1960's" (Ph.D. diss., Columbia University, 1973), pp. 302–9.
83. See Dean Schooler, Jr., *Science, Scientists and Public Policy* (New York: Free Press, 1971); and William Zimmerman, "Issues, Area and Foreign Policy Process," *American Political Science Review* 67, no. 4 (December 1973): 1204–12.
84. Franklyn Griffiths, "Images, Politics and Learning in Soviet Behavior toward the United States" (Ph.D. diss., Columbia University, 1972); Richard B. Remnek, *Soviet Scholars and Soviet Foreign Policy: A Case Study in Soviet Policy towards India* (Durham, N.C.: Carolina Academic Press, 1975).
85. The participation in the formation of Soviet policies for science and technology by specialists in social studies of science has not been documented in published sources, but unpublished research by this author supplies ample evidence of the development of such participation in the 1960s and its institutionalization in the early 1970s.
86. This conclusion may be inferred from Richard Judy, "The Economists," in *Interest Groups in Soviet Politics,* and Philip Stewart, "Soviet Interest Groups and the Policy Process: The Repeal of Production Education," *World Politics* 22, no. 1 (October 1969): 29–50.
87. See Remnek, *Soviet Scholars and Soviet Foreign Policy.*
88. As Raymond Bauer has written, "Busy men do not have the resources to treat many issues as salient . . . and their strategies for handling salient and nonsalient issues are probably quite different" ("The Study of Policy Formation: An Introduction," in *The Study of Policy Formation,* ed. Raymond Bauer and Kenneth Gergen [New York and London: Free Press, 1968], p. 17).
89. Donald Schon, *Beyond the Stable State* (New York: Random House, 1971), esp. pp. 123 and 128; James Q. Wilson, *Political Organizations* (New York: Basic Books, 1973), p. 330; Jack Walker, "The Diffusion of Knowledge and Policy Change: Toward a Theory of Agenda-Setting" (paper delivered at the 1974 meeting of the American Political Science Association).

Glossary of Untranslated Russian Words and Abbreviations

agitator disseminator of propaganda orally
agitprop the agitation and propaganda section of the Party (also used to describe the activities which this section sponsors)
aktiv the activist nucleus of the Party and other Soviet mass organizations
apparat the Party apparatus (refers both to personnel and organizational structure)
apparatchik a full-time Party functionary employed in the Party apparatus
chinovnik functionary or bureaucrat (now mildly pejorative, chin:rank)
edinonachalie "one-man control." The assignment of fundamental responsibility to a single director
gorkom city or town Party committee
ispolkom executive committee of a soviet
khozraschet a system of independent local-level economic accounting
kolkhoz "collective economy." Collective farm
kolkhoznik member of a collective farm
kafedra department (academic)
kontrol supervision or "checking" (does not mean control)
krai territory
kraikom territorial Party committee
MTS machine-tractor station (most were abolished in 1958)
MVD Ministry of Internal Affairs
NOT Scientific Organization of Labor
NKVD People's Commissariat of Internal Affairs, since renamed
nomenklatura list of appointments subject to Party initiation or ratification
obkom oblast Party committee
oblast region
oblispolkom executive committee of oblast soviet
obedinenie industrial association or amalgamation
otdel section
politinformator a propagandist more educated and specialized than an agitator
profilaktoriya dispensary
proverka check-up, examination
raiispȯlkom executive committee of a district soviet
raikom Party district committee
raion district
samizdat "self-publication." Materials, often of political significance, reproduced and distributed without approval of the censor
samogon home-brewed vodka

spravka certificate
subbotnik a gathering for collective work on free evenings or rest days (now rare)
zampolit deputy commander for political affairs (in a military unit), successor to the commissar
Zhdanovshchina the campaign against Western culture after World War II directed by A. A. Zhdanov

Index